CRACOW

Author:
Łukasz Ziółkowski

Chief Editor of the Series:
Katarzyna Marcinkowska

Editor:
Urszula Augustyniak

Map Editors:
Kartografika, Aneta Rupniewska, Krzysztof Radwański

Photography Contributors:
Katarzyna Marcinkowska
and Żydowskie Muzeum Galicja (p. 79), MOCAK Muzeum Sztuki Współczesnej
w Krakowie fot. Rafał Sosin (p. 109), ©Dreamstime.com/Riondt (p. 165),
© 108pictures – Fotolia.com (p. 166), ©Dreamstime.com/Cobretti (p. 169),
©Maria Brzostowska – Fotolia.com (p. 171), Kopalnia Soli „Wieliczka"/
Rafał Stachurski (pp. 172, 173), ©Bart Kwieciszewski – Fotolia.com (p. 175),
©wiktor bubniak – Fotolia.com (p. 176), ©rafafrancis – Fotolia.com (p. 177),
restauracja Wierzynek (pp. 178 top, 184), Jama Michalika/Piotr Kuliś (p. 197),
Teatr Słowackiego/Ryszard Kornecki (p. 200), Galeria Krakowska (p. 216),
Wielka Parada Smoków/Łukasz Malinowski (p. 229), Festiwal Kultury Żydowskiej (p. 230)

Translator:
Joanna Moczyńska

Proofreader:
Michelle Smith

Layout Designers:
Michał Zielkiewicz
Katarzyna Marcinkowska

Photo Editor:
Katarzyna Marcinkowska

Prepress Photo Editor:
Wojtek Radwański

DTP:
Michał Zielkiewicz

© **Copyright ExpressMap Polska Sp. z o.o.**
www.comfortmap.com

First edition, June 2012
ISBN 978-83-7546-489-4

CRACOW

ExpressMap

Table of Contents

About the Guidebook

This comprehensive, reader-friendly source of information on the city is enhanced with engaging stories of its past. No guidebook has ever been so simple and enjoyable to use.

The main part (white pages) consists of a detailed presentation of the sights to be seen. The ensuing sections (cream-coloured pages) cover food and drink, arts and entertainment, shopping, a calendar of festivals and events, as well as general traveller information. At the end of the book, the user will find a street atlas on a scale of 1:22 000 (1:12 000 for the city centre).

Rich content and a clear layout make this guidebook highly versatile to use, ensuring that it is easy to make one's choice in accordance with individual needs and interests. The book aims to satisfy all users: both those who look for basic streetwise knowledge and those keen on history and the present-day spirit of the city.

11 sightseeing chapters together present 99 places. The chapters are colour-coded. The most interesting sights are marked with an asterisk.

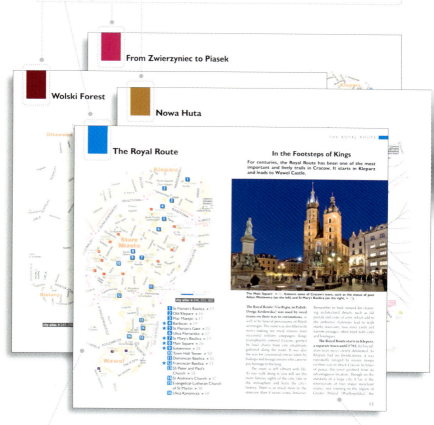

Each chapter begins with a map that shows the precise location of all the sights described in the pages that follow. Particular descriptions are easy to find thanks to colour-coded numbers and page references.

Chapters begin with a general introduction to the history and character of a given part of the city, including practical advice on visiting.

Practical details are separated from the main text, which makes it easier and quicker to check transportation connections, opening times, admission fees etc. You will find the symbol legend on the front jacket flap.

Cream-coloured pages focus on food and drink, arts and entertainment, and shopping. A list of cyclical events and a section on practical information for travellers is also included.

At the end of the book, you will find a street atlas with markings of all the places presented in the sightseeing chapters. The symbol legend is on the back jacket flap.

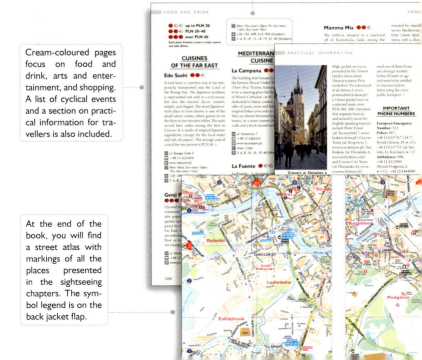

The City of Kings

Cracow is a city with two faces. It boasts a long history, a rich tradition and a lot of treasured historic monuments, but it is also greatly successful at moving with the times. The city is simply unique for its traditions and diversity.

A visit to Cracow is incomplete if you have not seen the Main Square (➤26), the Sukiennice (➤28) and a monument to Adam Mickiewicz, a celebrated Romantic poet.

Cracow is the second largest city in Poland and continues to expand all the time. Its eighteen districts together cover an area of over 300 square kilometres. The registered population amounts to about 750,000. Crowds of tourists and students flock to this cultural and arts centre, which is among the most important in the country. It was here that the first Polish national museum was established (see: The Sukiennice Gallery ➤29). 2011 saw the inauguration of the Museum of Contemporary Art (➤109). There are many theatres to choose from. The Cracow Opera House (➤205) and the Cracow Philharmonic (➤205) enjoy ever-increasing popularity. Cracow never sleeps on the weekends, holding a multitude of concerts and dance events. Its numerous bars are teeming with regulars, and squares such

as pl. Nowy (➤86) boast a great variety of eating and drinking places.

The centuries-old history of Cracow is best told through its many monuments. A diverse architecture chronicles the successive stages of the city's growth. You will find here Romanesque buildings: the Rotunda of the Blessed Virgin Mary in Wawel (see: The Lost Wawel ➤45), St Leonard's Crypt in Wawel Cathedral (➤46) and St Andrew's Church (➤37). There are also a number of Gothic edifices, mostly churches, e.g. St Mary's Basilica (➤23) and the Franciscan Basilica (➤33). The Renaissance proved a particularly fertile period for architectural gems, not to mention representative Baroque examples such as SS Peter and Paul's Church (➤35) and the Church of the Most Holy Trinity

(➤ 94). Successful showpieces of more recent architecture include the eclectic-style Juliusz Słowacki Theatre (➤ 54, ➤ 203) and the Art Déco-style National Old Theatre (➤ 67, ➤ 203). The Cracow Opera House (➤ 205), in turn, has given rise to controversy ever since it was commissioned in 2008. In order to understand this diversity, one needs to go back in time to the city's origins.

Cracow was first mentioned in written sources in 965. Abraham ben Jacob who travelled Europe wrote in his memoirs that it was an important centre of the region, which proves that the story of the settlement dates much further back in time. Indeed, the first vestiges of human presence near Cracow date from the Paleolithic Age (c. 200 000 BC). The remains of mammoth hunters have been found on the grounds of today's Zwierzyniec (➤ 140). Before 1000 BC, the area was populated by people of the Lusatian culture, and the 4th century BC saw the arrival of the Celts.

Wawel Hill (➤ 40) was the natural choice for the location of the settlement. It was inhabited as early as the Paleolithic Age. The Slavs already lived here in the 7th century. It was probably then that they built the mysterious mounds of the city's legendary founder, Krakus (➤ 113), and his daughter Wanda (➤ 138). In the 9th century, Wawel was a major centre of the Vistulans' state. Even before 1000 AD, however, it was taken over by the Polans, who gave Poland its name.

In 966, Christianity became the state religion. Soon afterwards, in 1000, a bishopric was founded in Cracow and the first Wawel Cathedral (➤ 46) was constructed. About 40 years later Cracow was made the capital city and remained so until 1609, when King Sigismund III Vasa (♔ 1587–1632) moved the royal seat to Warsaw.

In 1257, Cracow received municipal rights under the Magdeburg Law. The city was given a new urban layout, centred around the Main Square (➤ 26). The square featured two rows of

St Mary's Basilica (➤ 23) **is a Cracow icon.**

market stalls, which later evolved into the Sukiennice (➤ 28). The merchandise sold here today includes some interesting regional products, jewellery, and all kinds of souvenirs. The Main Square itself teems with florists and sellers of *obwarzanki* (Cracow bagels). The place is usually brimming with people: students are rushing to and from classes, pairs of lovers stroll leisurely, and party crowds meet up by one of the city's major landmarks – the statue of Adam Mickiewicz.

Even before 1257, Cracow boasted a number of remarkable buildings, such as the Romanesque-style St Mary's Basilica (➤ 23). The temple was later rebuilt in the Gothic style. Its greatest pride is a genuine masterwork of sculpture, a 15th-century altarpiece by Veit Stoss. Every hour, atop one of the towers, a trumpeter plays the so-called Heynal tune (➤ 24), which is one of the

Cracow has been expanding for centuries, but its centre has always been mighty Wawel Castle (➤40, above: the bastion named after King Vladislaus IV Vasa).

city's trademarks. Tourists and Cracovians alike stop for a moment to listen. Lifting their heads up high, they try to catch a glimpse of the trumpet sparkling in the sun.

The oldest Polish college was founded in Cracow under King Casimir III the Great (♛ 1333–1370). In 1364, the king was granted the Pope's permission to set up Cracow Academy (now the Jagiellonian University). This enhanced the prestige of the city and turned it into one of the major European cities of that time. One can still visit the oldest university building in Poland, the Collegium Maius (➤61). Academic traditions have survived to this day, even though the Nazis tried to annihilate the Polish *intelligentsia* during WWII (see: The *Sonderaktion Krakau* Operation ➤61). There are now about 20 higher education institutions in Cracow and over 200,000 students. They greatly add to the local colour, forming cabarets and music bands, organising long and loud parties, filling up bars and celebrating their festival called Juwenalia (➤228) every May.

Casimir the Great also founded a new town, Kazimierz (bearing the Polish name of the king). It was inhabited both by Christians (see: Christian Kazimierz ➤88) and Jews (see: Jewish Kazimierz ➤68). It is now one of the most intriguing districts in Cracow. The local Corpus Christi Basilica (➤90, founded by Casimir) is one of the city's most imposing buildings. The district has several synagogues. The historical burgher houses accommodate cult bars such as Singer (➤208) and Alchemia (➤206). When in Kazimierz, remember to try the famous bread pizzas sold in Okrąglak (see: Fast Food in Cracow ➤186).

The Renaissance was the golden age of Cracow. The Jagiellonian rule in the 15th and the 16th centuries significantly contributed to the development of the city. Wawel Castle (➤43) was extended to become a representative royal seat, and a large courtyard with the still impressive arcaded galleries was added. Other Renaissance gems include the fine Sigismund's Chapel in Wawel Cathedral, and the Decius Villa (➤157).

The city has been affected by many wars. During the invasion called the Swedish Deluge, enemy troops occupied Cracow for two years (1655–1657). A lot of buildings were damaged, and valuable items and works of art were looted. The 18th century proved even harder: the city was first pillaged by the Swedes, and then by the Russian army (1768–1772).

In 1793, during the Second Partition of Poland, vast territories were taken over by Prussia and Russia; Cracow came under Russian occupation. One year later, in the Main Square, Tadeusz Kościuszko started a Polish uprising. It failed, and in 1795 Poland was divided between Prussia, Russia and Austria, losing its independence for 123 years. Cracow came under the rule of Austria. The occupier had most of the walls around the Old Town pulled down, leaving only three towers and St Florian's Gate (➤20). The Austrians started to build a 19th-century system of fortifications called the Cracow Fortress, which included St Benedict's Fort (➤111) and the Mogiła Fort (➤139).

Poland regained independence in 1918, but it did not last long. During WWII, Cracow was occupied by the Nazis, and Wawel became the seat of the Governor-General Hans Frank. Cracovian Jews had to move to the ghetto in Podgórze (➤110), and were then murdered in pl. Bohaterów Getta (➤106) or deported to camps such as Płaszów (➤116).

After the war, the communist regime built a model socialist town, Nowa Huta (➤118), in the vicinity of Cracow. A conglomerate (see: Steelworks Administrative Centre ➤122) and housing estates were constructed. Inhabitants fought long for their first church (see: Lord's Ark ➤131), since Nowa Huta was originally planned as a working-class "town without God." The place is now visited for its original layout and the Socialist-Realist architecture of pl. Centralny (➤126) and al. Róż (➤127). ■

Romantics at heart will feel at home in Kazimierz (➤68).

On a one-day trip, see the Royal Route (➤12) and Wawel Hill (➤40). However, you may not be able to see all the castle's highlights since there are daily visitor limits, and tickets sell really fast. At the height of the season come before noon or book your ticket in advance.

On a three-day visit, allocate one day for the Old Town (➤50) and the Royal Route (➤12). The next day, go to Wawel Hill (➤40) and spend the evening enjoying the Cracow nightlife. Don't forget to treat yourself to a beer in one of the many bars, and try the local specialities – the famous Cracow bagel is the bare minimum. On the third day, visit Kazimierz, both Jewish (➤68) and Christian (➤88). Yet another idea is a trip to Podgórze (➤98), which can be combined with Kazimierz (a version for indefatigable tourists), or with a more leisurely day two in Wawel.

During a week's stay, take a trip to Nowa Huta (➤118), walk from Zwierzyniec to Piasek (➤140), or relax in an active way in Wolski Forest (➤154). It is a good idea to allocate one day for a trip to the surroundings of the city.

The Royal Route

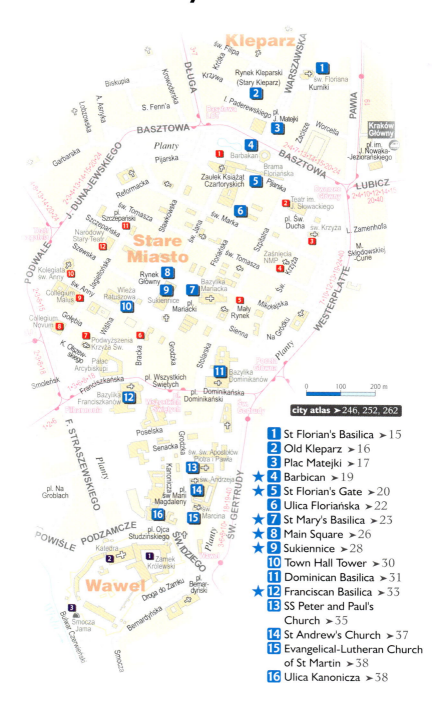

In the Footsteps of Kings

For centuries, the Royal Route has been one of the most important and lively trails in Cracow. It starts in Kleparz and leads to Wawel Castle.

The Main Square (➤26) features some of Cracow's icons, such as the statue of poet Adam Mickiewicz (on the left) and St Mary's Basilica (on the right, ➤23).

The Royal Route (*Via Regia*, in Polish: Droga Królewska) was used by royal trains on their way to coronations, as well as by funeral processions of Polish sovereigns. The route was also filled with merry-making for royal returns from successful military campaigns. Kings triumphantly entered Cracow, greeted by loud cheers from city inhabitants gathered along the route. It was also the way for ceremonial entries taken by bishops and foreign envoys who came to pay homage to the king.

The route is still vibrant with life. As you walk along it, you will see the most famous sights of the city, take in the atmosphere and learn the city's history. There is so much more to the itinerary than Cracow icons, however.

Remember to look around for charming architectural details, such as old portals and coats of arms, which add to the ambience. Gateways lead to wide murky staircases, nice inner yards and narrow passages, often lined with cafés and boutiques.

The Royal Route starts in Kleparz, a separate town until 1792. Its boundaries were never clearly delineated. As Kleparz had no fortifications, it was repeatedly ravaged by enemy troops on their way to attack Cracow. In times of peace, the town profited from its advantageous location. Though on the outskirts of a large city, it lay at the intersection of two major merchant routes: one running to the region of Greater Poland (Wielkopolska), the

St Adalbert's Church in the Main Square (➤ 26) **is one of the smallest in Cracow.**

test songs to the sound of the often out-of-tune guitars. There are also mimes, who freeze motionless and do not move until someone puts some coins in their buckets. The Main Square is where actor Krzysztof Falkowski puts on his marionette shows ("starring" Céline Dion, Michael Jackson and Elvis Presley, among others). From time to time, you can also listen to some live accordion music: the trio gives its virtuoso performances in the Main Square, often in the vicinity of St Mary's Basilica (➤ 23).

The last stretch of the Royal Route used to run by the settlement called Okół, the centre of which was the square in front of St Andrew's Church (➤ 37). Okół was a connecting area between Wawel Castle and Cracow; it received municipal rights in 1257. The village did not serve this function for long: it was already incorporated into the neighbouring town in the 14th century. Today, ul. Grodzka is one of the most lively streets in Cracow. It is walked by tourists on their way to Wawel, as well as Cracovians and students. The street is home to the Philosophy Department of the Jagiellonian University, and the adjacent SS Peter and Paul's Church (➤ 35).

In the summer, look for a singular match stall in the neighbourhood of ul. Grodzka. The seller wears old-fashioned clothes and drives a specially converted bike with a large goods compartment. Matchboxes vary in size; the largest ones considerably exceed the size of this guidebook. They can certainly serve as an original souvenir from Cracow. The street itself is home to a great number of shops and restaurants. However, it is enough to turn into ul. Kanonicza (➤ 38), which runs parallel to ul. Grodzka, to take a rest from the hustle and bustle. The city's oldest street also affords a nice view of Wawel Hill. ■

other to the city of Toruń. Kleparz thus had strong trade traditions, and the local square used to be a well-known horse market. Now half the original size, the marketplace is called Stary Kleparz (Old Kleparz ➤ 16). Colourful, fragrant piles of fruit and vegetables make it one of the most popular shopping places in Cracow.

The Royal Route runs through St Florian's Gate (➤ 20) **into the Old Town** (➤ 50), the city's most ancient part that came to incorporate the neighbouring villages. As soon as the first spring sunbeams start warming the Main Square (➤ 26), Cracow wakes up from its winter sleep. Sun-shaded pavement cafés spring up like mushrooms, and operate until the autumn rains come. Ul. Floriańska (➤ 22) and the Main Square are always teeming with interesting people. You can count on street musicians to sing *engagé* pro-

The best time to take a walk along the Royal Route is before noon, when the Main Square, the local streets and eating places are not yet filled with wearisome tourist crowds. The busiest time is Sunday. Visiting churches during services is unwel-

come, if not straightforwardly forbidden, but St Andrew's Church (➤37) and the Evangelical-Lutheran Church of St Martin (➤38) are open only for Sunday Masses. Remember that SS Peter and Paul's Church (➤35) holds Foucault's Pendulum demonstrations on Thursdays only. After dusk, most sights are illuminated, so an evening walk in the Main Square (➤26) is a must.

A leisurely walk along the route without visiting the sights takes about 90 minutes; when visiting all of them, about half a day.

There are many restaurants, bars and fast food outlets lining the route. Everyone can find something for oneself, regardless of financial resources. You can also try traditional Cracow bagels (the so-called obwarzanki), sold on most street corners.

Access by public transport:

1–6

🅑 124, 152, 424, 601, 608, 610, 618, 902 (Basztowa LOT)

🅣 2, 3, 4, 7, 13, 14, 15, 20, 24 (Basztowa LOT)

7–10

🅑 124, 152, 424, 502, 522, 601, 605, 608, 609, 610, 614, 618, 902, 904 (Dworzec Główny)

🅣 2, 4, 7, 10, 12, 13, 14, 15, 19, 20, 24, 40 (Dworzec Główny)

11–15

🅣 1, 3, 6, 8, 18 (Plac Wszystkich Świętych)

16

🅣 3, 6, 8, 10, 18, 19, 40 (Wawel)

1 St Florian's Basilica

The first church dedicated to St Florian was built towards the end of the 12th century, when the relics of the martyr were brought to Cracow. The site was indicated by... oxen.

In 1184, Duke Casimir the Just brought the relics of St Florian to Cracow. The bishop of the city had sought to obtain the relics since he believed that they could raise the status of Cracow and strengthen relations with the papacy. Legend has it that Pope Lucius III went to St Lawrence's Church in Rome to look for the holy relics to send to Poland. Two of the three saints buried in the church turned their backs on the Pope when asked if they wanted to go to Cracow. It was St Florian who handed him a note that read, "I'll go to Poland."

There is also an intriguing story behind the choice of location for the church. When pulling the cart with the holy relics of St Florian towards Wawel, the oxen suddenly stopped and could not be made to continue. Only when it was decided that the spot would become the site of a church dedicated to the martyr did the animals move on. The saint's body was interred in Wawel Cathedral, and St Florian's Church later came to hold the holy relics.

The construction had already begun in 1185. The exact consecration

St Florian's Basilica only got its Baroque-style lavishness in the 1900's.

Today, there is no trace left of the original Romanesque building. The present Baroque-style decoration dates from the beginning of the 20th century. The main altarpiece features a 17th-century painting showing St Florian against the background of Kleparz. Visit St Anne's Chapel with St John the Baptist's altar, brought here from St Mary's Basilica (➤23). The Baroque altarpiece of St Valentine, in turn, has a 1440 bas-relief picturing the Assumption of Mary.

The treasury of the church boasts genuine gems: three extremely valuable reliquaries. The pinnacle-shaped one was donated by the Polish and Lithuanian king Vladislaus Jagiello after he defeated the Teutonic Knights in the 1410 Battle of Grunwald, practically annihilating the Order's army and giving Poland the position of the region's military power (the 1365 reliquary had belonged to a Teutonic commander, Heinrich von Bode). The second, hand-shaped reliquary held the relics of St Florian, and the third one, of the Holy Cross. ■

The painting in the basilica's high altar depicts Florian, its patron saint.

date remains unknown; it took place some time between 1208 and 1216, and was celebrated by Wincenty Kadłubek, a famous Polish bishop and historian. The church was repeatedly ravaged by fires. St Florian himself is said to have helped in putting the flames out in 1528. The legend might have a grain of truth: the church was miraculously saved even though the whole Kleparz neighbourhood burnt down. Since that time, St Florian has been the patron saint of occupations connected with fire, e.g. firemen.

St Florian's Basilica (Bazylika św. Floriana)
✉ ul. Warszawska 1
@ www.swflorian.net
🕐 Mon–Sat 6am–6.30pm, Sun 6.30am–8pm
ℹ services: Mon–Sat at 6am, 6.30am, 7am, 7.30am, 8am, 9am, 6.30pm, Sun and holidays at 6.30am, 8am, 9.30am, 11am, 12.15pm, 3.15pm, 6.30pm, 8pm

2 Old Kleparz

In operation for over 800 years, Stary Kleparz is the city's oldest market. Merchandise included horses and citruses (rare in the 1980's); now it is fresh fruit, vegetables and dairy products.

Although Kleparz is just a stone's throw away from the Old Town, it was an independent settlement until 1792. In 1366, King Casimir the Great (👑 1333–1370) granted Kleparz municipal rights under the Magdeburg Law, but large numbers of people had come here to settle down two centuries previously, when St Florian's Church (➤15) was

constructed. King Casimir named the town Florencja, after the patron saint.

It was not until the 15th century that the town was called Kleparz. The name probably comes from the Polish word for making a deal; the local market was already thriving. Yet another possible derivation concerns staves used in the manufacturing of barrels.

The main square of Kleparz was originally much larger. It used to encompass the grounds of today's market place and pl. Matejki (➤17). It was famous for its weekly grain and horse markets. In the 1980's, Stary Kleparz offered many products that were largely unavailable in shops at that time. Cracovians searched here for quality baby food, fresh meat, and the then-rare delicacy – citrus fruit.

Today, people come to the Old Kleparz to buy fresh organic fruit and vegetables. Other goods to be commended include *charcuterie* and dairy products, as well as flowers. ■

Old Kleparz/ Kleparz Main Square (Stary Kleparz/ Rynek Kleparski)

🕐 *market: 7am–6pm daily, Sun: only some stalls are open, most of them until the early hours of the afternoon*

3 Plac Matejki

Matejko Square used to be part of the extensive main square of Kleparz. It remained undeveloped until the latter 19th century. Today, it affords a magnificent view of the Barbican, St Florian's Gate and the remains of the town walls.

The square centre is marked by a monument to the Battle of Grunwald. The Barbican (in the background, ➤19) and St Florian's Gate (➤20) are situated nearby.

The imposing 24-metre-high monument in the square centre commemorates the victory of Poles and Lithuanians over the Teutonic Order in the Battle of Grunwald (1410). The mounted figure is the triumphant King Vladislaus Jagiello (♛1386–1434). Below stands Vytautas, the Grand Duke of Lithuania, with the dead body of Grand Teutonic Master Ulrich von Jungingen at his feet. The monument was inaugurated in 1910, on the 500th anniversary of the battle. 150,000 people attended the ceremony. It was a dizzying crowd indeed: the population of Cracow alone was little more than 100,000

The recumbent figure in the Grunwald Monument depicts Ulrich von Jungingen.

inhabitants. Poland was under partitions back then, and the event soon turned into a patriotic demonstration. The people assembled in the square sang *Rota* for the first time (*Rota*, or *The Oath*, was written in protest against the occupiers' attempts at suppressing the Polish culture).

When WWII broke out and the Nazis entered Cracow, the Grunwald Monument was destroyed: the metal figures were melted and reused by the Nazi army. The monument was reconstructed only in 1976 by Marian Konieczny, a celebrated Polish sculptor and professor of the Academy of Fine Arts in Cracow. It took a helicopter to place the heavy, 5.5-metre-tall statue of the king atop the plinth. It flew for almost 100 km, and the event was televised.

In 1925, Cracow followed a fashion of the time and put up the Tomb of the Unknown Soldier. The symbolic grave was located in pl. Matejki right next to the Grunwald Monument, and shared its fate during WWII. However, the site of the dismantled tomb still held a place in the Polish national memory. In the 1960's, Cracow was offered portions of soil from WWII battlefields where Poles died fighting. The soil was put into an urn and placed on the spot of the pre-war Tomb of the Unknown Soldier. In 1976, during the reconstruction of the Grunwald Monument, the urn was moved to the basement under the present Tomb (a marble slab with a square-shaped metal burning lamp, lighted with gas during official celebrations).

The corner edifice at No. 13 is the seat of Cracow's Academy of Fine Arts, the oldest art college in Poland. Its story goes back to 1818, when the Jagiellonian University opened the School of Drawing and Painting. After 65 years, the School became an independent unit and changed its name to the School of Fine Arts. The headmaster at that time was Jan Matejko (1838-1893), a renowned historical painter who gave the name to the square and is now the patron of the Academy. Academic teachers included celebrated Polish painters, whose works can be seen in the museums of Cracow: realist Leon Wyczółkowski (1852–1936), modernist Stanisław Wyspiański (1869–1907), symbolist Jacek Malczewski (1854–1929) and postimpressionist Józef Pankiewicz (1866–1940). Today, the Academy educates future sculptors, painters, graphic artists, as well as stage and interior designers, and art restorers. ■

Plac Matejki

🏨 *Jarema restaurant* ➤ 181, *pl. Matejki 5* 🔴🔵🟢; *vegetarian bar: Glonojad* ➤ 191, *pl. Matejki 2* 🔴🔵🟢

Built in the 15th century, the Barbican has remained largely unchanged.

★ 4 Barbican

The shape of the Barbican has earned it the pet name of a "Saucepan" among the inhabitants of Cracow. Tourists should perhaps show more respect: it is one of the grandest and best-preserved fortified structures in Europe.

Towards the end of the 15th century the tribes of Turks, Tatars and Vlachs started to pose a real threat, venturing as far as the border of Lesser Poland (Małopolska), where Cracow is situated. King John I Albert (♔ 1492–1501) decided to strengthen the city's fortifications with an additional structure: a barbican. Its construction took only two years and ended in 1499.

The Gothic Barbican was modelled not only on European, but also Arab fortifications. The inside diameter is 24.5 m. The imposing walls, up to 3 m in width, are topped with seven watchtowers where marksmen were stationed. The towers could be climbed only by ladders. 130 embrasures are arranged in four rows in such a way that defenders could catch their enemy in the crossfire. Yet another defensive feature were machicolations: battlements projecting from the wall that have floor openings, still to be seen today. Machicolations allowed for one of the many grim ways of repulsing attacks: pouring boiling oil or molten lead down on enemy soldiers who stormed the Barbican.

The Barbican and St Florian's Gate (➤20) **were connected with a bridge.** It was called a "neck"; the main structure was surrounded by a moat, about 3.5 metres in depth. In order to prevent overgrowing with bull rushes, which could facilitate penetrating the defences by enemy troops, the bottom of the moat was covered with slabs of stone. The widest stretch of water, measuring over 20 m, used to be near today's ul. Basztowa. ■

Barbican (Barbakan)
- ✉ *ul. Basztowa*
- ☎ *+48 12 4229877*
- ⊙ *Apr–Oct: 10.30am–6pm daily*
- € *PLN 7 (PLN 5); combined ticket (Barbican and City Defence Walls): PLN 6 (PLN 4), valid for 7 days*

The rampart adjacent to St Florian's Gate resembles a small open-air gallery.

An 18th-century Kill Button

A shot fired by a Cracovian from the Barbican in defence of the city became a legend. However, the missile that mortally wounded an enemy soldier was allegedly not a bullet, but… a button.

In 1768, a Cracovian craftsman Marcin Oracewicz took a well-aimed rifle shot and killed the Russian commander. The incident happened during the uprising of the Bar Confederation, an alliance of Polish nobles against the expansionist politics of Russia and Stanislaus Augustus Poniatowski (👑 1764–1795), a Polish king considered to be a puppet in the hands of the Russian Empress Catherine the Great. It is believed that Oracewicz had run out of ammunition and shot a gilded button from off his garment instead. Before firing, he rubbed the missile against the painting of the Mother of God that can still be seen in the passageway of St Florian's Gate; unfortunately, there is no trace left of this miraculous event.

★ 5 St Florian's Gate

St Florian's Gate was the main entrance into the city, used by kings and parliament envoys on their way to Wawel Castle. It is now one of the icons of Cracow, admired by local residents and tourists alike.

Brama Floriańska is the only one of Cracow's eight gates that survives to this day. It was the city's main entry point, called the *Porta Gloriae* (Gate of Glory) for the fact that it was used by Polish monarchs. Built in stone at the turn of the 14th century, the building was given a brick top storey in the 15th century, when the Barbican was constructed. The Baroque cupola replaced the original one that was destroyed in the Swedish Deluge (1655–1660).

The tower's facade facing the Planty (➤ 53) features an eagle, the national emblem of Poland, as designed by Jan Matejko. The crown on the eagle's head is modelled on that of the Piasts, the first Polish royal dynasty. The bas-relief sculpture was made in 1882 by Zygmunt Langman, whose works can be seen in St Mary's Basilica (➤23) and Wawel Cathedral (➤46). On the opposite side, the wall facing ul. Floriańska (➤22) displays the figure of St Florian. Take a closer look at the portal, still bearing the traces of the guide bars for the so-called portcullis; the gate used to be closed with an iron grille.

Between 1901 and 1953, narrow-gauge electric trams ran through the Gate's passage. The opening of this line was not free of problems: it turned out that the vehicle which replaced horse-drawn trams was too high for the passage. The municipal authorities even considered the demolition of the tower itself. In the end, however, they opted for the less drastic solution of lowering the ground level in the passage. Nevertheless, trams needed to pull down pantographs when passing through the Gate.

Nearby, there are the remains of the ramparts and three towers, called Haberdashers' (Pasamoników), Joiners' (Stolarska) and Carpenters' (Ciesielska). Of the over 40 towers, they are the only preserved parts of the city's former fortifications. The first one is situated at the exit of ul. Szpitalna; the third one in the vicinity of ul. św. Jana. The names of the towers derive from the guilds that made sure they are in good condition. The construction of stone defences began in 1285 and ended in the early 14th century. In 1806, they were pulled down on the decision of Francis II, Holy Roman Emperor (♛ 1804–1835). Only the entreaties of Feliks Radwański, Professor of the Jagiellonian University and a politician, saved what is left to this day.

There is a tourist trail running along the preserved city defence walls. Tours cover the interiors of the towers, a walk on the wooden footbridge along the wall, and the chapel in St Florian's Gate. The external wall is hung with works by local painters and sculptors. It looks like an open-

St Florian's Gate is a fine remnant of Cracow's medieval fortifications.

air gallery. Although some Cracow inhabitants keep grumbling that so many pieces border on kitsch, this peculiar art fair is there to stay, greatly enhancing the local colour. ■

St Florian's Gate (Brama Floriańska)

✉ *corner of ul. Floriańska and ul. Pijarska*

☎ *+48 12 4211361*

⏱ *City Defence Walls (Mury Obronne) trail: Apr–Oct 10.30am–6pm daily*

€ *City Defence Walls: PLN 7 (PLN 5); combined ticket (Barbican and City Defence Walls): PLN 6 (PLN 4), valid for 7 days*

🍴 *Galicyjska restaurant, ul. Pijarska 9* 🔴🔴€

Ul. Floriańska is the city's most popular pedestrian precinct, full of restaurants and souvenir shops.

6 Ulica Floriańska

St Florian's Street, one of the oldest in Cracow, is special not only for its rich history and attractive burgher houses, but also up-to-the-minute bars, restaurants and shops. It is a place where the past meets the present.

The city's best-known street was laid out in the 13th century. Due to numerous conversion works and renovations, most of its historic tenements have lost their original character. However, there are many highlights left, such as Renaissance portals and figures on the facades. Ul. Floriańska is now the city's most popular place to take a stroll.

No. 45 accommodates Jama Michalika (➤ 197), one of the most famous artistic cafés. The name, which can be translated as Michalik's Den, derives from the fact that the café was first housed in one windowless room. It was founded in 1895 as Cukiernia Lwowska (Lviv Cake Shop) by Jan Apolinary Michalik, who had come from Lviv. The place soon became fashionable among the artistic and bohemian communities of Cracow. 1905 saw the establishment of a legendary literary revue called

Zielony Balonik (Little Green Balloon). Admission to the shows was free, but one needed a special invitation which was very hard to get. On New Year's Day, the café also staged puppet shows that satirised the vices of the bourgeoisie; the puppets are now displayed in the Red Room. Remember to take a look inside the Green Room to sense the spirit of the Young Poland (Młoda Polska), the modernist artistic movement. The room's Art Nouveau furniture, paintings and caricatures on the walls are illuminated by sunlight filtering though the stained-glass ceiling. The furnishings were designed by artists befriended by Michalik, who themselves spent a lot of time in the café.

No. 42 is now home to Hotel Polski. It used to be named after the emblem of the white eagle shown on the facade. Around the turn of the 20th century, this was a favourite meeting place of underground activists, as the city authorities had no interest in hotel guests. No. 14 houses another hotel, now called Hotel Pod Różą, whose eminent guests included Tsar Alexander I and Franz Liszt.

The 16th-century building at No. 41 was the birthplace of Jan Matejko (1838–1893). It was here that one of Poland's most renowned painters lived from childhood to adulthood. He worked here, and even redesigned the facade. In 1880, Matejko was visited by Emperor Franz Joseph (♛ 1848–1916). The historic building is now the artist's museum, displaying his paintings, drawings, personal belongings and documents, e.g. a school report, marriage and death certificates.

Nightlife enthusiasts will love ul. Floriańska. Its many bars, restaurants and discos welcome all-night clubbers. Amateurs of small atmospheric bars should try Święta Krowa at No. 16; look for its inconspicuous signboard on the right while walking towards the Main Square (➤ 26).

Ul. Floriańska is also a cluster of shops and boutiques. Here, you will find fashionable clothes, shoes, luxury watches and jewellery. Lower-priced souvenirs can be bought in stalls located in interior courtyards. Ornaments prevail, from Chinese beads to curious handmade earrings. ∎

St Florian's Street (Ulica Floriańska)

🏨 pubs: Łódź Kaliska ➤ 193, ul. Floriańska 15 🔴🔴€, Pauza ➤ 194, ul. Floriańska 18 🔴🔴€; bar: Święta Krowa, ul. Floriańska 16 🔴🔴€ restaurants: Chaczapuri ➤ 190, ul. Floriańska 26 🔴€€, Carlito, ul. Floriańska 28 🔴🔴🔴; café: Jama Michalika ➤ 197, ul. Floriańska 45 🔴🔴🔴

Jan Matejko Museum (Dom Jana Matejki)

✉ ul. Floriańska 41
☎ +48 12 4225926, +48 12 4230408
🕐 Tue–Sat 10am–6pm, Sun 10am–4pm
€ PLN 8 (PLN 4), free on Sun (permanent exhibitions)

★ 7 St Mary's Basilica

Every hour, the Heynal tune is played on the trumpet from the taller of the two towers at St Mary's Basilica. Come inside to see the famous altarpiece by Veit Stoss, one of the greatest pieces of artwork of the late Middle Ages.

A church dedicated to St Mary was built before 1257, the year that Cracow was granted municipal rights. The evidence is the fact that the building is situated diagonally in respect to the Main Square (➤ 26); the Magdeburg Law would require it to be placed perpendicular to the square. The remains of the first Romanesque temple of 1222 are now 2.5 m under ground level. Demolished in Tatar raids, it was rebuilt in brick and consecrated in 1320 as a three-nave Gothic hall church (with the central nave and side aisles of equal height). In the mid-14th century, a wealthy Cracovian merchant Mikołaj Wierzynek financed a new chancel, and the end of that same century saw the alteration of the main body of the church, based on a basilica plan (with the central nave higher than the side aisles). Chapels were added between 1435 and 1446. There have been no major architectural changes since then.

The most valuable item inside is the altarpiece by Veit Stoss. It took 12 years before it was completed in 1489. The result is an imposing (11 m wide and 13 m high) pentaptych, which is an altarpiece consisting of the central panel and two side wings, one of them foldable. It features about 200 figures, the tallest of which are almost 3 m in height. They were carved in the wood of 500-year-old

The Heynal Tune

A live trumpet signal, one of Cracow's trademarks, is played every hour from the taller tower of St Mary's Basilica. It stops abruptly halfway through…

Sounding the tune has become the city's tradition. It is believed to have served as a signal to open or close Cracow's gates in the distant past. Later, it was used to raise the alarm against fire and enemy attacks. Legend has it that, during the 1241 Tatar raid, the trumpeter atop the tower spotted the approaching invaders and tried to warn the city inhabitants by sounding the alarm. He was soon hit by an arrow shot from a Tatar bow, which is when the sound stopped. To commemorate this legendary event, the Heynal tune is interrupted halfway, allegedly on the very same note.

Since 1874, the tune has been played by professional firemen. They work 24-hour shifts in pairs atop the Heynal tower (*Hejnalica* in Polish). Each of the two firemen plays the tune 48 times during one shift (every single time, the Heynal is sounded four times, in all directions).

St Mary's Basilica has the Heynal tower (82 m) and the bell tower (69 m).

linden trees. The central panel depicts the scene of the Assumption (hence the full name of the church, the Basilica of the Assumption of Our Lady). St Mary is represented as a young woman at the moment of fainting, no pain showing on her serene face. She is supported by James the Greater, surrounded by the other Apostles. Representations are so vivid that one can diagnose the ailments suffered by Stoss' models, such as arthritis. For this masterpiece Stoss was paid the dizzying sum of 2,800 florins, an equivalent of the city's annual budget. During WWII, the altarpiece was looted and deposited in Nuremberg. After the war, it was brought back, renovated and reinstalled in 1957.

The walls were painted in polychrome by Jan Matejko. The highlight is the chancel vault, resembling the sky. The 84-metre-long and 28-metre-high central nave is mostly decorated with heraldic motifs, mainly guild coats of arms.

The facade is dominated by two towers of varying heights. According to a legend, they were built by two brothers. They competed to see whose structure would be taller. One brother stabbed the other to death when he saw that he was losing. Guilt-ridden, he confessed to the crime, climbed the tower and pierced his heart with the very same knife.

The church used to have a cemetery. Its borders are marked by stone slabs different in colour than those of the Main Square (➤26). It closed at the turn of the 18th century, when the Rakowice Cemetery (➤25) was founded. ∎

The wooden altarpiece carved by Veit Stoss is the pride of the Basilica.

Rakowice Cemetery

The necropolis was founded by the Austrian authorities. They had the city's church graveyards closed down, including the one by St Mary's Basilica.

At the turn of the 19th century, burying the dead in the vicinity of densely built-up residential areas was already known to be a possible cause of epidemic outbreaks. The first funeral in the then-suburban Rakowice Cemetery took place in 1803. Since then, over 400,000 people have been buried here.

The cemetery is the final resting place of some well-known Polish personages, such as Nobel Prize-winning poet Wisława Szymborska (1923–2012). Among the most original tomb monuments is the one that commemorates visual artist Tadeusz Kantor (1915–1990): a boy sitting at a school bench next to a bending cross, like in a scene from Kantor's world-famous theatre piece, *Dead Class* (1975). The tombstone of Piotr Skrzynecki (1930–1997), the founder of the Piwnica pod Baranami (➤ 207), features a replica of the metal bell that he used to start the shows.

Along the axis of the main alley are located the tombs of historical painters Jan Matejko (1838–1893) and Wojciech Kossak (1856–1942). Other famous people buried here include actress Helena Modrzejewska (1840–1909), known as Modjeska in America where she starred after leaving Cracow, and philosopher Roman Ingarden (1893–1970), a student of Husserl and a friend of Edith Stein.

Rakowice Cemetery (Cmentarz Rakowicki)
✉ *main entrance from ul. Rakowicka*
🕐 *Apr–Sept 7am–8pm, Oct–Mar 7am–6pm*
🚌 *124, 184, 424 (Cmentarz Rakowicki)*
🚊 *2 (Cmentarz Rakowicki)*

St Mary's Basilica (Bazylika Mariacka)
✉ *pl. Mariacki 5*
@ *www.mariacki.com*
🕐 *visiting (entry through the side doors):
Mon–Sat 11.30am–6pm, Sun 2pm–6pm;
tower: May–Aug Tue, Thu, Sat 9am–11.30am, 1pm–5.30pm;*
prayer (free entry through the main doors): 6.30am–6.30pm
€ *visiting: PLN 6 (PLN 3); tower: PLN 5 (PLN 3)*
ℹ *Veit Stoss' altarpiece is open 11.50am–6pm. Try to be there at 11.50am to see the unfolding of the panels.*

★ 8 Main Square

Cracow's Main Square was the largest, and – according to some sources – also the finest square of medieval Europe. Laid out on the plan of a square with an edge of 200 m, it is the size of five football pitches.

Poet Adam Mickiewicz proudly inspects the Main Square from his pedestal.

Cracow's Main Square is the place that never sleeps. Bustling with activity in the daytime – teeming with florists and street artists who demonstrate their many talents – it is vibrant with life at night as well: local bars and discos offer endless opportunities for all-night partying, and the finely illuminated historic monuments attract photo enthusiasts. Before setting off on a pub crawl, Cracovians meet by the 1898 statue of the 19th-century poet Adam Mickiewicz. The monument is one of the city's most recognisable sights.

Today, the best view of the Main Square is from the side of ul. Szewska; you will see the Sukiennice (➤28), the

The Underground Trail

There is more to Cracow's Main Square than meets the eye. Now everyone can discover its secrets walking along a tourist trail – 4 metres underground.

On the Underground Tour, you will learn that the original 12th-century settlement was founded on the site of an old burial ground. A lot of ancient tombs have been found, including "vampire" ones where corpses were arranged so that the dead could not rise (they were tightly bound, or the heads were chopped off and placed at their feet). You can also trace the gradual changes of the square's architecture and usage. The trail runs partly among the remainders of the original 13th- and 14th-century walls as well as merchants' stands; the pavement level was lower by several metres back then. This underground museum is one of the most up-to-date in Poland with its 600 3D digital reconstructions, multimedia presentations, touchscreens and holograms.

"Following the traces of the European identity of Cracow" („Śladem europejskiej tożsamości Krakowa")

✉ *Rynek Główny 1 (entrance through the Sukiennice)*

☎ *+48 12 4265002, +48 12 4265004*

🕐 *Apr–Oct Mon 10am–8pm, Tue 10am–4pm, Wed–Sun 10am–10pm, Nov–Mar Tue 10am–4pm, Wed–Mon 10am–8pm; closed on the 1st Tue of the month*

€ *PLN 17 (PLN 14), free on Tue*

ℹ *audio guide (in English, German, French, etc.): PLN 5; last admission 60 minutes before closing time*

Town Hall Tower (➤30), St Mary's Basilica (➤23) – and the inevitable pigeons. Although the effect these birds have on houses and pavements is a thorn in the side of local residents, they have

The inconspicuous Romanesque St Adalbert's Church is as old as the Main Square itself.

become a trademark, and are said to be enchanted knights.

Laid out on the occasion of the city foundation in 1257, the Main Square served as a marketplace right up to the 19th century. Salt, fish, coal, bread, and barrels, among other items, were sold here. At the end of the 18th century, there were already more than 300 stands. The square witnessed many historic events. It was here that Albert, Duke of Prussia and the last Grand Master of the Teutonic Knights, paid homage to Polish king Sigismund I (♛ 1506–1548) in 1525. Two centuries later, Tadeusz Kościuszko took an oath to liberate the Polish nation and began an uprising against Russia and Prussia, the countries that participated in the Second Partition of Poland. The uprising failed, which resulted in the Third Partition of 1795 and the loss of the country's independence for 123 years.

Back in the Middle Ages, the Main Square was where justice was administered to criminals. Minor offences were punishable by caging or shaving one's head. More serious misdemeanours entailed bodily mutilation (e.g. thieves had their hands cut off). The gravest crimes resulted in a death sentence, the fact emphasised by the metal knife by the Sukiennice's middle exit on the side of the Mickiewicz statue and St Mary's Basilica. Some say, though, that this was the murder weapon of the brothers that built the Basilica's towers.

One cannot miss St Adalbert's Church (Kościół św. Wojciecha). This small Romanesque building at the exit of ul. Grodzka was erected at the turn of the 12th century on the site of the earlier wooden structure. Although remodelled in the Baroque style, the church has kept one of its Romanesque windows and the entrance portal. Inside, see the Gothic crucifix on the rood screen (where the nave meets the chancel). ■

Main Square (Rynek Główny)

🍴 restaurants: *Szara* ➤ 190, *Rynek Główny 6* 🔴🔴🔴; *Wesele* ➤ 184, *Rynek Główny 10* 🔴🔴🔴; *Wierzynek* ➤ 184, *Rynek Główny 15* 🔴🔴🔴; *Hawełka* ➤ 181, *Rynek Główny 34* 🔴🔴🔴; *Wedel Chocolate Lounge* ➤ 199, *Rynek Główny 46* 🔴🔴🔴; *Chłopskie Jadło restaurant* ➤ 180, *ul. św. Jana 3* 🔴🔴🔵; *Cafe Camelot* ➤ 196, *ul. św. Tomasza 17* 🔴🔴🔴

The characteristic arcades of the Sukiennice date from the 19th-century conversion.

★ 9 Sukiennice

The appearance of the Drapers' Hall has changed considerably, yet its commercial character remains. The place is still crowded and humming with activity, as it did centuries ago, but instead of fabrics it now sells knick-knacks and souvenirs.

The name of one of Cracow's most recognisable buildings derives from the draperies that were once sold here. Back in the Middle Ages, elegant fabrics were a luxury product much in demand. Drapers were considered members of the trading elite. They put their goods up for sale in a special market hall while dealers in ordinary merchandise had to trade in the open all around the Main Square.

Originally, the Sukiennice consisted of two rows of stone stalls. Built at the time of the city foundation, they formed a sort of a little narrow street at the very heart of the square. In the 14th century, Casimir the Great (♛ 1333–1370) – the king famous for commissioning brick fortifications throughout the country – had the Sukiennice rebuilt. The two rows of stalls were inte-

grated into one building, with the alley roofed over. The Gothic vestiges of that modernisation can still be seen. The most characteristic feature are the pointed-arch arcades, which have served as the hall's entrances for 600 years.

The Sukiennice building was damaged in the fire of 1555; the reconstruction involved adding the upper floor and the attic (an ornamental wall above the cornice). It features mascarons, weird faces of chimeras made up of human and animal traits. The loggias above the entrances also date from that time.

For many years, the Renaissance splendour of the building was eclipsed because of outside stalls and stands which were chaotically integrated in the structure. When the Sukiennice needed a complete refurbishment in the 19th

The market hall is still flourishing; the shine of the trinkets alone can make one dizzy.

The Sukiennice Gallery

It was not in the capital city of Warsaw, or in Cracow's Wawel Castle, but in the Sukiennice that the first Polish national museum was established.

In 1879, Józef Ignacy Kraszewski, a renowned Polish writer, celebrated the 50th anniversary of his artistic career. On this grand occasion, painter Henryk Siemiradzki gave to the city one of his monumental paintings, *Nero's Torches* (*Pochodnie Nerona*, 27 m^2). Other artists followed suit. The art works that were thus collected "for the nation" were the beginning of the National Museum, then located on the Sukiennice's first floor.

Today, the hall is home to one of the branches of Cracow's National Museum (➤151), the Gallery of 19th-century Polish Art. 2010 saw the completion of a major refurbishment. The gallery displays 195 paintings and 19 sculptures. The multimedia room transports visitors into the 19th century, and touch panels present the story of the Sukiennice, the museum, and the collection.

National Museum, the Sukiennice branch (Muzeum Narodowe – Sukiennice)
🕐 *Tue–Sat 10am–8pm, Sun 10am–6pm*
💶 *PLN 12 (PLN 6)*
ℹ️ *audio guides in English, German, Russian and Polish: PLN 5*

century, the task was entrusted to an architect recommended by the famous historical painter Jan Matejko. The renovation of the Sukiennice and restoring the Main Square as the city's visual showpiece involved pulling the stands down and lining the walls with arcades. Wooden stalls were installed inside. The Sukiennice has changed very little since then.

The place is still used for commerce. The merchandise consists mostly of Cra-cow souvenirs and regional products. On offer are jewellery and items made from leather and wood. Come inside and try to imagine what the place looked like 100, 400 or 700 years ago. ∎

Drapers' Hall (Sukiennice)
✉️ *Rynek Główny 1*
🍴 *Noworolski café ➤ 198, Rynek Główny 1 (Sukiennice) 🔴🔴🔴; Cafe Sukiennice restaurant, Rynek Główny 1-3 🔴🔴 ☺*

🔟 Town Hall Tower

Cracow boasts its own leaning tower, the remnant of the old Town Hall. It leans at half a metre from the vertical and features a viewing platform as well as a clock famous for its unparalleled accuracy.

The tower is the only surviving structure of the 14th-century Town Hall.

The **70-metre-tall tower that rises in the Main Square** (➤ 26) **is what remains of the old Town Hall,** built at the beginning of the 14th century. The first written mention of the tower dates back to 1383. The Town Hall was adjoined by municipal granaries, pulled down once they were on the verge of collapsing. During the works, the structure of the Town Hall itself was damaged, which resulted in its final demolition in 1820.

The tower entrance is guarded by two lions. These 19th-century statues were brought here from a palace in Pławowice to replace the original ones, worn out by the rains. The ground floor hall boasts Europe's unique assemblage of house marks – medieval signatures by masons who worked on the Town Hall Tower, dating from 1444. There are as many as 14 house marks, and it is this impressive number that makes them particularly rare and valuable.

The tower has an extremely accurate clock. It is controlled by radio signals emitted by the Mainflingen transmitter, set by an atomic clock that is only one second slow in one million years. Those who climb up to the last visitor-accessible floor can take a closer look at the tower clockwork. You can also observe the Main Square from up here, though only through a glazed window.

The Town Hall basement has served a number of purposes. Some of the rooms were home to a famous cellar called Piwnica Świdnicka. The name derives from the fact that the beer served here was bought from members of the Świdnica town council. The cellar was reportedly frequented by women of questionable virtue. An adjacent room, tellingly called *tortoria*, belonged to the torturer who extracted testimonies from prisoners detained in the Town Hall's dungeon. He usually succeeded, aided by a whole arsenal of ingenious instruments of torture.

It is possible and even recommended to go down to the tower's basement via a separate entrance to have a coffee or lunch in a small atmospheric restaurant by a branch of the People's Theatre (➤130, ➤202). Called Scena pod Ratuszem, it holds evening performances of the world's classics and contemporary works in an original setting of old mighty walls – an experience that is not easily forgotten. ∎

Town Hall Tower (Wieża Ratuszowa)
✉ *Rynek Główny 1*
☎ *+48 12 6192318*
🕑 *Apr–Oct 10.30am–6pm daily*
€ *PLN 7 (PLN 5)*
🍴 *Ratuszowa restaurant on site* 🔴🔴 €

🔢 Dominican Basilica

The gloomy-looking church, devoted to the Holy Trinity, impresses with its lofty silhouette and an austere interior. Within the Gothic walls, the locals look for words of wisdom from Dominican friars, the so-called "Order of Preachers."

Every Sunday, homilies delivered by the Dominicans attract crowds of Cracovians. The noon Mass has been unremittingly popular for many years. However, it is the Mass at 8.20pm that is attended by the greatest number of believers. Students come here even from the furthest corners of the city. If you arrive at the last minute, there will be no seats left and you will have to settle for a standing place at the very back of the church.

The Order of Preachers has been present in Cracow since 1222. Named after the founder, St Dominic, the friars came to the city together with St Hyacinth. Iwo Odrowąż, the bishop of Cracow, offered them a small church. After it was destroyed by the Tatars in 1241, the Dominicans began the construction of a Gothic hall church. This building was converted many times throughout the centuries. The central nave was already made higher in the second half of the 14th century, which gave the church its present basilica form. In the Renaissance and Baroque periods, side chapels were added and the décor was changed.

The great fire of 1850 ravaged the interior almost completely. Nave vaults and the supporting pillars collapsed. Only some chapels survived. The church and the adjoining monastery fell into such disrepair that it was suggested to the Dominicans that they move. They

The interior of the Dominican Basilica is crowned with Gothic vaults.

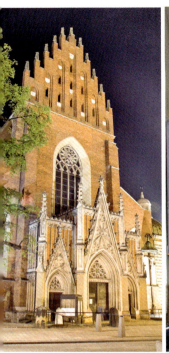

The cloisters of the Dominican Basilica have witnessed 800 years of history.

decided to stay and rebuild their church; it was consecrated again in 1884.

The interior harmonises with the lofty form. Since the last fire, the décor has been kept very modest. The walls and pillars that support 22-metre-high vaults are not covered with any paintings. The neo-Gothic altar of the Holy Trinity, the choir stalls and confessionals date from the 19th century.

The oldest visitor-accessible part of the monastery are the cloisters. The northern stone wing features vestiges of the original church, built before 1222. The site is now a refectory. The stone epitaphs set in the cloister walls are worth a look; the oldest come from the 14th century. There is also an entrance to the chapter house, where the friars hold various meetings and conferences.

The monastic cell of St Hyacinth has been replaced with his chapel. If you want to visit it, climb the staircase to the left of the nave. The chapel is the final resting place of the saint, canonised in 1594; he became the patron of the Polish Dominican Province. The sarcophagus with the statues of angels, carved at the turn of the 18th century, is the work of sculptor Baldassare Fontana.

The altar of the Rosary Chapel (Kaplica Różańcowa) features a replica painting of Our Lady of the Snow from the Santa Maria Maggiore Basilica in Rome. In 1921, Archbishop Adam Sapieha crowned the miraculous image with Papal crowns. The mother and one of the brothers of King John III Sobieski (♕ 1674–1696) are buried in the crypt. The 19th-century polychrome paintings on the ceiling depict the mysteries of the rosary. ■

Dominican Basilica (Bazylika Dominikanów)
- ✉ *ul. Stolarska 12*
- @ *www.krakow.dominikanie.pl*
- ⏱ *Mon–Fri 6.30am–7.30pm, Sun 6am–9.30pm*
- 🍴 *Siesta Cafe* ➤ 198, *ul. Stolarska 6* 🔴🔴 €

★ 12 Franciscan Basilica

Polychromes and stained glass windows by famous artist Stanisław Wyspiański, a faithful copy of the Turin Shroud, the relics of Blessed Aniela Salawa: the Gothic walls of the Franciscan monastery hold vestiges of the last 800 years.

The rainbow-coloured polychromes and golden stars in the ceiling of the basilica were painted by Stanisław Wyspiański in 1895. The right side of the chancel shows Our Lady with child, wearing traditional Cracovian attire, and the Charity – two cuddling girls surrounded by irises. Floral motifs characterise Wyspiański's work, and abound on the basilica's walls as well. Lilies, nasturtiums, pansies, field poppies ornament a large part of the nave, stressing the Franciscan love of nature. The founder of the order, St Francis of Assisi, is even the patron saint of ecology.

Pope's Window

The yellow-painted building opposite the main entrance of the Franciscan Basilica is the Cracow Archbishop's Palace. It features the best-known window in Poland.

Pope John Paul II appeared in the window above the entrance gate to talk to young people, assembled below, on every visit to Poland between 1979 and 2002. Such meetings at ul. Franciszkańska 3 were never part of the official schedule, but both sides could always count on them. The youth used to wait for hours for John Paul II to open the window and talk to them. During these evening get-togethers, the Pope talked not only about important issues, but also made jokes and reminisced about his youth.

The window now usually displays a large photo of John Paul II. Young people gather here to pray together on the anniversary of Pope's death (April 2nd). The pavement and walls opposite the window are lined then with long rows of cemetery lights.

The back wall of the basilica boasts the best-known and the largest stained glass window by Wyspiański, entitled *God the Father – Become!* This dynamic depiction of the world's creation has a personal note to it: the model for the figure of God was the painter's uncle. Wyspiański's stained glass windows can also be found around the altar. Their symbolic representation of the power of the elements is quite remarkable. The lilies, nasturtiums and water lilies stand

John Paul II used to speak to Cracovians from a window in Archbishop's Palace.

33

The Franciscan Basilica is worth a visit for its impressive decoration.

for water, while the flame trees and red flowers opposite signify fire.

The pride of the basilica is a faithful copy of the Turin Shroud. The replica of the linen cloth with the image of a man commonly identified as Jesus is displayed on the altar of the 15th-century Passion Chapel (Kaplica Męki Pańskiej). After the fire of 1655, the chapel lost its original Gothic décor. The present Baroque-style interior is adorned with 14 *Via Dolorosa* paintings by Józef Mehoffer. A small white altar under the window in the north wall holds the relics of Blessed Aniela Salawa (1881–1922), a Franciscan nun and mystic beatified by John Paul II.

The Franciscan monastery in Cracow is the only one in Poland that has continued to exist ever since its foundation. The friars came to settle here in 1237. The first Provincial Chapter meeting took place in 1249, which is believed

to be the date of the church consecration. The building has undergone several alterations and burnt down as many as four times. When Nazi occupiers closed down Wawel Cathedral during WWII, it was in the Franciscan Basilica that the bishops of Cracow celebrated the Eucharist. John Paul II visited the basilica twice during his pontificate.

The monastery is also home to the Archconfraternity of the Lord's Passion (Arcybractwo Męki Pańskiej), founded in 1595. Its motto is a chanted refrain, *Memento homo mori* ("Remember, man, about death"). The members wear black pointed hoods. Before the city became part of the Austrian partition in 1796, every Holy Thursday saw the Archconfraternity ransoming debtors from prison and pleading with the monarch or the city authorities to pardon one criminal sentenced to death. The Archconfraternity members have included both clerics and laymen; the black robes and hoods with only two slits for eyes continue to ensure anonymity. The hooded medieval-looking figures can be seen during services that they celebrate on Lent Fridays at 5pm in the Passion Chapel. Their procession is a memorable sight. Even though the membership is still largely anonymous, it is well known that a famous Polish photographer, Adam Bujak, is part of the Archconfraternity. ■

Franciscan Basilica
(Bazylika Franciszkanów)
✉ *pl. Wszystkich Świętych 5*
@ *www.franciszkanska.pl*
⏱ *Mon–Sun 6am–7.45pm, visiting (no guided tours are offered): Mon–Fri 9.45am–4.15pm, Sunday and holidays 1.15pm–4.15pm*
🍴 *Polakowski self-service restaurant ➤ 182, pl. Wszystkich Świętych 10* ● ● ●

The pride of the Franciscan Basilica is a fine stained glass window depicting God.

13 SS Peter and Paul's Church

The oldest Baroque church in Cracow has an additional tourist attraction: it stages an interesting experiment that confirms the Copernican theory of the rotation of the Earth.

Come to SS Peter and Paul's Church to see with your own eyes proof that the Earth rotates on its axis. Every Thursday before noon, you can witness an experiment conducted with the help of the so-called Foucault Pendulum. A 25-kilo bob, suspended on a 47-metre-long rope, is set in a pendulum swing. It moves at first along the line that is marked on the floor. However, since the floor under the pendulum moves together with the Earth, the path of the swinging bob skews at a rate of 1 degree per 6 minutes. The Coriolis force that works on the mechanism as a result of the Earth's rotation makes the bob move in a curving pattern, which is visualised by a rosette-like figure "drawn" by the pendulum.

The Jesuits came to Cracow in 1579. They already enjoyed a reputa-

tion for their pastoral and educational activities. The two churches that they used after settling down in the city soon turned out to be too small. A square by ul. Grodzka was picked out as the ideal location for a new church that would surpass the surrounding architecture with its splendour and modern design. The foundation stone was laid in 1597, and the completed building was consecrated in 1635.

The Jesuit episode of SS Peter and Paul's Church did not last long, and its history took a dramatic turn. In 1773, Pope Clement XIV suppressed the order by a bull entitled *Dominus ac Redemptor* (the Society of Jesus survived in Russia; it was reinstated all through the Catholic Church in 1814). The Jesuits left the building that later changed hands many times and gradually fell into decline.

The facade of SS Peter and Paul's Church is modelled on Il Gesù Church in Rome. The square in front of the building features a statue of Piotr Skarga, a Jesuit preacher.

Between 1809 and 1815, it was used by the Orthodox Church; since 1824, it has belonged to a Catholic parish.

In front of the church entrance there is a stone wall with the figures of the twelve apostles. These are the modern replicas of the original statues of 1723, which were damaged by acid rain. The facade is modelled on Il Gesù Church in Rome. The portal is topped with the Jesuit emblem and, above, the coat of arms of King Sigismund III Vasa (♛ 1587–1632), the founder of the church. The niches hold saint figures.

The white-painted interior seems ascetic at first sight, but the colour only adds to its monumental character. Take a look at the 1735 altar with a painting that depicts Christ giving the keys to St Peter. The niches of the dome shelter the figures of the Four Evangelists.

The crypt holds the remains of Piotr Skarga, a 16th-century Jesuit preacher and political activist. It was thanks to his endeavours that Sigismund III Vasa agreed to finance the church construction in the first place. The monarch thought so highly of Skarga's rhetorical skills and intellect that the Jesuit was appointed to be the court preacher for 24 years. His *Sejm Sermons* (*Kazania sejmowe*), a warning to the Polish Parliament against the fall of the state, became particularly popular for their relevance at the turn of the 19th century – the time of the Partitions of Poland. ■

SS Peter and Paul's Church
(Kościół św. św. Apostołów Piotra i Pawła)

✉ *ul. Grodzka 52a*

@ *www.apostolowie.pl*

🕐 *Mon–Fri 9am–7pm, Sat 9am–5.30pm, Sun 1.30pm–5.30pm*

€ *free, crypts and Foucault Pendulum demonstrations: a voluntary donation*

🍴 *restaurants: Balaton ➤ 189, ul. Grodzka 37 €€€, Miód Malina ➤ 182, ul. Grodzka 40 €€€; milk bar: Pod Temidą, ul. Grodzka 43 €€€; pizzeria: Trzy Papryczki ➤ 189, ul. Poselska 17 €€€*

ℹ️ *Foucault Pendulum demonstrations: Thu 10am, 11am, noon; services: Mon–Sat at 7am, 6pm, Sun and holidays at 8am, 9.30am, 11am, 12.30pm, 6pm*

14 St Andrew's Church

Anyone who crosses the threshold of this centuries' old church will be astonished by the great contrast between the austere and simple Romanesque silhouette and its lavish Baroque interior.

This is one of Cracow's oldest churches and a fine example of Romanesque architecture. It was originally built in the years 1079–1098, but the transept and the towers most probably date from the 12th century. The most eye-catching features are the small windows that were characteristic of the epoch. The defensive function of the building is best manifested in the thickness of its white stone walls (up to 1.6 m). They were strong enough to protect the city inhabitants from Tatar invaders in 1241.

The sumptuous interior is the exact opposite of its plain Romanesque facade. It was given its Baroque-style decoration at the turn of the 18th century, when it gained its stucco ornaments created by an Italian stuccoer, Baldassare Fontana, and the *Last Judgement* polychrome by a Swedish painter, Carl Dankwart. The black marble main altarpiece depicts Blessed Salomea. The highlight is a curious pulpit in the shape of a boat, dating from the third quarter of the 18th century. You can see a similar structure in the Corpus Christi Basilica (➤ 90) in Kazimierz.

For over 700 years, St Andrew's Church has remained in the care of the Order of Saint Claire. King Vladislaus the Short entrusted the church to the Poor Claires in 1320, and a few years later the living quarters were built in the direct vicinity. Sisters of Saint Claire live in enclosed convents, which means that they do not leave their residence and are allowed to meet people from the outside world only in exceptional circumstances. They devote their lives to prayer and contemplation. ■

The convent of St Claire by St Andrew's Church has a strict monastic rule.

St Andrew's Church (Kościół św. Andrzeja)
✉ *ul. Grodzka 56*
⏱ *before services*
ℹ *services: Mon–Sat 7am, Sun 7am, 10am*

15 Evangelical-Lutheran Church of St Martin

The 17th-century Baroque Church of St Martin is the only Evangelical-Lutheran place of worship in Cracow. The city's Protestant parish has existed since 1557.

In 1517, Martin Luther posted his *Ninety-Five Theses* on the door of a Wittenberg church in an attempt to reform Catholicism. Among others, he taught the doctrine of justification which says that man can be saved not by good works, but by faith in Jesus and God's grace. Thus Luther started the Reformation movement in Europe, which led to divisions within Christianity.

The first Lutheran service in Cracow was celebrated in 1557. That event marked the beginning of Cracow's Protestant congregation, which gathered in many different places, also outside the city. It was only in 1816, at the time of a partially autonomous city-state called the Free City of Cracow (Wolne Miasto Kraków), that Reformed Protestants were granted a church in ul. Grodzka, which had stood empty since Discalced Carmelite nuns had left it in 1787.

St Martin's Church was built between 1637 and 1640. It stands on the site of the old 12th-century temple. The Baroque-style facade is similar to the one of the nearby SS Peter and Paul's Church (➤35). The most important element of the white-painted interior is the altar in the form of a Communion table. The painting above dates from the end of the 19th century and depicts the scene of Christ calming a storm. The painter was Henryk Siemiradzki, who also created the impressive curtain of the Juliusz Słowacki Theatre (➤54, ➤203). The Gothic crucifix above the painting (c. 1370) is very valuable as well. ∎

St Martin's Church (Kościół św. Marcina)
✉ ul. Grodzka 58
@ www.ewangelicy.krakow.pl
⏱ Sun before the 10am service

16 Ulica Kanonicza

It is believed to be the oldest street in Cracow. The name derives from the canons of the Cracow Chapter who served in Wawel Cathedral. They settled at the foot of Wawel Hill and built their houses here from the latter 14th century.

Around the turn of the 19th century, under Austrian rule, No. 1 housed the Investigation Office (Inkwizytoriat): a law court and a prison. It is now home to the Architecture Faculty of the Cracow University of Technology; you can also grab a bite in Literacka café. A stone window on the ground floor of No. 7, which does not fit in the Gothic and Renaissance styles of the facade, is a medieval relic. It has survived since the

original construction in the latter 14th century. Another remarkable feature is the Gothic metal door to La Campana restaurant, a replica of the original 16th-century structure. It was once the entrance to a café which was a gathering place of the Fraternity of Wawel Bell-Ringers (Bractwo Dzwonników Wawelskich). The team members came here after work and each of them drank from his own beer mug, numbered for clarity.

The future John Paul II lived in ul. Kanonicza in the 1950's (Wawel ➤ 40 in the background).

It is said that, in order to chime the best-known Polish bell called Zygmunt (13 tonnes), as many as 12 bell ringers need to pull the ropes simultaneously.

No. 16 once lodged Nicholas Copernicus, and (centuries later) Prince Charles of Wales and American President George W. Bush. It is now a luxurious hotel, named after Copernicus.

Karol Wojtyła, the future Pope John Paul II, lived in the so-called St Stanislaus House (Dom św. Stanisława) at No. 19 in the years 1952–1958. When he was made a bishop, Wojtyła moved to the Dean's House (Dom Dziekański) at No. 21. Nos. 19 and 21 now accommodate the Archdiocesan Museum (Muzeum Archidiecezjalne) with Wojtyła's fully-furnished room and a collection of 400 mementoes of the late Pope, as well as valuable paintings, sculptures and liturgical vessels. The arcaded courtyard with a Baroque statue of St Stanislaus in the centre is also worth a look.

At the end of the 14th century, the corner building at No. 25 housed royal baths. They were supplied with water from the Rudawa River, which then flowed along today's ul. Podzamcze. The building was altered by Wawel canons, its subsequent owners. From 1453, it was home to Jan Długosz, a Polish chronicler; that is why it is called the Długosz House. Another famous person who lived in the building was writer and painter Stanisław Wyspiański; his father, a sculptor, had his studio here in the latter 19th century. The place now accommodates the Rector's Office of the Pontifical University of John Paul II. ∎

Ulica Kanonicza

🍴 *Literacka café, ul. Kanonicza 1 😊😊 €; La Campana restaurant ➤ 188, ul. Kanonicza 7 😊😊😊; Bona. Książka i Kawa café and cultural centre ➤ 196, ul. Kanonicza 11 😊😊 €*

John Paul II Archdiocesan Museum (Muzeum Archidiecezjalne Kardynała Karola Wojtyły)

✉ *ul. Kanonicza 19–21*
☎ *+48 12 4218963*
@ *www.muzeumkra.diecezja.pl*
🕐 *Tue–Fri 10am–4pm, Sat–Sun 10am–3pm*
€ *PLN 5 (PLN 3)*

Wawel Hill

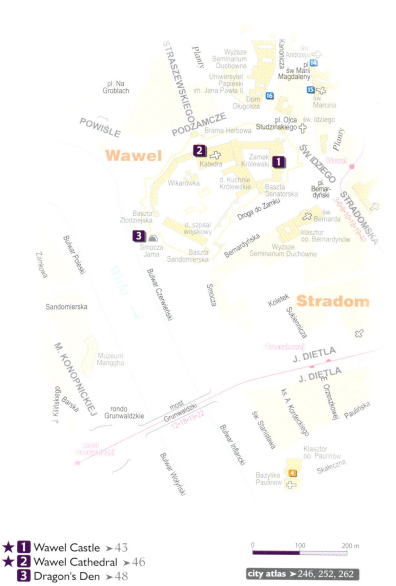

0   100   200 m

city atlas ➤246, 252, 262

The Heart of Cracow

Wawel Hill is the icon of Cracow and the symbol of the Polish nationhood. Wawel Castle used to be the seat of kings, and Wawel Cathedral was the site of their coronations and burials.

The reflection of the illuminated Wawel Castle in the Vistula is a sight to remember.

Wawel is the name of the hill that rises 25 metres above the waters of the Vistula River, flowing at its foot. The hill was formed about 150 million years ago, when the earth was still populated by dinosaurs. It consists of calcareous rock, vulnerable to erosion. The karst processes (dissolution and washing out of carbonate rock by water) led to the creation of one of Poland's best-known caves: the Dragon's Den (➤48). Every Polish child has probably heard the legend of the Wawel dragon that lived there, spreading terror among the local population.

The vestiges of the original settlement on the hill date from the Paleolithic Age. Surrounded by marshes and overflow areas, it was a perfect site for a hamlet. The spot was found convenient by the Slavs, who inhabited the hill from the 7th century. Wawel became the political centre of the Vistulans' state, and then kept its significance under the first Polish royal dynasty, the Piasts. The dynasty was represented, for example, by Duke Mieszko I (c. 922–992), the first Polish ruler to be baptised thus starting the Christianisation of his people, and Boleslaus the Valiant (♔ 992–1025) – the first Polish king, crowned in 1025. It was during the Piasts' reign that Wawel Castle (➤43) became one of the state's most important centres of power, and was even named the capital of the kingdom under Casimir the Restorer (♔ 1034 and c. 1040–1058).

From the 14th century, Wawel hosted the coronations of successive rulers. Crowning ceremonies took place in Wawel Cathedral (➤46), one of Poland's best-known churches. Royal coronations and funerals continued to be held here even after Sigismund III Vasa (♔ 1587–1632) moved the royal seat to Warsaw in 1596.

The grand Gothic Wawel Cathedral (➤ 46) is over 600 years old.

Manggha Centre of Japanese Art and Technology

The museum, founded in 1994 by film director Andrzej Wajda and his wife Krystyna Zachwatowicz, has already become an integral feature of the city's landscape – the cultural one as well. Its location affords a fine view of Wawel Hill.

The centre holds cyclical temporary exhibitions on Japanese and Asian art and culture, as well as presentations of artistic works influenced by Eastern aesthetics. The museum's mission is not only to display but also to interest and teach, hence the many demonstrations, lectures and workshops (e.g. in the art of *ikebana*), and Japanese language courses.

The building, conspicuous from Wawel Hill, was designed by Japanese architect Arata Isozaki so as to harmonise with the surroundings. The wavy contours, inspired by a Hokusai woodcut of a boat on waves, fit with the Vistula River that separates the centre from the castle.

Manggha Centre of Japanese Art and Technology (Muzeum Sztuki i Techniki Japońskiej Manggha)

✉ *ul. M. Konopnickiej 26*
☎ *+48 12 2672703,*
  +48 12 2673753
@ *www.manggha.krakow.pl*
🕐 *Tue–Sun 10am–6pm*
€ *PLN 15 (PLN 10), free on Tue*
ℹ *guided tours in English, German, Japanese (PLN 100)*

Wawel was also used as a headquarters by Cracow's occupiers. After Poland lost its independence, Austrian forces were stationed here until 1911 (with breaks). The castle served as barracks, and the damage done to the historic building came to light only after the soldiers had left. A decision to renovate the practically devastated castle was taken. The works unearthed remnants such as the Rotunda of the Blessed Virgin Mary (see: The Lost Wawel ➤ 45). In September 1939, when the castle renovation was almost completed, Cracow came under the Nazi rule. Wawel was taken over as the office for the Governor-General Hans Frank, who resided here up to his flight from the approaching Red Army in 1945.

Today, Wawel Hill is a popular walking destination for Cracovians and tourists alike, with couples, lovers, and families with kids. It affords a magnificent view over Cracow and the Vistula Boulevards, and hosts many cultural events. Every year, the castle courtyard becomes a venue for summer opera festivals and other concerts. ∎

You should allocate at least half a day to see most of what Wawel Hill has to offer; a visit to one exhibition alone takes about 1 hour. A must-see is Wawel Cathedral (➤ 46): the Royal Tombs make a memorable impression. Other interesting places worth visiting include the State Rooms and the Royal Private Apartments in Wawel Castle (➤43). If you run out of time, you can skip the Lost Wawel (➤45), an exhibition that mainly targets history enthusiasts. The Dragon's Den can be visited on the way out from the castle if you choose the exit through the cave, not the main gate.

Access by public transport:

1-3

🚋 3, 6, 8, 10, 18, 19, 40 (Wawel)

🍴 Na Wawelu restaurant, ul. Wzgórze Wawelskie 9 ●●●; Kompania Kuflowa bar ➤ 182, ul. św. Gertrudy 26–29 ●● ♿

★ **1** Wawel Castle

One of Poland's greatest Renaissance-style courtyards, unique collections of Arras tapestries, sabres and armour, state rooms and private royal apartments… Wawel Royal Castle boasts many visitor attractions.

Stone buildings were originally erected on Wawel Hill by the first Polish rulers, the Piasts, at the turn of the 11th century. They included a ducal seat – the so-called *palatium* – and the Rotunda of the Blessed Virgin Mary (see: The Lost Wawel ➤45). Their vestiges can still be seen today. The decades up to the 16th century saw many alterations to the castle. Fortifications, towers and other buildings were constructed around the courtyard. The Gothic stronghold survived until 1499, when it burnt down in a great fire.

In the **Royal Private Apartments (Prywatne Apartamenty Królewskie), you can see how the Polish monarchs used to live.** That part of the castle also had guest apartments and retinue quarters. The so-called Hen's Foot Tower (Kurza Stopka), an intriguing 14th-century structure, once held the bedroom of King Sigismund the Old (👑 1506–1548). Also Ignacy Mościcki, the President of Poland in the years 1926–1939, stayed in the tower's rooms. Remember to stop at one of the windows to take in a magnificent view over Cracow.

The best-known hall of the State Rooms (Reprezentacyjne Komnaty Królewskie) is the Envoys' Room (Sala Poselska). Its wooden coffer ceiling is adorned with 30 carved human heads. The sculptures date from the 16th century, when there were as many as 194 of them. Crane your neck and try to find the

The Castle Courtyard

The Arcaded Courtyard is the most recognisable sight of Wawel Castle.

The 16th-century alteration changed the castle into a Renaissance residence. The works were supervised by Italian architects, Bartolommeo Berrecci among others. The finest and highest rooms and chambers are located on the castle's second floor. In order to provide them with enough light and appropriate splendour, columns were lengthened while their slenderness was kept, which highlights the loftiness of the building topped with a steep roof. The courtyard used to sparkle with colours: multicoloured roof tiles shimmered in sunlight, the second storey was covered in polychromes, the columns had a burgundy shade. The present look dates from the early 20th century. Though not all the architectural details could be restored, and the columns are only a reconstruction of the original, the Renaissance feel of the place has been preserved.

head with a piece of cloth over its mouth. Legend has it that it cried out to Sigismund Augustus (👑 1548–1572) to be just when he was passing sentence. The insolence of the carved head made the king so angry that he had it gagged.

The museum exhibition includes part of the famous collection of 16th-century Arras tapestries. They resemble Gobelins, heavy ornamental

The castle's Arcaded Courtyard is modelled on Italian Renaissance architecture.

The Szczerbiec Sword

The Polish royal coronation sword is one of the most valuable medieval items of its kind in Europe. For centuries, it was a symbol of the power and sovereignty of Poland.

The sword was made around the 12th century. Its first recorded use took place in the coronation ceremony of Vladislaus the Short (♔ 1306–1333). Today, the sword can be seen in the Crown Treasury of Wawel Castle. The gilded ornamental hilt is particularly impressive.

The name of the artefact, the "Jagged Sword," derives from a notch that allegedly appeared during a Russian expedition of Boleslaus the Valiant. The Polish king was said to have hit the sword against Kiev's Golden Gate to indicate taking the city over. It cannot be but a myth: the gate was most probably built in 1037, which was 12 years after the king's death.

fabrics depicting scenes woven with woollen, silk and golden threads. Their size reaches up to 45 m² – a surface area of a two-room flat! The collection is one of a kind. The tapestries were all made in about 10 years on a commission from King Sigismund Augustus, and constitute an artistic whole. This is what makes the 136-piece collection in Cracow one of Europe's most valuable, even though it is not among the largest. The biblical scenes, landscapes, and royal initials are over 450 years old, but still delight the eye with exquisite workmanship and vivid colours.

The Polish Hussar wings and tournament armour, sabres and swords, shotguns, and even cannon barrels: all this can be seen in the Armoury (Zbrojownia). From the 14th century on, the Crown Treasury (Skarbiec) guarded the insignia of royal power, used for coronations: orbs, sceptres and crowns. In 1795, they were looted and destroyed by the Prussian army. Now, the highlight of the collection is a coronation sword called Szczerbiec.

The castle also holds an exhibition of Oriental Art (Sztuka Wschodu), displaying the trophies taken from the Turks defeated by John III Sobieski in the Battle of Vienna (1683), Chinese ceramics and Japanese porcelain.

To see a great view of the city, go up the 137 steps of Sandomierska Tower (Baszta Sandomierska). It was erected in the 15th century as the southern fort. It was an artillery tower, called a fire tower since the city defenders could fire shots at the enemy from up there. ■

The Lost Wawel

The exhibition presents the beginnings of the settlement on the hill. Those interested in Romanesque architecture can count on an exciting journey through time, and admire the relics of the over millennium-old Rotunda of the Blessed Virgin Mary (Rotunda Najświętszej Marii Panny).

The rotunda is one of the oldest pre-Romanesque structures in Poland. It can be seen in the basement of a building erected by the Nazis in the 1940's on the site of the 13th-century coach house and the 16th-century kitchen (their remains, which are also worth seeing, are located along the visiting trail). The rotunda probably served as the first castle chapel. It was built before 1000 AD on a four-leafed plan: a central circle with four round side apses.

On display are also other archaeological treasures, such as medieval articles of daily use and early coins found in Wawel Hill. The oldest ones date from the latter 11th century.

The Lost Wawel (Wawel Zaginiony)
☎ +48 12 4221697
🕐 Apr–Oct: Mon 9.30am–1pm, Tue–Fri 9.30am–5pm, Sat–Sun 10am–5pm; Nov–Mar: Tue–Sat 9.30am–4pm, Sun 10am–4pm
€ Apr–Oct: PLN 8 (PLN 5), free on Mon; Nov–Mar: PLN 7 (PLN 4), free on Sun

Wawel Royal Castle (Zamek Królewski na Wawelu)
☎ +48 12 4221697
@ www.wawel.krakow.pl
🕐 Wawel Hill: from 6am until dusk; State Rooms, Royal Private Apartments: Apr–Oct Tue–Fri 9.30am–5pm, Sat–Sun 10am–5pm, Nov–Mar Tue–Sat 9.30am–4pm (State Rooms also Sun 10am–4pm); Crown Treasury and Armoury, Oriental Art exhibition: Apr–Oct Tue–Fri 9.30am–5pm, Sat–Sun 10am–5pm (Crown Treasury and Armoury also Mon 9.30am–1pm), Nov–Mar Tue–Sat 9.30am–4pm; Sandomierska Tower: Apr, Sept, Oct 10am–5pm (Oct only on weekends), May–June 10am–6pm, July–Aug 10am–7pm; last admission: one hour before closing time (30 minutes for the Arcaded Courtyard)

The Thieves' Tower is one of Wawel's three preserved bastions.

€ Wawel Hill, Arcaded Courtyard: free; State Rooms: Apr–Oct PLN 18 (PLN 11), Nov–Mar PLN 16 (PLN 9), free: Nov–Mar on Sun; Royal Private Apartments: Apr–Oct PLN 25 (PLN 19), Nov–Mar PLN 21 (PLN 16); Crown Treasury and Armoury: Apr–Oct PLN 18 (PLN 11), Nov–Mar PLN 16 (PLN 9), free: Apr–Oct on Mon; Oriental Art exhibition: Apr–Oct PLN 8 (PLN 5), Nov–Mar PLN 7 (PLN 4); Sandomierska Tower: PLN 4; Apr–Oct: with tickets to three exhibitions (State Rooms, Royal Private Apartments, Crown Treasury and Armoury), you will pay only PLN 1 for a ticket to the fourth one (Oriental Art or Lost Wawel ➤ 45)

ℹ tickets can be bought in the Visitors Centre and the ticket office by Herbowa Gate; daily admission limits apply (except for the Oriental Art exhibition and the Dragon's Den); ticket reservation in English and French at the Visitor Information Desk (+48 12 4225155); reservation of tickets to the State Rooms and the Crown Treasury for a fee of PLN 16 (up to 9 people); tickets are timed and dated; Royal Private Apartments: guided tours only, also in English (included in the ticket price); on free-admission days, remember to collect your free ticket at a ticket office; bags and backpacks should be left in the luggage room at Bernardyńska Gate, small backpacks, umbrellas and strollers – in the one at the Arcaded Courtyard

45

★ 2 Wawel Cathedral

Kings were crowned and important personages were buried in this "mother of Polish churches." The high altar holds the relics of St Stanislaus the Martyr, the patron saint of Poland.

The courtyard in front of Wawel Cathedral (in the background) features a scale model of the castle.

The construction of the first church in Wawel Hill started around 1000 AD. It was the centre of the then-founded Cracow bishopric. For reasons that remain unclear, this original church did not last long, and its layout and appearance have never been established. The building was replaced with a cathedral, consecrated in 1142, the construction of which probably started under the reign of Duke Vladislaus Herman (♔ 1079–1102) – hence the name: Herman's Cathedral (katedra Hermanowska). The three-nave basilica church had towers and crypts. The lower part of the Silver Bells Tower (Wieża Srebrnych Dzwonów) and St Leonard's Crypt (Krypta św. Leonarda) have survived to this day; the rest burnt down in the 1305 fire.

The first king to be crowned in Wawel Cathedral was Vladislaus the Short (♔ 1306–1333). The ceremony took place in 1320 in the burnt-out Herman's Cathedral. From then on, all Polish rulers except for Stanislaus Leszczyński (♔ 1704–1710, 1733–1736) and Stanislaus Augustus Poniatowski (♔ 1764–1795) were crowned in Wawel.

Today's cathedral is the third church erected on the site. After the above-mentioned fire, a new Gothic building of a three-nave basilica church was constructed and consecrated in 1364. The rectangular chancel is surrounded by an ambulatory. Apart from the addition of chapels, the structure of the cathedral has not changed much, unlike the internal décor.

The heart of the church is marked by the Confession of St Stanislaus (c. 1035–1079) – a canopied tomb. The sepulchre holds a coffin with the relics of the saint who was killed and quartered by King Boleslaus the Bold. The description of the event in the famous chronicle by Wincenty Kadłubek (c. 1150–1223) suggests a particularly gory mutilation and dismemberment of the innocent bishop. Legend has it that the pieces of the body miraculously grew back together, and thus became the symbol of national unity. Some historians say that the bishop was murdered as revenge for the king's excommunication. Others claim that the clergyman might have taken part in a plot against the king.

The cathedral is the final resting place of many Polish kings. Remember to take a look at the sarcophagi of Vladislaus the Short and of Casimir the Great (made of red marble). The tomb of Vladislaus of Varna (♛ 1434–1444) dates from 1906, and is only symbolic: the body of the king, killed by the Turks in the Battle of Varna, has never been found. Another 20th-century tomb is the sarcophagus of St Jadwiga the Queen (♛ 1384–1399). It is also empty: in 1987, her remains were moved from here as holy relics to the black marble altarpiece on the east side of the ambulatory.

The black altar also holds a miraculous limewood crucifix through which Christ spoke to Jadwiga when she was in her teens. During her prayers, she was summoned by God to bring Christianity to Lithuania. So she did, by marrying a much older Lithuanian Duke Vladislaus Jogaila, later King Vladislaus Jagiello (♛ 1386–1434), who accepted Christianity. In 1997, Jadwiga was canonised by John Paul II.

Among the many chapels, the most noteworthy is Sigismund's Chapel (Kaplica Zygmuntowska), considered to be the finest example of Polish Renaissance architecture. It was founded by King Sigismund the Old after the death of his first wife, Barbara Zápolya (1495–1515); the architect was Italian-born Bartolommeo Berrecci. The chapel was consecrated

The entrance to the cathedral is flanked by Gothic chapels.

in 1533. The dome is covered with golden shingles, sparkling in the sun. Inside, in the contrasting pink and black marble décor, rich gildings and sculptures dazzle with splendour. There is also the intricately carved sepulchre of Sigismund Augustus (♛ 1548–1572) and Sigismund the Old (♛ 1506–1548). Visitors should know, however, that the remains of these kings and the succeeding monarchs entombed in Wawel were buried in the crypts of the cathedral.

The crypts are the burial vaults of the rulers as well as other distinguished Poles. The Crypt of the National Poets (Krypta Wieszczów) holds the remains of Adam Mickiewicz, Juliusz Słowacki, and the urn with soil from the cemetery in Montmorency (France), where Cyprian Kamil Norwid was interred.

In the crypt of the Silver Bells' Tower (Wieża Srebrnych Dzwonów), the body of Marshal Józef Piłsudski was laid to rest; his heart was buried in his mother's tomb in Vilnius' Rasos Cemetery. The vestibule is the final resting place of President Lech Kaczyński and his wife, who died in the Smolensk plane crash in 2010. All 96 people on board, political and military officials among them, died on impact. They were travelling to commemorate Polish POWs killed by the Soviet NKVD in Katyń forest in 1940.

The oldest part of the underground church is St Leonard's Crypt, a remnant of the 12th-century Herman's Cathedral and one of the best-preserved examples of Romanesque architecture in Poland. It has remarkable stone columns and the 13th-century floor in front of the altar. People buried here include King John III Sobieski (♛ 1674–1696) and famous commanders: Tadeusz Kościuszko (1746–1817) and Władysław Sikorski (1881–1943). The future John Paul II celebrated his first Mass in this austere interior.

End your visit by climbing the tower of Poland's best-known bell, called Sigismund (Zygmunt). It chimes only a few times a year, on major national and church holidays. It was believed that touching the clapper helped maidens to find a suitable candidate for a husband.

The Cathedral Museum (Muzeum Katedralne) is located nearby. The museum's four rooms display funerary emblems of Polish rulers, items from the Cathedral treasury, and keepsakes of John Paul II. Highlights include St Maurice's spear, a gift to the first Polish king Boleslaus the Valiant from Holy Roman Emperor Otto III, and items from a 12th-century bishop's grave, such as liturgical vessels: a chalice and a paten. ∎

Wawel Royal Cathedral of St Stanislaus and St Wenceslaus (Katedra Królewska na Wawelu p.w. św. Stanisława i św. Wacława)

☎ *visitor information: +48 12 4299515; ticket office: +48 12 4299515*

@ *www.katedra-wawelska.pl*

🕐 *Cathedral: Apr–Sept Mon–Sat 9am–5pm, Sun 12.30pm–5pm, Oct–Mar Mon–Sat 9am–4pm, Sun 12.30pm–4pm; Cathedral Museum: Apr–Sept Mon–Sat 9am–5pm, Oct–Mar Mon–Sat 9am–4pm*

€ *Cathedral: free; Sigismund Bell Tower, Royal Tombs and Cathedral Museum: PLN 12 (PLN 7)*

ℹ️ *audio guides in English, French, German, Russian etc.: PLN 7 (PLN 5); tickets to the crypts and the Sigismund Bell are available in the Cathedral Museum*

3 Dragon's Den

The cave was believed to have been inhabited by a dragon that plagued the local population and demanded to be fed cattle. Today, you no longer need to fear to enter the cave: instead of the beast, you will find a tourist trail.

The entrance to the Dragon's Den (Smocza Jama) leads through a former well: the brick tower was a 19th-century water intake for the castle, used by Austrian occupiers. It has 135 steps running down to one of the underground chambers. The den is 270 metres in total length. A convenient visiting trail is 81 metres long and spans three rooms. The other passages are narrow and muddy, some are even filled with water, and therefore accessible only to experienced cavers. Little ponds inside the cave are populated by a very rare crustacean species, *Niphargus tatrensis*.

The cave once served purposes that were far from holy. In the 17th century, it housed a drinking den that must have turned a considerable profit,

You can still see the legendary creature by the exit of the Dragon's Den.

The Legend of the Wawel Dragon

Visiting the cave at the foot of Wawel Hill is no longer as risky today as it is said to have been centuries ago. Back then, the daredevils who approached it had to be prepared to face the beast.

In the far-away past, the den was allegedly the lair of a dragon – the terror of the town. Every day, the locals had to offer cattle to the dragon, otherwise the angered beast would devour people. A decision was taken to kill it by resort-ing to a ruse: sheep's skin stuffed with sulphur, sawdust and conifer needles. The legend does not specify whether the "filling" was already burning when the dragon swallowed the fake sheep or if it got ignited afterwards. Some say that the beast was killed by flames. Others claim it tried to extinguish the fire by gulping down water from the Vistula River until it burst. To honour Krakus (c. 7th century), the ruler who got rid of the blight, the town was called Kraków. The 16th-century variant of the legend says, however, that the dragon was poisoned by a cobbler called Skuba.

since the money earned that way was enough to pay the castle servants. It was also rumoured that the place was a brothel. Reportedly, the den was also famous abroad, but it remains unclear if that was for the quality of food and drink served there, or for any of the other pleasures on offer.

The dragon still breathes out fire. It is located on a boulder at the exit from the cave, by the Vistula Boulevards. The bronze statue was made by a Cracovian artist, Bronisław Chromy. The beast stands on its hind legs and has its jaws wide open; from time to time, flames burst out from its throat. ■

Dragon's Den (Smocza Jama)

🕐 *Apr: 10am–5pm; May–June: 10am–6pm; July–Aug: 10am–7pm; Sept–Oct: 10am–5pm*

💶 *PLN 3*

ℹ️ *the visiting trail is a one-way route, it exits onto the Vistula Boulevards (Bulwary Wiślane)*

Old Town

The Heart of the City

The area within the Planty (a greenway on the site of the former ramparts) is the city's central district. Its unique atmosphere is created by the many churches, theatres, bars and university buildings. The past merges with the present.

In the summer, the marble seats in Mały Rynek (➤ 57) are very popular among tourists and locals alike.

The layout of the Old Town (**Stare Miasto**) is over 750 years old. The city received municipal rights under the Magdeburg Law in 1257, in the reign of Boleslaus the Chaste. The rectangular-shaped Main Square (➤ 26), together with a network of roads branching out, was planned in the very centre of Cracow. Although many burgher houses have not survived to this day, the layout has been kept unchanged.

The Magdeburg Law assumed that streets should lie at right angles to the square, but ul. Bracka (➤ 58) and ul. Grodzka do not follow the rule. It goes to show that the town was not the first one to be founded on the site, but replaced the already existing settlement. Some important buildings must have been already there, and the munici-

pal authorities had probably decided to grant them a privileged place in the town plan. This much is confirmed by Abraham ben Jacob in his note of 965. On his visit to the Slavic territories, the Jewish traveller got as far as Cracow and called it the centre of the region in his Arabic-language memoirs. Hence, we may conclude that it was already a settlement of major significance back then.

The Old Town holds the most important buildings of Poland's oldest university. Cracow Academy was established in 1364 by King Casimir the Great (👑 1333–1370) as one of the first colleges in Central Europe. At the beginning, the courses were given in Wawel Castle (➤ 43). It was only the financial help of Queen Jadwiga (👑 1384–1399), who bequeathed

51

The neat greenery and a humming fountain make the Planty a nice place to relax.

her personal property to the Academy, that the academic seat moved to the Collegium Maius (➤61). Around that time, the Pope granted it the right to open the theology faculty, and the university in Cracow came to rank among West European institutions of that type. Previously, there were only three faculties: of medicine, law, and liberal arts (grammar, rhetoric, logic, arithmetic, geometry, astronomy, music).

The academy was also popular among foreign students, who accounted for about 40 percent of the student group in the years 1433–1510. The present name of the Jagiellonian University has been in use since 1817. The building of the Collegium Novum (➤60) is also relatively new. It was there that Cracow professors were arrested by the Nazis during WWII (➤61).

Put the guidebook aside for a moment to wander around the Main Square and the adjacent narrow streets. Do not worry about the map, the Planty (➤53) will prevent you from straying too far from the Old Town whatever direction you take. Strolling about is the best opportunity to

see the continuity and harmony of the 750-year-old Cracow architecture and appreciate the uniqueness of the city.

The Old Town is also a cultural centre. Cracow's leading theatres are located here: the paramount National Old Theatre (➤67, ➤203) and the Juliusz Słowacki Theatre (➤54, ➤203), housed in the city's finest theatre building. It is also a district of smart clubs. For live jazz, visit U Muniaka (➤210); for a cabaret show, go to the Piwnica pod Baranami (➤207); for a beer and a dance, drop in at one of the city's oldest student clubs, Pod Jaszczurami (➤206). The many bars often hold concerts and *impromptu* jam sessions.

There is no way to visit all the local bars during one night. One thing is for sure: everyone will find something there to enjoy, whether they are connoisseurs of Polish and world cuisines, or just like savouring good wine and beer. Those who like to talk the night through in the semi-darkness of a bar as well as those who prefer looking for adventure in multi-coloured dance floors will all be welcome. The Old Town never sleeps. ■

The suggested itinerary takes about 3 hours. A visit to the Collegium Maius is an additional hour. Allocate about 15 minutes for each of the churches. In the evening, take a look at pl. Szczepański (➤66) and its illuminated fountain. You can also have a drink in one of the pavement cafés in Mały Rynek (➤57) or enjoy the night time atmosphere of ul. Bracka (➤58). The Old Town is a pedestrian precinct (only local residents are exempt).

Access by public transport:
1–5

124, 152, 424, 502, 522, 601, 605, 608, 609, 610, 614, 618, 902, 904 (Dworzec Główny)

2, 4, 7, 10, 12, 13, 14, 15, 19, 20, 24, 40 (Dworzec Główny)

6–9

304, 522 (Filharmonia)

1, 3, 6, 8, 18, (Plac Wszystkich Świętych); 1, 2, 3, 6, 8, 18 (Filharmonia)

10–12

124, 152, 304, 424, 502, 522, 601, 608, 618, 902 (Teatr Bagatela)

2, 3, 4, 8, 13, 14, 15, 20, 24 (Teatr Bagatela)

★ **1** Planty

It takes just a few steps to move from the bustling Main Square to the verdant Planty, shaded by wide-stretching trees. One of the city's most popular parks is situated on the site that was occupied by fortifications 200 years ago.

It is hard to imagine that town walls once rose on the site of the Planty alleys.

At the beginning of the 19th century, Cracow's town walls were pulled down, with only a small part left for posterity (see: St Florian's Gate ➤ 20). Feliks Radwański, an architect and professor of the Jagiellonian University, suggested that the grounds of the former ramparts should be turned into a public park. The residue of the fortifications, the embankments and the moat, overgrown with weeds, were a breeding ground for all types of vermin. Leaving the terrain as it was would have posed a grave health hazard to the city inhabitants. A decision was taken to clean and level the grounds (*splantować* in Polish, hence the name of Planty for the park around the Old Town). It was a difficult and time-consuming task. The works lasted from 1822 to 1830.

The Planty were damaged during WWII. The Nazis cut down most trees and devastated the agave and dracaena gardens. The occupiers also took away the metal ornamental railings lining the alleys. These were reconstructed after the war, but the full-scale restoration started only after 1989.

Walking in the Planty, you can follow the course of the former walls and see where defence towers used to be. Just look for low stone walls and information boards along the alleys.

The intersection of ul. Franciszkańska and ul. Straszewskiego features an interesting fountain. It is dedicated to Frederic Chopin, a Polish-French composer. Inaugurated in 2007, the fountain was actually designed in 1947 by Maria Jarema, a painter, sculptor and stage designer who worked with Tadeusz Kantor at his Cricot theatre, among others. The abstract-style sculpture shows four piano hammers hitting the "water strings." The fountain is worth seeing at night, since it is seen at its best when illuminated. ■

Planty
ℹ *open to the public free of charge*

2 Juliusz Słowacki Theatre

At the end of the 19th century, municipal councillors were faced with a dilemma whether to finance a national theatre or a waterworks. The former was given priority, but the construction of its edifice aroused bitter controversy.

The Juliusz Słowacki Theatre represents a truly imperial splendour.

The matter of contention was the intended location of the theatre. It had been formerly occupied by the Holy Ghost Church, the adjoining graveyard and a few medieval burgher houses. Protests came to nothing: the buildings were demolished and the theatre's construction started in March 1891. One of the people who did not accept this decision was painter Jan Matejko. He renounced the Freedom of the City of Cracow, and wore his regular working clothes for the official inauguration on October 21, 1893. He also did not exhibit his works in Cracow until his death. In 1909, the theatre was named after a Polish Romantic poet Juliusz Słowacki.

It was the city's first building equipped with electric lighting; in the late 19th century, Cracow was lit by gas lanterns. A little power station was constructed behind the main building especially to meet the theatre's needs. This so-called Machine House (Dom Machin) now accommodates the Small Stage (Scena Miniatura) that can seat 100 spectators.

The dress circle of the Large Stage (Duża Scena) is dubbed the Imperial Box. The fact is, however, that the Emperor of Austria, Francis Joseph, never visited the theatre, despite frequent invitations. The Imperial Box was used by the leader of the Second Polish Republic Józef Piłsudski; during WWII, by Hans Frank and other Third Reich officials. It is one of the two circles around the amphitheatrical auditorium, illuminated by a huge crystal chandelier.

The eclectic-style building consists of three parts. The division, modelled on the French National Opera in Paris, can be clearly seen from pl. św. Ducha. First, there is a spacious vestibule, a foyer called the Mirror Hall (Sala Lustrzana) and staircases. The second part is crowned with a green dome and holds the auditorium, and the third shelters the stage and the rehearsal room above.

While waiting for a show to start, take a closer look at the impressive curtain created in 1894 by painter Henryk Siemiradzki. The oil painting on linen canvas measures 11.9 m x 9.6 m and does not fold: the stiff framework is still moved up and down manually, as it was one century ago. The figures depicted in the centre are the ancient-style representations of Inspiration, Beauty and Truth. You will also recognise the personification of Comedy, holding a theatrical mask, and Tragedy wearing a piece of black cloth. ■

Juliusz Słowacki Theatre (Teatr im. Juliusza Słowackiego)

✉ pl. św. Ducha 1

☎ +48 12 4244525 (guided tours), +48 12 4244526 (box office)

@ www.slowacki.krakow.pl

🕐 box office: Mon 10am–2pm, 2.30pm–6pm, Tue–Sat 9.30am–2pm, 2.30pm–7pm, Sun 3pm–7pm (only on show days)

€ shows: PLN 30–50 (PLN 25–35)

🍴 Café Foyer in the basement, entrance from pl. św. Ducha ● ● ●

ℹ group guided tours on prior arrangement; spectators are let in 30 minutes before show time; the building is closed to the public during the day and opens only for shows

3 Holy Cross Church

The Gothic structure of the tile-roofed building has survived to this day largely unchanged. For that reason, the small church is one of most treasured monuments in Cracow.

The ceiling of the main nave is supported with only one pillar. The centrally located column, like a tree, branches out into twelve ribs of a palm vault. The feature has a symbolic significance, drawing on the call of the church: for Christians, the Holy Cross is the Tree of Life. This architectural gem is extremely rare, the only one in Cracow. The nave and the pillar date from the end of the 14th century (as does the church in general), but the vault had to be slightly repaired after a fire of 1528.

The nave is decorated with 16th-century frescoes, the most intriguing of which is located on the eastern side and depicts a naked old man sitting on a chair. This 1580 painting represents the Sinner's Mirror (Zwierciadło Grzesznika). The swords that pierce the man symbolise the devil, sin, death, and bad word. It is the only painting of that type in Poland. The church also boasts… a hole in heaven. Until the 16th century, the aperture in the ceiling served to haul up the statue of Jesus on Ascension Day, and of the Virgin Mary on Assumption Day.

The austere Holy Cross Church is a fine example of Gothic architecture.

The oldest part of the church is the stone chancel, visible from the side of the Planty (➤ 53). It was built with limestone blocks around 1300 AD. The original cross ribbed vault was destroyed in the great fire of 1528 that razed a large section of the city. The net vault you can see today was reconstructed in 1533.

The Baroque central altarpiece dates from the 17th century, and the oil-painted wooden choir stalls from about 1722. The Renaissance 16th-century confessional is one of the oldest in Cracow; it stands in St Sophia's Chapel (Kaplica św. Zofii), added on the south side of the nave. In 1838, painter Jan Matejko was baptised here; the 1423 font that remembers the event is a very valuable historical item. There is no other Gothic bronze artefact with such rich ornamentation anywhere else in Cracow. ■

Holy Cross Church (Kościół św. Krzyża)
✉ pl. św. Ducha 2
@ www.krzyzkrakow.pl
🕐 Mon–Sat 7.30am–6pm, Sun 9am–9pm
🍴 restaurant: U Babci Maliny ➤ 183, ul. Szpitalna 38 🔴🔴◎; pubs: Nic Nowego ➤ 193, ul. św. Krzyża 15 🔴🔴◎; House of Beer ➤ 193, ul. św. Krzyża 13 🔴🔴◎; Non Iron ➤ 193, ul. św. Marka 27 🔴🔴◎
ℹ services: Mon–Sat at 7.30am, 6pm; Sun at 9am, 10.30am, noon, 1.15pm, 6pm, 7.15pm, 9pm

4 Orthodox Church of the Assumption

The Orthodox Church is housed on the first floor of a 14th-century burgher house. It has a small golden dome and the Orthodox cross above the entrance. The building used to be a dwelling house, a synagogue, and even a workshop.

You will recognise the Orthodox Church building by a characteristic icon painting.

The synagogue of *Ahawat Raim* (**Love of the Neighbour**) was founded in Cracow around 1900. When the city was taken over by German forces during WWII, it was turned into a workshop, probably the carpenter's. The alterations were so vast that soon there was no trace left of the former use of the building. In 1940, the house came to accommodate an Orthodox parish office, in search of a new seat after the Nazis evicted it from the barracks in pl. na Groblach. The former synagogue building was thus renovated and altered to suit its new purpose.

The Orthodox Church is located on the first floor. The white-painted interior is adorned with icon paintings and banners, some of which were brought here from churches no longer in existence. The gilded iconostasis, for example, comes from the church in Miechów.

Icon enthusiasts should not miss the refectory on the second floor. The wooden interior is all covered with icons

Mały Rynek has changed beyond recognition, from a marketplace to a sheltered oasis of peace.

painted by Jerzy Nowosielski (1923–2011). The artist developed his own distinct style of icon painting, based in the Orthodox tradition but not limited to its standard conventions. He often used strong vivid colours. In the Cracow church, one of his paintings in particular attracts the eye: the majestic Transfiguration of Jesus, depicted against three rings, wearing white robes. The effect is made complete with a wooden iconostasis in a dark blue colour scheme, contrasted by the red halos of the saints. ■

Orthodox Church of the Assumption of St Mary (Cerkiew prawosławna Zaśnięcia Najświętszej Marii Panny)

✉ *ul. Szpitalna 24*

@ *www.krakow.cerkiew.pl*

🕐 *Mon–Fri 11am–3pm (ask the lady in the shop by the entrance to open the grill); closed in the summer (you can try asking the priest to let you in; the intercom is in the corridor to the left of the stairs)*

ℹ️ *services: Wed at 6pm, Sat at 9am and 5pm, Sun at 10am; you can tour the church before the service*

★ 5 Mały Rynek

A meat marketplace up to the 19th century, Mały Rynek was once called the Butcher's Square. These times are long gone. Mały Rynek is now a remarkably charming place.

For over 700 years, Mały Rynek served as a marketplace that supplemented the Main Square (➤26). At first, the squares were not even separated. Butchery stalls were located on the site of today's vicarage of St Mary's Basilica (➤23). The construction of the building in the 18th century, and then the closure of the adjoining graveyard, allowed the creation of a separate square. The marketplace came to an end in 1902, when a tram line was laid through the square. In the mid-20th century, the tracks were dismantled and Mały Rynek was used mainly as a car park until 2007.

The recent refurbishment of Mały Rynek was a complete makeover. The square is now almost completely closed to vehicles, there are marble benches popular with locals and tourists alike. If there is no free seat left, visit one of the pavement cafés along the eastern frontage, sip a glass of wine and watch colourful facades and the passing crowds. The square's fountain has been jokingly dubbed the "wet stairs" since water is not spurted out, but flows down the brown marble steps. The square also looks great at night, when it is lit with the golden light of ornamental lanterns, and the fountain is finely illuminated. The site holds various cultural events, from concerts to the annual Pierogi Festival (➤231). There is also a small gallery inside the Lamelli House – a fine corner building by ul. Mikołajska, now the seat of the Old Town Community Centre. ∎

St James' Way

Mały Rynek is an important stop on a Polish stretch of St James' Way, the pilgrimage route to the Cathedral of Santiago de Compostela in Spain.

The Christian tradition of going on the Way of St James has existed for over 1000 years. There is no one definite route, but a network of trails from different European locations, all leading to the tomb of St James and marked with the Shell of St James – scallop shell signs that can be found on walls, pavements, posts or information boards. Pilgrims carry the so-called *credencial*, a form of passport for keeping a record of their journey. In Mały Rynek, *credencials* can be stamped in Księgarnia Hiszpańska (Spanish bookshop) at No. 4.

Little Square (Mały Rynek)

restaurants: Szoberowska, Mały Rynek 6 ⬤⬤⬤; *Aperitif, ul. Sienna 9* ⬤⬤€; *U Stasi* ➤184, *ul. Mikołajska 16* ⬤€€; *Green Way vegetarian bar* ➤191, *ul. Mikołajska 14* ⬤€€; *clubs and bars: Paparazzi* ➤194, *ul. Mikołajska 9* ⬤⬤€; *Pierwszy Lokal na Stolarskiej po lewej stronie idąc od Małego Rynku* ➤194, *ul. Stolarska 6/1* ⬤⬤€; *Siesta Cafe* ➤198, *ul. Stolarska 6* ⬤⬤€

6 Ulica Bracka

The street runs from the Main Square to the Franciscan Basilica; the order is called Friars Minor (Bracia Mniejsi), hence the name: "Friars' Street." The leisure opportunities offered by the place, however, are far from ascetic.

Ul. Bracka is among the most charming streets in the Old Town. Its picturesque gentle curve seems to suggest that the city's urban planning project of 1257 incorporated some earlier buildings. The street is a perfect destination for an evening walk in between fine historic houses and the flickering lights of the many bars, clubs and restaurants. Every day after dusk, the building at No. 2 is used as a screen for the projection of a new poem from writer Michał Zabłocki, the author of the lyrics to Grzegorz Turnau's *Bracka* – the song that made it one of the best-known streets in Poland. ∎

Friars' Street (Ulica Bracka)

restaurants: Sempre Bracka ➤189, *ul. Bracka 3-5, 1p.* ⬤⬤€; *C.K. Dezerter, ul. Bracka 6* ⬤⬤€; *Nowa Prowincja café-bar* ➤207; *ul. Bracka 3-5* ⬤⬤€; *Cafe Botanica, ul. Bracka 9* ⬤⬤€; *Cieplarnia Art Cafe, ul. Bracka 15* ⬤⬤

Ul. Bracka, a street of unique atmosphere, is teeming with social life.

7 Uniat Church of the Feast of the Cross

While walking along ul. Wiślna, it is easy to miss the Uniat Church. Its facade does not make one think of a sacred building, and the entrance is right next to a grocery.

Throughout the years, the building has changed hands many times. It was erected between 1636 and 1643 as the Baroque St Norbert's Church, and remained in the care of Premonstratensian nuns until 1803. Five years later, the Austrian authorities allocated the church to Greek Catholics. The parish survived to 1947, when it was suppressed by the communist regime. Handed over to the Missionaries of La Salette, it became a Roman Catholic church again. Greek Catholics returned here after more than 50 years, in 2001.

Inside, the most prominent feature is the iconostasis from the end of the 19th century, designed by renowned Cracovian architect Tadeusz Stryjeński. The icons were painted by Władysław Rossowski, a pupil of Jan Matejko; Rossowski based them on his master's sketches. After WWII, the iconostasis was dismantled and put back only in 2001 by Greek Catholics. Today, it can once again be seen in all its glory.

The room by the porch boasts yet another iconostasis, created by painter Jerzy Nowosielski (1923–2011) in the 1970's. It was used by Greek Catholic believers while the church was in the hands of the Missionaries of La Salette. The Eastern Orthodox Eucharist was celebrated in one of the chapels at St Catherine's Church, run by the Augustinian friars. ■

Uniat Church of the Feast of the Cross (Cerkiew greckokatolicka Podwyższenia Krzyża Świętego)
✉ ul. Wiślna 11
☎ +48 12 4292861
@ www.krakow.cerkowgr.pl
🕐 visiting on Sundays before services
🍴 Bordo restaurant ➤ 180, ul. Gołębia 3 ●●€; Camera Cafe ➤ 196, ul. Wiślna 5 ●●●
ℹ services: Sun at 10am, periodically at 8.30am and 5pm – see the website for details

The stately edifice of the Collegium Novum is the pride of the Jagiellonian University.

8 Collegium Novum

This monumental red-brick building is the seat of the authorities of the Jagiellonian University – the oldest institution of higher education in Poland. Academic courses and conferences are held here.

Go inside for a moment, if only to take in the atmosphere of Cracow's university life. The place is very busy during the academic year: students are rushing to and from classes, up and down the huge splendid stairwell, designed on a grand scale. It is topped by white diamond vaults, very popular in the late Gothic period. However, do not be fooled by architectural features and the dignity of Poland's oldest university: the neo-Gothic edifice itself was built in the years 1883–1887, and opened on the 500th anniversary of the institution's foundation.

The most representative room of the Collegium Novum is its Lecture Hall (**Aula**). It holds public defences of doctoral dissertations, as well as lectures and official meetings. The blue seat upholstery contrasts with the red shade of the walls, on which hang sizeable paintings. The best-known among them was created by Jan Matejko. It shows Nicholas Copernicus, who also studied in Cracow. The famous astronomer is depicted talking to God. Even with such grand decoration, the hall did not escape criticism. It proved already too small for university assemblies at the time of its inauguration. ■

Collegium Novum at the Jagiellonian University (Collegium Novum Uniwersytetu Jagiellońskiego)
🕐 *Oct–June during classes (c. 8am–6pm)*

The *Sonderaktion Krakau* Operation

The main building of the Jagiellonian University, usually bustling and teeming with students, witnessed a sombre WWII episode in the history of the Polish *intelligentsia*.

When Cracovian university professors congregated in the Collegium Novum on November 6, 1939, little did they know what awaited them. The Nazis had told Polish academics to come to a meeting under the pretence of presenting a new model for the education system in occupied Poland. However, once SS Obersturmbannführer Bruno Müller entered room No. 66 (now 56) at noon, it immediately became apparent

that talks were not on the agenda. The 183 professors were arrested and detained in Montelupich prison. Then, they were sent to Sachsenhausen concentration camp near Berlin. This form of oppression was unprecedented. It gave rise to a considerable international protest, which eventually led to the release of the surviving scholars and scientists over 40 years of age. The younger ones were transported to other camps and then gradually released. The operation had tragic consequences: 13 academics died in Sachsenhausen lone, some succumbed soon after the relaease, many never recuperated. These events are commemorated today with a plaque set in a wall of room No. 56.

★ 9 Collegium Maius

This is the oldest university building in Poland. The first lecture here was given in 1400. The edifice houses the museum of the Jagiellonian University, which displays works of art, scientific instruments, and even an Oscar statuette.

The Collegium Maius has kept its old medieval appearance: the present building would still be perfectly recognisable to students and professors of Cracow Academy at the turn of the 16th century. Courses started at dawn and lasted until the evening. Rooms were overcrowded. At first, students brought their own seats. It was only later that the rooms were furnished with wooden benches, and panes of glass replaced bladder membranes in the windows (yet another solution were sheets of paper thickly smeared with fat). After their lectures, professors would come together for a common meal in a refectory, the Stuba Communis, which also held social gatherings and debates on the Academy's future. Damaged in WWII, the hall was renovated in the 1950's. The present Baroque look was designed by Professor Karol Estreicher, an art historian and son to Stanisław, a professor of history killed in the *Sonderaktion Krakau* operation (see above).

Honorary degrees are awarded in a fine Assembly Hall called Aula Jagiellońska.

61

The courtyard of the Collegium Maius is surrounded by diamond-vaulted cloisters.

The motto of the university, "Let reason prevail over force," is inscribed in Latin on the portal of the Assembly Hall, the so-called Aula Jagiellońska. It hosts graduation ceremonies for postdoctoral and honorary degrees. In 1983, John Paul II received the *Honoris Causa* Doctorate here. At the end of the 18th century, the hall was used as a corn storehouse by the Austrian troops, which resulted in its complete devastation. The present interior décor is relatively new. Professor Karol Estreicher managed, here as well, to restore the old look and atmosphere of this historic place.

The Collegium Maius boasts treasures from various eras: from drawings by Veit Stoss to an Academy Award statuette. The Oscar was donated by Andrzej Wajda, who received it as an award for his lifetime achievement. The museum collection includes two more prizes awarded to the director: a Palme d'Or won at the Cannes Film Festival, and a Berlin Bear. You will also see Veit Stoss' handwritten design project for the altarpiece at Nuremberg. Yet another treasured exhibit is the 16th-century

Jagiellonian globe, one of the oldest in the world to show America. All these valuable items are displayed in the Treasury (Skarbiec).

The building used to be home to Poland's oldest library, dating back to the beginnings of Cracow Academy. At first, the Collegium Maius held mostly philosophical and theological books. 1515 saw the establishment of a reading room, which was the main seat of the Jagiellonian Library (Biblioteka Jagiellońska) until 1940. The room is called Libraria, and holds meetings of the University Senate on the last Wednesday of each month. At other times, it is accessible to visitors. Take a look up to the Gothic ceiling: it consists of 30 segments, painted in clouds. There are also the portraits of lecturers and three reconstructed scientific instruments used by Nicholas Copernicus. A larger exhibition dedicated to the famous astronomer is presented in the so-called Copernicus Room (Pokój Kopernika). The items put on display include an 11th-century Arabic astrolabe. You can also take a look at the re-

The hall called the Libraria is where the University Senate meets once a month.

decorated former Professors' Chambers (Pokoje Profesorskie).

The collection comprises many interesting scientific appliances, some used by the lecturers and students of the university, other bought especially for the museum. Of particular interest are the instruments that once belonged to physicist and chemist Karol Olszewski, including the one he used for the pioneering experiment of liquefying oxygen. The museum also displays a considerable collection of wooden sculptures, mostly Madonnas.

A tourist attraction that targets mainly children is an interactive exhibition, the World of Senses (Świat Zmysłów). Visitors can carry out simple experiments and take measurements on their own, but the staff is always ready to help.

If you do not have the time for a visit inside the Collegium Maius, at least take a look into the courtyard. It is surrounded by Gothic arched cloisters, and there is a historic well in the centre. The courtyard features a unique clock. Every two hours, a procession of important university figures moves by to the accompaniment of courtly music. These figures include Queen Jadwiga and her spouse, King Vladislaus Jagiello. ∎

Collegium Maius at the Jagiellonian University (Collegium Maius Uniwersytetu Jagiellońskiego)

✉ *ul. Jagiellońska 15*

☎ *+48 12 4220549, +48 12 6631307*

@ *www.maius.uj.edu.pl*

🕑 *permanent exhibition (Libraria, Stuba Communis, Treasury, Professors' Chambers, Copernicus Room, Assembly Hall): guided tours only, every 20 minutes Jan–Feb, Nov–Dec Mon, Wed–Fri 10am–2.20pm, Tue 10am–3.20pm, Sat 10am–2.40pm, Mar–Oct Mon, Wed, Fri 10am–2.20pm, Tue and Thu 10am–5.20pm, Sat 10am–2.40pm; guided tours of the permanent exhibition, the exhibition of scientific instruments and the sculpture gallery on prior arrangement, Mon–Fri at 1pm (in English), Fri at 11am (in Polish), the World of Senses: Mon–Sat 9am–1.30pm*

€ *permanent exhibition: PLN 12 (PLN 6), free guided tours: Nov–Mar Tue 2pm–3.20pm, Mar–Oct Tue 3pm–5.20pm; the permanent exhibition, the exhibition of scientific instruments and the sculpture gallery: PLN 16 (PLN 12); the World of Senses: PLN 7 (PLN 5)*

ℹ *due to great popularity, tickets to all the exhibitions should be booked in advance*

With its stuccoes, paintings and gilding, the Collegiate Church of St Anne is an example of Baroque style at its finest.

🔟 Collegiate Church of St Anne

The church has cultivated its academic links for 600 years. Eminent priests provide university chaplaincy services. The church is a Baroque gem, resounding with the period's organ music.

The first church dedicated to St Anne was built on the site at the end of the 14th century. Back then, the neighbourhood was the Jewish quarter. The church stood in the vicinity of a synagogue and a *mikveh* (ritual baths); today's ul. św. Anny was called ul. Żydowska (Jewish Street). This cohabitation was not always peaceful. In 1407, a rumour was started that Jews had committed a ritual murder on a Christian child and used its blood to make *matzah* (a kind of bread). The accusation was absurd, but sadly proved to be enough to stir up the crowds. The situation soon got out of control. According to the chronicle of Jan Długosz, Jewish houses were burnt down to stop the wave of violence and plundering. The chronicler does not specify who actually started the fire. It spread quickly and destroyed St Anne's Church, which was later reconstructed.

The present church building was erected in the 17th century on the initiative of the lecturers at Cracow Academy, closely linked with St Anne's Church since 1418. That was the year that the Gothic edifice (built after the fire of 1407) was pulled down, and a new one was constructed. Its lavish design was meant to surpass that of SS Peter and Paul's Church (➤ 35). A fact that adds spice to the whole affair is that the church architecture was modelled on the church of San Andrea della Valle in Rome, which was in the care of the Theatines, a religious order that competed with the Jesuits. The Academy itself competed with the Jesuits in the field of education, so the choice does not appear to have been accidental. The construction was commissioned to Tylman van Gameren, a Dutch-born designer of many Polish architectural gems (located mainly in Warsaw). Works started in 1689, and the church was consecrated in the early 18th century.

The Collegiate Church of St Anne is one of the finest examples of Baroque architecture in Poland. The interior of the three-nave basilica is covered with multi-coloured frescoes by Carl Dankwart, and stucco ornaments by Baldassare Fontana. The latter also designed the high altar, displaying the painting of St Anne with the Virgin Mary and Child.

The right side of the transept holds a coffin with the holy relics of St John Cantius (1390–1473), the patron saint of the Jagiellonian University. He was canonised in 1767. The figures that support the sarcophagus stand for the four faculties of the university: law, philosophy, theology and medicine. The most remarkable votive offerings are the Turkish Bunchuks (yak-tail standards), taken by King John III Sobieski (♔ 1674–1696) in the Battle of Vienna.

The church also features a statue of Nicholas Copernicus, erected in 1823 – before his *De Revolutionibus* was dropped from the Index of Prohibited Books in 1828.

Music lovers can hear for themselves what organ music sounded like back in the times of Johann Sebastian Bach. The organ, constructed in the years 1723–1726, has preserved its original form and thus constitutes one of the most valuable historic items of its type in Poland.

Above all, the Collegiate Church of St Anne serves as the university's place of worship. It is used for university chaplaincy services, such as Masses for the inauguration of the academic year. One of the canons was Karol Wojtyła, the future Pope John Paul II. Yet another

The Collegiate Church of St Anne was designed by Tylman van Gameren.

eminent person connected with the church was the late Father Józef Tischner, a professor in philosophy and the author of many publications. He was a chaplain of the Solidarity movement and a critic of Polish religiosity. His thought-inspiring sermons drew crowds. ■

Collegiate Church of St Anne (Kolegiata św. Anny)

✉ *ul. św. Anny 11*

@ *www.kolegiata-anna.katolicki.eu*

🕐 *7am–7.30pm daily*

🍴 *Chaczapuri restaurant* ➤ *190, ul. św. Anny 4* ●● ⊜

ℹ️ *services: Mon–Sat at 7am, 8am, 7.30pm, Sun at 7.30am, 9am, 10am, 11am, noon, 1pm, 7.30pm, 8.30pm, 9.30pm*

11 Plac Szczepański

Not so long ago, this peaceful square with benches was a car park. Today, it is a popular recreation spot for locals: children are attracted by a fountain, their parents can see open-air photo exhibitions held here from time to time.

In pl. Szczepański, evenings belong to admiring the fountain in front of the Palace of Art.

The colourful features of the square echo the Viennese Art Nouveau style. An eye-catching object is a bizarre wooden bench, twisted into the infinity symbol (a horizontal eight). The green bicycle racks, newsagent kiosks, and even litter bins imitate 19th-century design. In addition, the square is paved with red porphyry.

Pl. Szczepański is one of the newest squares in Cracow. It was created at the beginning of the 19th century, after the demolition of St Stephen's Church and the adjacent buildings (hence the name, St Stephen's Square). At first, it served as a marketplace, and then as a car park until its renovation in 2010.

Come here in the evening to see Cracow's illuminated music fountain. The lighting colours, as well as water jets, are synchronised with music. The evening shows enjoy great popularity. The fountain surpasses the architectural constraints: water is also ejected by nozzles installed in the pavement in front of the fountain pond. The structure is a controversial topic for the locals. Some are delighted with it, others find it a bit too kitschy.

The building behind the fountain is called the Palace of Art (Palac Sztuki). It is home to an art gallery and the seat of the Society of Friends of Fine Arts. Auctions are organised here from time to time. The building itself is worth a visit. It was constructed between 1898 and 1901, and is modelled after the famous Secession Hall in Vienna.

No. 3 accommodates another gallery, the so-called Art Bunker (Bunkier Sztuki). The name of the gallery describes its outside appearance quite accurately: the building is one of the very rare Polish examples of brutalist architecture. The style flourished between the 1950s and '70s; it is characterised by concrete or rough-hewn stone structures, bulky and angular in shape. The Art Bunker is mostly dedicated to contemporary art. The winning works of the prestigious World Press Photo Contest are exhibited here every year.

Yet another example of the square's varied architecture is the 7-storey Art Déco building at No. 5. The tallest edifice in the Old Town, it was even called the "Cracow skyscraper" before WWII. ■

St Stephen's Square (Plac Szczepański)

🍴 *Cafe Bunkier, pl. Szczepański 3* 🔴🔴€; *Morskie Oko restaurant and pub, pl. Szczepański 8* 🔴🔴€

The Palace of Art is decorated with busts of celebrated Polish artists.

12 National Old Theatre

The building with an Art Déco frieze houses Poland's second oldest theatre, founded at the end of the 18th century. Long traditions go hand in hand with modernity.

The story of the theatre dates back to 1781. It was then that Mateusz Witkowski, a Warsaw actor, was granted permission from Cracow authorities to stage regular performances here. Under his directorship, the theatre did not have its own seat, and used the rooms at No. 34 in the Main Square (➤ 26). It was only in 1799 that the theatre moved to the present building, which is a combination of three smaller houses. The Art Déco look was added during a complete refurbishment at the beginning of the 20th century. The stucco frieze that incorporates plant motifs also dates from that time.

The theatre was not always open for performances. In 1893, the team of actors moved to the Municipal Theatre, now called the Juliusz Słowacki Theatre (➤ 54, ➤ 203), and only returned here after 1945. See also: ➤ 203. ■

Helena Modjeska National Old Theatre (Narodowy Stary Teatr im. Heleny Modrzejewskiej)

✉ *ul. Jagiellońska 1*

☎ *+48 12 4224040 (box office and ticket reservations), +48 12 4284700 (tickets for Scena Kameralna)*

@ *www.stary.pl*

🕐 *box office: Tue–Sat 10am–1pm, 5pm–7pm and two hours before shows*

Jewish Kazimierz

city atlas ➤246–247, 253, 262–263

A Town Within the City

The history of Kazimierz is inextricably linked with Polish Jews. For centuries, this was their religious and cultural centre. The Jewish population in Kazimierz was so large that the district soon became dubbed the "Jewish town."

The backstreets of Kazimierz have preserved the atmosphere of the old Jewish quarter.

Jews came to live in Cracow as early as the 13th century. At first, they settled down in the Old Town (➤ 50); today's ul. św. Anny was actually called ul. Żydowska (Jewish Street). The decision to banish Jews from Cracow was taken by King John Albert (♔ 1492–1501). The supposed pretext was accusing Jews of starting the fire that consumed a large part of the city. Most probably, they were expelled because of the conflicting interests of Jewish and Christian merchants.

In 1495, Jews of Cracow moved to Kazimierz, a town that was granted municipal rights in the first part of the 14th century by King Casimir the Great (♔ 1333–1370). It already had a Jewish community of unknown beginnings, with their ritual baths and a Jewish mar-ketplace. The local populace must have been numerous and thriving. However, it was only after Cracow's Jews moved to Kazimierz that the district became truly distinct, to the point of gaining the name of the *oppidum Iudaeorum* (the Jewish town).

The 15th- and 16th-century persecution of Jews in Europe caused an influx of even more inhabitants. Kazimierz turned into an important centre for European Jews, who shaped the life and appearance of the district. This much can be gathered, for example, from the architectural form of the Old Synagogue (➤ 78), modelled on those in German and Czech territories. The spine of the "Jewish town" was ul. Szeroka (➤ 73) with as many as four places of worship (only three survive to this day: the

If you get peckish at night, go to Okrąglak's fast food bars in pl. Nowy (➤ 86).

Remuh Synagogue ➤ 75, the Old Synagogue ➤ 78 and the Popper Synagogue ➤ 77), ritual baths (*mikveh*), and a cemetery. The growth of the community brought it closer to the part inhabited by Christians. Jewish Kazimierz extended as far as ul. Bożego Ciała, new tenement houses and synagogues were also built in the neighbourhood of today's pl. Nowy (➤ 86).

Kazimierz suffered great damage in the foreign invasion of the Swedish Deluge (1655–1660). The town was plundered and destroyed by enemy forces. The 18th century was not much better: the Partitions of Poland and the resulting turmoil effectively prevented Kazimierz – both the Jewish and the Christian sectors – from restoring their former glory. WWII put a dramatic stop to the life of the "Jewish town." In 1941, the Nazis established a ghetto in Podgórze and had the Jews of Kazimierz move there, then killed them or deported them to the death camps. Those who remained alive were transferred to the Płaszów Camp (➤ 116) in 1945.

Less than 10 percent of 60,000 Jews that inhabited Kazimierz before 1939 survived the war, and many left Poland in the succeeding years.

At present, the old Kazimierz is slowly coming back to life. The Jewish community consists of only 150 members, but already boasts its own, hand-written Torah. Regular services are held in Cracow's oldest Remuh Synagogue (➤ 75) and the Isaac Synagogue (➤ 81). There is also the seat of orthodox Jews associated in the Chabad Lubavitch Hasidic movement. You can see its members in the street from time to time, long-bearded and wearing their characteristic black suits and hats. The district has its Centre for Jewish Culture (➤ 87) with rich cultural offerings that attract also those Cracovians who do not have Jewish roots. Yet another meeting place is the recently opened Jewish Community Centre (➤ 85). The Jewish Culture Festival (➤ 230), organised every year, also enjoys great popularity.

Kazimierz is now one of the trendiest places in Cracow. There are

The Old Synagogue (➤78) **presents a historic exhibition on the Jews of Cracow.**

so many different bars to choose from that everyone will find something to suit their tastes. Most places have a unique ambience, hiding many nooks and crannies, all in semi-darkness and furnished with vintage equipment. The flickering candlelight and mismatched sets of chairs, as if straight from a flea market, add even more charm. Such places include the cult bars called Alchemia (➤206), Singer (➤208) and Eszeweria (➤193). Free seats are hard to find there on practically any day of the week. Sometimes, late-night conversations last until the morning. Those who prefer modern interiors will enjoy a night at Nova Resto Bar (➤190) or Le Scandale, among others. Dance freaks cannot miss Stajnia (➤212) and Ulica Krokodyli (➤195).

Kazimierz also offers a multitude of small shops. Ul. Józefa (➤220) is lined with many small design and second-hand shops. There is a growing number of boutiques, also with clothes that are not brand-new, usually retro in style. Tourists looking for some really interesting souvenirs should be par-

ticularly alert to unexpected opportunities for finding remarkable items, for example, at an antique fair held every Saturday in pl. Nowy (➤86). ■

Jewish Kazimierz should be visited twice. First, allocate an entire morning to a sightseeing tour. Better make sure it is not on a Saturday: on the Sabbath, almost none of the synagogues are accessible to visitors. Then, come back to Kazimierz in the evening to see the contrast between the historic past and the fun-loving present at its most striking. A night out at the local bars is a good time and a memorable experience.

In the district's cemeteries and synagogues (especially those that are still operational) male visitors must wear a head covering. At some places (e.g., the Remuh Synagogue ➤75 and the Tempel Synagogue ➤83) paper kippahs are available at the entrance.

Access by public transport:

1–5 7–13

Ⓣ 7, 9, 11, 13, 24, 50, 51 (Miodowa)

6

Ⓣ 7, 9, 11, 13, 24, 50, 51 (św. Wawrzyńca)

71

The oldest tombstones in the Jewish Cemetery are over 200 years old. Their engravings are overgrown with moss, but the memory of those buried here is still cultivated.

1 Jewish Cemetery

The forest of *matzevot* (Jewish tombstones) looks its best in the autumn sunlight. Enveloped in a nostalgic atmosphere, it makes one think back to the scenes from the life of Polish Jews depicted in old photographs, and their later tragic fate.

This cemetery was founded around 1800, when the Remuh Cemetery (➤ 75) was closed down. Most burial plots were soon sold and, from 1932 on, the deceased were laid to rest in the cemeteries by ul. Jerozolimska and ul. Abrahama. During WWII, both these burial grounds found themselves in the Nazi labour and concentration camp in Płaszów (➤ 116), and were consequently devastated and desecrated. The cemetery in ul. Miodowa also sustained considerable damage. The *matzevot* made of precious stone got sold to tombstone carvers, and the rest became building material for the camp's roads. After the war, the cemetery was used again for burials. Because the Jewish community is not very large, there are not many funerals taking place.

Take a look at the symbols engraved in *matzevot*. The crown stands for the Torah: it signifies that the tomb is the resting place of a well-respected man. Hands joined in benediction mark a person from a rabbinic family, usually the rabbi himself. The candle symbol stands for a woman, since it was mostly a woman's task to light the Shabbat candles. The eminent people buried here include Osias Thon (1870–1936), a rabbi and an MP for the Polish Sejm, Kalonimus Kalman Epstein (1754–1832), a Hasidic mystic, and Maurycy Gottlieb (1856–1879), a painter and a pupil of Jan Matejko.

Ul. Szeroka is one of the district's main thoroughfares. It features a monument commemorating the Jewish inhabitants of Kazimierz who were killed in WWII.

A large building by the entrance is a pre-funeral house. It was constructed in 1903. Bodies of the deceased are laid here on a special bench and prepared for burial by a funeral organisation, the Chevra Kadisha. It is a charity group, working for free (Jews have a strong belief that an act of kindness towards a person who cannot return the favour is particularly commendable). ∎

Jewish Cemetery (Cmentarz żydowski)
✉ *ul. Miodowa 58*
🕐 *Mon–Fri, Sun 9am–5pm*
€ *free*

★ 2 Ulica Szeroka

Once the spine of Jewish Kazimierz, Broad Street is now among the most popular places in Cracow. Trace the vestiges of the past, try Jewish cuisine, and have some wine in one of the many restaurants that line the street.

Every year at the end of June and the beginning of July, ul. Szeroka fills up with hundreds of dancing and singing merrymakers. The street is then the venue for the finale of the Jewish Culture Festival (➤ 230). The great open-air concert called Shalom in Szeroka Street gathers artists from all over the world. Late at night, you can hear the strains of klezmer music. When the concert is over, crowds move to bars and restaurants to enjoy themselves until the crack of dawn. Weekends are also busy. When the weather is fine, pavement cafés fill with people. Some restaurants resound with Jewish music, and the street is walked up and down by Cracovians and tourists alike.

Ul. Szeroka is brimming with places serving Jewish cuisine (above, Ariel ➤ 185).

The street once constituted the centre of the "Jewish town." It had a marketplace with kosher shambles, imposing tenements and places of worship: the Old Synagogue (➤ 78), the Remuh Synagogue (➤ 75), the Popper Synagogue (➤ 77) and the Auf'n Bergel Synagogue. The greenery hemmed in with a metal fence is the former burial ground, probably part of the Remuh cemetery. It now features a stone obelisk commemorating the Jewish inhabitants of Kazimierz, killed during WWII. No. 6 housed a *mikveh* (ritual baths). It was reached by going down a few dozen stone steps, since the source that supplied it with water had its outlet deep underground. The building is now home to a café and a bookshop, with very few traces left of the baths. Today, devout Jews use the *mikveh* at the Eden Hotel (ul. Ciemna 15). ■

Ulica Szeroka

🍴 restaurants: ethnic Arka Noego, ul. Szeroka 2 🔴🔴🟢; Klezmer Hois ➤ 185, ul. Szeroka 6 🔴🔴🟢; Awiw, ul. Szeroka 13 🔴🔴🟢; Ariel ➤ 185, ul. Szeroka 18 🔴🔴🔴; Polish-Jewish

The Auf'n Bergel Synagogue

The Synagogue on the Hill (Polish: Synagoga Na Górce) at No. 22 has been replaced with another building, but there is still a light burning in one of the top windows. This continuity is not accidental.

The loft of the former synagogue was the abode of a renowned rabbi and cabbalist, Natan Spira (1585–1633). It was rumoured that he talked face to face with the prophet Elijah himself. The rabbi was a pious man and spent his nights exploring the mysteries of the Torah and Cabbalah by candlelight. Today, a loft window is lit up to commemorate this eminent figure. The synagogue was destroyed during WWII, reportedly in search of gold; the hearsay about the hidden treasure, however, proved to be wrong.

Ester ➤ 185, ul. Szeroka 20 🔴🔴🔴; *Szara Kazimierz* ➤ 191, ul. Szeroka 39 🔴🔴🔴; *Ulica Krokodyli bar* ➤ 195, ul. Szeroka 30 🔴🔴🟢

The spiritual life of the Jewish community centres around the Remuh Synagogue.

★ 3 Remuh Synagogue and Cemetery

At present, this is the main synagogue in Kazimierz. It holds regular services and guards the Torah. On Jewish holidays, the interior resounds with prayers – just as it used to in the past.

The Remuh was once called the New Synagogue, which is odd given the fact that the shul was built on the site as early as 1553. It was, however, the second synagogue ever constructed in Kazimierz, and its name was meant to differentiate it from the Old Synagogue (➤ 78). During WWII, the Nazis devastated most of the furnishings and turned the interior into a storehouse for body bags. The synagogue was also used for storing fire brigade equipment.

The heart of the synagogue is marked by a metal *bimah* – an elevated place for reading the Torah aloud and leading the prayers. It is surrounded by a metal grille. The original structure vanished in WWII, but the present one is its faithful replica. One of the few surviving furnishings is the original Renaissance-style *Aron Kodesh* (a stone closet for keeping the Torah scrolls). The Torah ark is traditionally located by the wall closest to Jerusalem; in Poland, it is always the eastern wall.

Adjacent to the synagogue is Cracow's oldest preserved Jewish cemetery, one of the first founded in Poland. Interments started c. 1551, when victims of the plague were buried here. The cemetery was closed down in 1800 by the Austrian authorities on the strength of the regulation prohibiting burials close to dwelling houses. Around that time, a new cemetery was established in ul. Miodowa (➤ 72). However, occasional funerals took place by the Remuh Synagogue until the mid-19th century.

The Remuh Cemetery is the oldest preserved Jewish burial ground in Cracow.

During WWII, the Nazis wrecked the cemetery and turned it into a rubbish dump. The damage was massive. Most tombstones were broken, a lot were pushed over. To this day, some have still not been found and put back. The pieces of broken-up *matzevot* were incorporated within the interior side of the so-called Wailing Wall (Ściana Płaczu) around the cemetery. The name refers to the only remnant of the Jewish Temple in Jerusalem, also known as the Western Wall. ■

Remuh Synagogue and Cemetery
(Synagoga i cmentarz Remuh)
✉ *ul. Szeroka 40*
@ *www.remuh.jewish.org.pl*
🕐 *Mon–Fri, Sun 9am–6pm*
€ *PLN 5 (PLN 2)*
ℹ *on Fri, open until dusk (the beginning of Shabbat)*

A Renaissance Man

The name of the synagogue derives from the Remu – the popular name for Rabbi Moses Isserles. The tomb of this eminent Talmudist is a pilgrimage destination for devout Jews.

The Remu lived in the 16th century. He studied the Torah and Jewish Law, as well as geometry, physics and philosophy. The rabbi was laid to rest at the back of the synagogue. His tombstone was one of the very few to survive WWII almost intact. Legend has it that the Nazi who tried to raise his hand to destroy the tomb of the God-beloved wise man was struck dead on the spot. The place is still visited by pious Jewish pilgrims who leave here so-called *kvitelach* – notes with petitionary prayers to God. They believe that the Remu will give them his blessing and act as an intermediary.

The gate in ul. Szeroka reminds passers-by of the former sacral use of the Popper Synagogue.

4 Popper Synagogue

When first built, the Wolf Popper Synagogue was among the best-equipped shuls in Kazimierz. The building, tucked away at the far end of a courtyard, now houses a youth cultural centre and has almost completely lost its old feel.

The construction of the synagogue was financed in the early 17th century by Bocian (the Stork). Such was the nickname of Wolf Popper, which he earned for his habit of freezing into a bizarre stork-like position, with one leg up, when lost deep in thought. Popper was one of the wealthiest people in Europe of that time: he had made a fortune in trade and maintained wide business contacts. Towards the end of his life, he decided to found a synagogue.

The interior was highly impressive, which contrasted with the plain, simple exterior structure. The old décor has not been preserved. The fact that the building used to be a synagogue can be gathered from a plaque by the entrance. The form of the building and the characteristic shape of the windows on the side of ul. Dajwór are tacit traces of its old purpose. The place is now home to the Old Town Youth Cultural Centre (Staromiejskie Centrum Kultury Młodzieży). ■

Popper Synagogue (Synagoga Poppera)
✉ *ul. Szeroka 16*
ℹ️ *if the place is open for activities, ask to be let in to see the main hall – visitors are usually allowed to come in*

The name of the **Old Synagogue** is not accidental: this was the first shul built in Kazimierz.

5 Old Synagogue

One of the first synagogues built in Poland, it is the oldest to survive to this day. It now houses a museum with a collection of *judaica*, telling the story of the daily life of the Jews in Cracow and their celebrations.

A massive red-brick edifice at the end of ul. Szeroka cannot be overlooked. This was the first synagogue ever constructed in Kazimierz. The extensive square in front of the synagogue annually holds the grand concert called Shalom in Szeroka Street, the finale of the Jewish Culture Festival (➤ 230).

The architects of the synagogue were probably Czech, judging from the architectural similarities between equivalent structures erected earlier in that territory and the Old Synagogue. There are also some German influences. The interior is divided into two naves, which was rare in medieval Jewish architecture. Similar layouts can be found only in Prague, Regensburg and Worms. The ribbed vault is supported by two slender columns.

The synagogue was first built as a Gothic structure in the 15th century. Destroyed in a great fire of 1557, it was reconstructed in the Renaissance style. The synagogue burnt down several times, but the gravest damage was done during WWII, when the Nazis used it as a storehouse. In the 1950's, the edifice was restored, and the Jewish community handed it over to the Historical Museum of the City of Cracow. Today's exhibitions tell the story of the Jewish inhabitants of Cracow, their daily life and traditions. The collection includes a divorce document and a circumcision knife. Remember to take a look at *Aron Kodesh* curtains and coats used to decorate the Torah. ∎

Old Synagogue (Stara Synagoga)
✉ *ul. Szeroka 24*
☎ *+48 12 4220962, +48 12 4310545*
🕐 *Apr–Oct: Mon 10am–2pm, Tue–Sun 9am–5pm; Nov–Mar: Mon 10am–2pm, Tue–Thu, Sat–Sun 9am–4pm, Fri 10am–5pm*
€ *PLN 8 (PLN 6), free on Mon*
🍴 *Czajownia ➤ 199, ul. Józefa 25* 🔴🔴 €

The modern Galicia Jewish Museum is set in a pre-WWII mill building.

6 Galicia Jewish Museum

The museum has been in operation since 2004, but it has already become an inherent part of Kazimierz. The local exhibitions and events enjoy great popularity, and the bookshop offers a wide selection of publications.

The permanent exhibition is entitled "Traces of Memory." This is the fruit of a long-term collaboration between Chris Schwarz (1948–2007), a photographer, the founder and first director of the museum, and Jonathan Webber, an Oxford lecturer and the then holder of the UNESCO Chair in Jewish and Interfaith Studies. Their large-scale project was meant to collect the vestiges of the Jewish culture in Poland. The 1990's research resulted in truly intriguing photographs. Particularly evocative are the shots of old synagogues: closed, long-forgotten, as well as ruined, roofless, with dense thickets slowly overgrowing the peeling walls. The museum also holds numerous temporary exhibitions.

The interior of the museum is an interesting example of integrating modern design and post-industrial space. The building is a renovated mill from the interwar period. The wood and glass décor elements harmonise with the open interior space within the old structure of the building.

The museum is a happening place. It holds a number of regular events, such as family activities on the first Sunday of each month. Fridays see Shabbat in Galicia, organised by the Reform Jewish community (7pm until midnight), and on Saturdays there are concerts of Di Galitzyaner Klezmorim band (from 7pm). The café on site offers kosher wine. ■

Galicia Jewish Museum
(Żydowskie Muzeum Galicja)
✉ *ul. Dajwór 18*
☎ *+48 12 4216842*
@ *www.galiciajewishmuseum.org*
🕐 *10am–6pm daily*
€ *PLN 15 (PLN 10)*
🍴 *café on site ●●◐; Cosa Nostra restaurant, ul. Dajwór 25 ●●●*
◎ *activities and workshops for children, Family Sundays, a special play area next to the café*
ℹ *a bookshop with Jewish-themed literature on site*

The High Synagogue in ul. Józefa is a unique example in Jewish sacral architecture, since shuls usually had only one storey.

7 High Synagogue

The austere facade of the synagogue is enclosed by massive buttresses. The main prayer hall is located not on the ground floor, but upstairs, which is unique in Poland.

The original one-storey building accommodated a number of shops. The upper storey with a prayer hall was probably added later. This architectural solution was unique, since synagogues were not supposed to be higher than Catholic church buildings. The reason for this breach of convention may have been the constraints of space in the flourishing district; it could also have been the fear of attacks, as the synagogue stood in the immediate vicinity of Christian houses. The High Synagogue, the third shul that appeared in Kazimierz, was constructed between 1556 and 1563. The interesting thing is that a twin structure was built in Prague soon afterwards.

The majestic bulk of the synagogue has remained unchanged since its construction. The predominant features on the facade in ul. Wąska are the four massive buttresses that support the structure and the characteristic tall round-arched windows. The only modern addition is a glazed pyramid at the top. Not much has been preserved of the interior. The almost 10-metre-high hall used to be roofed over with an interesting barrel vault. In the renovation of 1969–1972, the vault was replaced with a plain ferroconcrete ceiling. This lack of sophistication is all the more surprising as the works were carried out for the Atelier for the Conservation of Historic Monuments, which was seated here.

An item that luckily escaped the ravages of time is a stone Renaissance *Aron Kodesh*, the oldest one in Poland. Yet another highlight are the remnants of wall paintings, which will give you the idea of what the synagogue once looked like. It was adorned with the signs of the zodiac and other motifs.

The rooms of the former shops on the ground floor are now occupied by a bookshop. It offers a very wide range of titles on the Jewish culture, history and tradition. It also sells interesting albums, modern fiction, and CDs of klezmer music, the sounds of which fill the bookshop. ■

High Synagogue (Synagoga Wysoka)

✉ ul. Józefa 38

🕐 Apr–Oct: Mon–Fri, Sun 9am–7pm; Nov–Mar: Mon–Fri, Sun 9am–5pm

€ PLN 7 (PLN 5)

🍴 Portofino restaurant ➤ 189, ul. Wąska 2 ●●; Cheder Cafe ➤ 197, ul. Józefa 36 (entrance from ul. Jakuba) ●●

8 Isaac Synagogue

This is the city's second oldest synagogue that still holds regular prayers and services. Its construction in 1644 was financed by Isaac Jakubowicz. One just cannot miss this imposing structure.

The lavish interior of the synagogue was a tempting target for robbers. Legend has it that, when the Jewish inhabitants of Kazimierz learnt about some plunderers' plans to break into the synagogue, they closed all the city gates so that the only way in was through the Remuh Cemetery (➤ 75). Wearing white nightgowns, Jews were waiting there for the robbers, who fled in panic when they saw the eerie apparitions wandering among tombstones in the middle of the night. However, the synagogue's moment of glory did not last long. The anecdotal criminals may have been scared away, but the Swedish invaders of 1656 looted the valuable furnishings of the prayer house. Over 20 years later, during an epidemic that decimated the population of Kazimierz, Jews themselves transported the rest of the items to the synagogue in Opatów; they were never brought back.

The 20th century did not spare the synagogue either. During WWII, it was devastated by the Nazis. 1939 saw the execution of Maximilian Redlich, a Jewish official, by the entrance to the shul: he was shot dead when he refused to destroy the Torah scrolls. In the 1950's, the building was assigned to the association

The Hidden Treasure

There is a legend on how Isaac Jakubowicz (d. 1653) – also known as reb Ayzik reb Jekeles – came into a great fortune that allowed him to found a synagogue.

One night, he had a dream about Prague and heard a voice saying that he would find a treasure under the city's bridge over the Vltava River. Upon waking, he made his way there. While he was looking for the riches, he was arrested by soldiers. The officer could not believe that Ayzik came all that way just because of a dream. "If I believed in such fantasies," he said, "I would go to Cracow myself, since I dreamt about a treasure buried under the stove of an Isaac Jakubowicz." And so, Isaac went back home, found the treasure under his stove, and spent half of it on building the synagogue.

of Polish visual artists. It was returned to the Jewish community after 1989.

The Baroque-style synagogue was designed by Giovanni Trevano, a famous Italian architect. His other projects included the facade of SS Peter and Paul's Church (➤ 35) and the reconstruction

The Isaac Synagogue, the largest shul in Cracow, is still an active place of worship.

of Wawel Castle (➤43) after the fire of 1595. The interior of the imposing synagogue is truly noteworthy. Of particular interest are the vestiges of the original wall paintings, restored during the renovation of 1994. These are mostly quotations from Jewish prayers.

The synagogue holds prayers and services. Its Torah was brought here from the Remuh Synagogue (➤75). The place of worship is mainly used by the Orthodox Hasidic Jews of the Chabad Lubavitch movement.

The square in front of the synagogue was once used as a fish market. It was in operation until the outbreak of WWII, becoming a recognisable landmark of Kazimierz and an integral part of the local colour. ■

Isaac Synagogue (Synagoga Izaaka)
✉ *ul. Kupa 18*
🕑 *Apr–Oct: Mon–Thu, Sun 9am–6pm, Fri 9am–2pm; Nov–Mar: Mon–Thu, Sun 9am–4pm, Fri 9am–1pm*
💶 *PLN 7*
🍽 *Kosher Delight restaurant, ul. Kupa 18, 1st floor* 🔴🔴 €
ℹ️ *a kosher shop nearby*

9 Kupa Synagogue

Linked with the nearby hospital for the poor, the synagogue served the destitute. After the Tempel Synagogue, it is the second most-decorated shul: polichromes cover the wooden barrel vault and the balustrades of the women's gallery.

The word *kupa* in the name of the synagogue comes from Hebrew. It stands for contributions that Jews paid the *qahal* (a Jewish community or its government), or for its treasury. This is the money with which the construction of the Kupa Synagogue was financed. In the past, it was dubbed as the "poor" or "hospital" synagogue. The first nickname refers to the material situation of the worshippers: the Kupa Synagogue was mostly visited by the poorest. The other nickname comes from the old Jewish hospital, once situated in pl. Nowy (➤86).

The synagogue, completed in 1643, was a very plain structure. On the outside, it was only the characteristic round-arched windows that indicated the purpose of the building. The floor was originally almost one metre below its present level, which made the synagogue completely sheltered by the adjoining city walls (a remnant of the 14th-century ramparts can be seen at the intersection of Warszauer and Kupa streets). When the fortifications fell into disuse, the synagogue was altered: it was made taller, and a wooden barrel vault and an annexe were added.

The facade of the Tempel Synagogue features the motif of the tablets with the Ten Commandments (they can be seen below the risalit).

After WWII, one of the rooms accommodated a kosher poultry slaughterhouse. It was open until the death of Abraham Lesman, the last kosher butcher, in 1985. For decades, the building also housed a shoe factory. The synagogue regained its former character when returned to the Jewish community, but it rarely holds services. The building is used rather as a venue for exhibitions and concerts.

The interior is decorated with multi-coloured paintings that date back to 1925. Particularly noteworthy are the signs of the Zodiac on the balustrades of the women's section: this motif is rare to find. Polychromes ornament the ceiling as well, depicting Jerusalem, the Western Wall, and the Flood. ▪

Kupa Synagogue (Synagoga Kupa)
✉ *ul. Warszauera 8 (entrance from ul. Miodowa)*
🕐 *Mon–Fri, Sun 10am–3.30pm*
€ *free*
🍴 *Kuchnia u Doroty, ul. Miodowa 25* 🔴€€; *Vanilla patisserie* ➤ *198, ul. Brzozowa 13* 🔴€€; *Absynt pub* ➤ *192, ul. Miodowa 28* 🔴🔴€

★ 🔟 Tempel Synagogue

The prayer house was the meeting place of those Jewish inhabitants of Cracow who wished to assimilate and break with orthodoxy. The finest synagogue in Kazimierz becomes a concert venue during the Jewish Culture Festival.

The synagogue interior delights the eye with a feast of colour. Sunbeams filtering through the stained glass windows illuminate the stucco decoration and vegetation ornaments (look up at the ceiling). The ornamental chandeliers also add lustre to the interior. The white marble *Aron Kodesh* in a semicir-

The interior of the Tempel Synagogue is decorated in the Moorish Revival style.

cular apse is truly impressive. Other noteworthy features include the supports of the women's gallery.

During the Jewish Culture Festival (➤230), the Tempel Synagogue is vibrant with life. It hosts concerts of many types of music, given by artists of different generations. The synagogue has seen performances from, for example, one of the last prewar klezmer musicians, Leopold Kozłowski, and an American-born Hasidic reggae musician, Matisyahu. A good concert in this fine setting is an unforgettable experience. Be quick: tickets sell like hot cakes!

The story of progressive Judaism in Poland goes back to the 19th century. The concept came from Germany, and involved a break with orthodoxy, and the cultural assimilation of Jews. A novelty that offended traditionalists was celebrating services in the local language. In the Tempel Synagogue, the weekly sermons were delivered in Polish and German; Osias Thon (1870–1936),

a rabbi famous for his sermons, was buried in the Jewish cemetery in ul. Miodowa (➤72). A mixed choir was introduced, which was disliked by orthodox Jews and aroused controversy.

The Reformist Jews of Cracow had to wait almost 20 years for their own synagogue. They were not welcome among the largely orthodox population of Kazimierz, and they first met for prayers in a private house. It was only in 1860 that they were granted permission to build a synagogue, which was completed two years later. It served religious purposes until WWII. After the Nazis took over Cracow, the synagogue was ravaged and used as a storehouse and a stable. Services were celebrated here again in the period between the end of the war and 1968. This was the year that a large number of Jews left Poland after the political witch-hunt of citizens of Jewish origin, conducted by the communist regime. A thorough renovation of the building took place in the 1990's, and restored the splendour it boasted before WWII. ▪

Tempel Synagogue (Synagoga Tempel)
✉ ul. Miodowa 24
🕐 Mar–Oct: Mon–Fri, Sun 10am–6pm;
Nov–Feb: Mon–Fri, Sun 10am–4pm
€ PLN 5 (PLN 2)

🍴 restaurants: Pieprzne Kawałki,
ul. Miodowa 20 ●●€; Edo Sushi
➤ 188, ul. Bożego Ciała 3 ●●€;
Absynt pub ➤ 192, ul. Miodowa 28 ●●€

11 Jewish Community Centre

The five-storey building at the back of the Tempel Synagogue is the venue of cultural events and a meeting place for the Jewish community of Cracow. Everyone is welcome to attend courses of Hebrew or Jewish dancing.

The JCC owes a lot to the Prince of Wales. On his visit to Cracow in 2002, Prince Charles came to Kazimierz and met the representatives of the Jewish community. When he learnt that they had no cultural centre of their own, he promised to help – and he kept his word. Soon, Cracow was visited by members of the World Jewish Relief, an organisation under the patronage of Prince Charles. They financed the construction of the JCC, and the patron himself was present at the inauguration in 2008. He affixed a *mezuzah* – a small box with the parchment bearing a section of the Torah as the blessing to the house – to the doorframe, in line with the Jewish tradition.

The mission of the JCC is the integration of the city's Jewish community. However, it is open to absolutely anyone interested in Jewish culture, religion and tradition, not to mention tourists to Cracow. The Centre offers a number of courses and workshops. One can learn foreign languages here, not only Hebrew or Yiddish, but also Spanish and Russian. There are also dancing, singing, and even yoga workshops. The classes range from sewing, through belly dance and basketball, to the Introduction to Judaism course conducted by Tanya Segal – the first woman Rabbi in Poland and an active member of the Jewish artistic community in Cracow.

The JCC holds celebrations of Jewish holidays and festivals. *Rosh Hashanah* (the Jewish New Year), *Pesach* (the Passover, which commemorates the Israelites' exodus from slavery in Egypt), and the multicoloured and joyous feast of *Purim* are only a few of the occasions attracting the city's inhabitants. The weekly Friday dinner gathers all those who want to celebrate the beginning of Shabbat and taste kosher food.

The Centre does not forget about its youngest visitors. They will have a good time in the play area on the second floor, with its many toys, books and drawing materials. The JCC provides nursery care for infants under 3 twice a week and during holiday celebrations. There is also a programme of regular activities for children, including classes in Israeli dance and a Sunday School.

The building is home to Cracow's only Jewish public library. The collection comprises about 2,000 publications, including the Torah and religious literature, as well as albums, contemporary Israeli prose fiction, and even comic books. ■

JCC – Jewish Community Centre in Cracow (Centrum Społeczności Żydowskiej w Krakowie)
✉ ul. Miodowa 24
☎ +48 12 3705770
@ www.jcckrakow.org
🕐 Fri 10am–4pm, Mon–Thu, Sat–Sun 10am–6pm
€ yoga workshops: PLN 15 per session; PLN 50 per month
🧸 a play area on the 2nd floor, occasional nursery care for children under 3

Popular souvenirs and choice beer are the trademarks of pl. Nowy.

★ 12 Plac Nowy

The rotunda in the centre of the New Square used to house an abattoir. It now sells the city's best French bread pizzas. The square is full of bars and great party opportunities.

Almost every house in the square accommodates several bars where you can have a beer and a talk. Pl. Nowy is one of the most fashionable places on the map of Cracow, and a popular destination for colourful party crowds. Here, the weekend spirit starts on Thursday, and often lasts all week. The place is a bit – but only a bit – quieter during the day. The air is filled with smells of vegetables and fruit sold in stalls; young men buy flowers on the way to their dates.

The centre of the square features the so-called Rotunda (Okrąglak). It has grocery shops selling dairy and meat products. Try one of the local fast food items served here (see: A Quick Bite ➤ 186). From 1927, the building was owned by Jews and housed a poultry slaughterhouse. Domestic fowls were killed in a ritual fashion so that all the blood ran out and the food stayed kosher (the Jewish law prohibits consuming blood). The slaughterhouse was closed down after the Nazis entered Cracow in 1939. ■

New Square (Plac Nowy)
🍴 *many eating places in the rotunda, e.g. the Oko bar 🔴 € €) and the Endzior bar 🔴 €); restaurants: Studnia Życzeń, pl. Nowy 6 🔴🔴 €); La Fuente ➤ 188, ul. Bożego Ciała 14 🔴 € €); Nova Resto Bar ➤ 190, ul. Estery 18 🔴🔴 €); pubs: Omerta ➤ 194, ul. Warszauera 3 🔴🔴 €), and Eszeweria ➤ 193, ul. Józefa 9 🔴🔴 €)*

Pl. Nowy features the popular Okrąglak building (see: Fast Food in Cracow ➤ 186).

13 Centre for Jewish Culture

The objective of the Judaica Foundation, seated in the Centre, is to preserve the heritage and traditions of Polish Jews. Visitors can see exhibitions, listen to concerts, or simply enjoy a coffee and a roof-top view over Kazimierz.

This building by the bustling pl. Nowy was once home to a Jewish prayer house (*Bejit ha-midrash*). Organised religious life came to a halt with the outbreak of WWII. After the war, the building was used as a storehouse, a carpenter's shop, and was then abandoned to fall into disrepair. The early 1990's saw its renovation.

The **Centre for Jewish Culture hosts concerts, themed events and exhibitions.** There are also book promotions and meetings with authors. Every year, from September to November, the Centre holds the *Bajit Hadash* programme: the Encounters with Jewish Culture, accompanied by a variety of events. Remember to visit the Centre's café. ■

Judaica Foundation – Centre for Jewish Culture
(Fundacja Judaica – Centrum Kultury Żydowskiej)

✉ *ul. Meiselsa 17*
☎ *+48 12 4306449, +48 12 4306452*
@ *www.judaica.pl*
🕐 *Mon–Fri 10am–6pm*
€ *free, most concerts are ticketed (PLN 25–50)*
🍴 *café on site ⊖⊖ ∈; Sara café ➤ 198, ul. Meiselsa 17 ⊖⊖ ∈*

Christian Kazimierz

Stradom

Berka Joselewicza
Brzozowa
Pod-brzezie
Centrum Społeczności Żydowskiej
Miodowa
STRADOMSKA
J. DIETLA
12·22
3·6·8·10·18·19·40
Synagoga Tempel
10
11
Synagoga Remuh
Miodowa
Synagoga Poppera
Synagoga Kupa
J. Warszauera
Jakuba
Szeroka
Synagoga Izaaka
Estery
8
Stara Synagoga
Dajwór
Koletek
św. Agnieszki
Meiselsa
Bożego Ciała
pl. Nowy
12
Nowa
Izaaka
Izraela
Kupa
Ciemna
pl. Bawół
9
Sukiennica
Orzeszkowej
Stradom
Miodowa
13
Centrum Kultury Żydowskiego
Józefa
Synagoga Wysoka
Wąska
Bartosza
Żydowskie Muz. Galicia
J. DIETLA
12·18·19·22
Meiselsa
Bazylika Bożego Ciała
św. Wawrzyńca
1
KRAKOWSKA
3·6·8·10·40

Kazimierz

ks. A. Kor-deckiego
E. Orzesz-kowej
Paulińska
św. Stanisława
Skałeczna
św. Kata-rzyny
św. Katarzyny Aleksandryjskiej
5
Augustiańska
Węgło-wa
pl. Bonifraterska
Bocheńska
Gazowa
pl. Wolnica
Ratusz Muz. Etnograficzne
2
Bazylika Paulinów
4
Piekarska
pl. Wolnica
Mostowa
Trynitarska
Skawińska
H. Wietora
A. Chmie-lowskiego
Trójcy Przenajświętrzej
3
PODGÓRSKA
Bulwar Kurlandzki
Ojca Bernatka
kładka
Bulwar Inflancki
Rybaki
most Piłsudskiego
3·6·8·10·40
Przy Moście
Celna
Staro mostowa
LEGIONÓW
pł. Sud-skiego
Wisła →
most Retmański
K. Rollego
Władysława Warneńczyka
Sokolska
Planty Nowackiego

0   100   200 m

city atlas ➤ 246, 262–263

The Town of King Casimir

Even though Kazimierz is now mostly associated with its Jewish inhabitants and landmarks, the story of the district (once a separate town) has been linked with the Christian population as well.

Pl. Wolnica (➤ 92) **boasts the most important building in Kazimierz: the Town Hall.**

In 1335, King Casimir the Great (👑 1333–1370) established a new town that was called by his Polish name of Kazimierz. The significance of the town was best indicated by the surface area, not much smaller than Cracow on its foundation. It thus appears that Kazimierz was a rival centre to the then capital of Poland, and was certainly among the most important towns under the rule of its founder. The original settlements that were the beginning of Kazimierz existed on the site at least 300 years before the town. They were located along the salt route which ran from the Wieliczka salt mine and Bochnia through Cracow to Hungary and Rus.

Kazimierz used to be an "island" in an overflow area, surrounded by marshes and rivers. It was washed on two sides by the Vistula River, the old branch of which flowed on the site of today's ul. Dietla. This river bed was only filled in the 19th century.

Different landform features and the fact that Kazimierz was encircled with ramparts make it perhaps easier to imagine that today's district (only one kilometre away from Cracow's Main Square) was once a separate town.

It is here that Casimir the Great wished to build Cracow Academy. The reasons for abandoning these plans remain unknown, and so does the site where it was supposed to be built. Historians wrangle over the precise place, indicating ul. Szeroka, or the neighbourhood of today's ul. Gazowa, or pl. Wolnica (➤ 92) – the main square of Kazimierz. The house at No. 11 has a plaque saying that the alleged foundations of the university were found here in 1868.

The glory of Kazimierz lasted until the 17th century. Considerable damage was done by the Swedish invasion (1655–1657), and then again during the Partitions of Poland. The town was

Part of the Altar of the Three Millennia by the Basilica on Skałka Hill (➤ 95).

After WWII, Kazimierz was a deserted district with poignantly empty buildings. The restoration is still in progress. It appears to advance more quickly in the "Jewish town," now among the most popular visiting places in Cracow (see: Jewish Kazimierz ➤ 68). The Christian part of the former town is less-known and attracts fewer tourists, but it is certainly worth seeing, especially for its old churches. Of particular importance for Polish Catholics is the Pauline Basilica on Skałka Hill (➤ 95), where St Stanislaus was reportedly killed. It is also a pantheon of distinguished Poles. The soaring Corpus Christi Basilica (➤ 90) makes a great impression with its austere Gothic walls, and the Baroque Church of the Most Holy Trinity (➤ 94) should be visited for illusionistic frescoes in the ceiling. ■

A leisurely walk in the former Christian part of Kazimierz, combined with visiting the sights, takes about 3 hours. The suggested route is a perfect extension of the preceding one that leads through Jewish Kazimierz. This relatively small area is home to as many as four churches, which is why Sunday is not a good day for visiting: the places of worship hold many Mass celebrations then.

Access by public transport:
1–5
304, 522, 614, 904 (Plac Wolnica)
3, 6, 8, 10, 40 (Plac Wolnica)

repeatedly ravaged by fires, which spread quickly in its dense, mostly wooden housing. In 1800, the declining Kazimierz was incorporated into Cracow. The early 19th century saw the demolition of the wall around the "Jewish town": Jews were now allowed to settle in the district's Christian sector.

★ 1 Corpus Christi Basilica

The most important Christian temple in Kazimierz was founded as the new town's parish church. When Mass is celebrated, the intriguing interior resounds with music played on the city's largest organ.

Upon entering the church, visitors are struck by the darkness of the interior. The windows in the high walls let in only scanty light. After a moment, however, you will find the semi-darkness quite appealing. It adds a sense of dignity to the over 600-year-old church, and puts visitors in a meditative mood.

The soaring Gothic austerity contrasts with more decorative and much newer Baroque furnishings, made after the church was plundered in the Swedish invasion of the 17th century. The side altars look to have been built with a new, different set of building blocks. At first glance, they seem not to match the rest of

The Gothic silhouette of the Corpus Christi Basilica stands out among the architecture of Kazimierz.

the interior, but they make for an interesting combination with the brick walls.

The highlight is the "boat" – an original late-Baroque pulpit (a similar one can be seen in St Andrew's Church ➤ 37). It was made with particular attention to detail, sails spread on masts and sirens supporting the structure.

The church boasts the largest organ in Cracow. It was designed for 84 pitches, of which 75 have been installed so far (one pitch is a separate rank of pipes). The organ consists of two parts: the main one (in the organ gallery) and the side one (in the chancel). They are synchronised so that one person can play both instruments simultaneously.

The basilica is the final resting place of St Stanislaus of Kazimierz. The preacher lived in the 15th century. He dedicated his life to helping the town's poor and needy. He was canonised in October 2010.

Legend has it that today's site of the basilica is where a Eucharist box was once found. It had been stolen from the Church of All Saints (no longer in existence) and thrown away once the thieves realised it was not gold, but only gilded. King Casimir the Great commissioned a church on the site so as to propitiate God for the desecration of the Eucharist.

The construction took a long time, even by medieval standards. It began in the mid-14th century and proceeded in stages up to 1405. At that time, the church was placed in the care of the Canons Regular of the Lateran, who have had their monastery here to the present day. ■

Corpus Christi Basilica of the Canons Regular of the Lateran (Bazylika Bożego Ciała Zakonu Kanoników Regularnych Laterańskich)

✉ *ul. Bożego Ciała 26*

@ *www.bozecialo.net*

🕐 *7am–7pm daily*

🍴 *Eszeweria pub ➤ 193, ul. Józefa 9* 🔴🔴 ⓔ

ℹ️ *services: Mon–Fri at 6.30am, 8am, noon, 7pm; Sun at 6.30am, 8am, 9.30am, 11am, 12.15pm, 4pm, 7pm*

The square in front of the Town Hall is popular with the feathered inhabitants of Cracow.

★ 2 Plac Wolnica and the Town Hall

Pl. Wolnica used to be the main square of Kazimierz. Marking the centre of the town, it had the town's weighing scales and market stalls. The dominant building is still the Town Hall, now home to the Ethnographic Museum.

Pl. Wolnica is slowly developing a big-city ambience. The frontages accommodate an increasing number of shops, bars and restaurants. More and more beer gardens start to spring up in the summer. This place simply seems destined to become fashionable in the near future. Take a closer look at the fountain, which represents three musicians: a trumpeter, a violinist and a cellist. The sculpture was designed by a Cracow-based artist, Bronisław Chromy.

The name of the square has been in use since the 13th century and is connected with the trade activity that took place here. *Wolny* means "free" in Polish,

and *wolnica* could refer to the freedom of commerce: one day a week (probably on Saturday) meat could be sold freely, unlike at any other time when this activity was prohibited outside shambles.

The main square of Kazimierz used to be much bigger, and ul. Krakowska ran through its middle. The town's official weighing scales were there so that traders could use them. The market stalls were closed only in the 1940's.

The most important building in the square was the Town Hall. The vestiges of the original Gothic structure can now be found only in the basement. Over the years, the Town Hall was

The *Three Musicians* Fountain, designed by Bronisław Chromy, stands next to the Town Hall.

altered many times and served many different functions. However, it lost its prestige when Kazimierz was incorporated into Cracow. The abandoned and decaying building came to house a school. After WWII, the Ethnographic Museum was moved here and can still be visited today.

The museum holds an outstanding folk art collection, one of the largest of its type in Poland. It includes a traditional bunch carried in rustic wedding ceremonies, a headdress worn by young wives in today's south-eastern Polish countryside in the early 20th century, toys for kids, and a hand-painted scarf of a reservist from the 1980's (what one might call army folklore). Visitors can see Polish countryside wear – both Sunday and everyday clothes – as well as get to know folk customs, traditions and workmanship. Rooms devoted to Cracow and the Podhale region display faithful and evocative reconstructions of 19th-century peasant cottage interiors. Wandering among the exhibits, one can easily picture life in the Polish countryside of two centuries ago. ■

Town Hall – Ethnographic Museum (Ratusz – Muzeum Etnograficzne)

✉ *pl. Wolnica 1 (permanent and temporary exhibitions), ul. Krakowska 46 (temporary exhibitions)*

☎ *+48 12 4306023*

@ *www.etnomuzeum.eu*

🕑 *Tue–Wed 11am–7pm, Thu 11am–9pm, Fri–Sat 11am–7pm, Sun 11am–3pm*

€ *permanent exhibition: PLN 9 (PLN 5), free on Sun; temporary exhibitions: PLN 8 (PLN 5)*

🍴 *Cafe Młynek, pl. Wolnica 7 €€€; Horai oriental restaurant, pl. Wolnica 9 €€€; Just Salad's, pl. Wolnica 13 €€€*

ℹ *guided tours in English, German, French, Russian and Swedish: PLN 65 for one person, PLN 5 for every additional person*

3 Church of the Most Holy Trinity

The Brothers Hospitallers of St John of God are famous for their herbalist skills. In Kazimierz, they look after the Church of the Most Holy Trinity – a late-Baroque edifice with an enormous illusionistic painting in the ceiling.

The interior walls of the church are decorated with fine Baroque frescoes.

For most Cracovians, herbalism has an automatic association with the order's name. The Brothers Hospitallers of St John of God have acquired their knowledge of natural medicine over centuries. The tradition combined with up-to-date medicine and diagnostics is quite efficient. No wonder the monastery's clinic attracts crowds from Cracow and neighbouring towns. The consultation is free, but donations are welcome.

The church was built by the Order of the Holy Trinity, but did not remain in their hands for long. The consecration took place in 1758.

The order was dissolved about 40 years later, and the church was used as a storehouse. The Knights Hospitallers came 15 years later and stayed in Kazimierz until the end of the 18th century.

The most characteristic remnant from the time of the Trinitarians is the polychrome painting on the vault of the nave. It depicts the founder of the order, St John de Matha, ransoming Christian prisoners from the Turks. The scene was not randomly chosen: freeing prisoners was part of the Trinitarians' mission. Go up to the high altar to take a closer look at the miraculous figure of Jesus of Nazareth, dating from the mid-18th century.

The slender late-Baroque facade of the church soars high above the rooftops of the neighbouring buildings. The third storey is higher up than the church ceiling and is purely ornamental, which you can see when walking along ul. Krakowska. Next to the church and the monastery stands a hospital, inaugurated in 1906. It soon became one of the best medical institutions of its type in Poland. After WWII, like many other private possessions, it was nationalised by the authorities of the Polish People's Republic. When the communist regime ended, the order demanded the return of their former property. The hospital was given back to them in 1997; it was the first privately-owned hospital after the fall of communism. ∎

Church of the Most Holy Trinity of the Brothers Hospitallers of St John of God (Kościół Bonifratrów p.w. Trójcy Przenajświętszej)

✉ *ul. Krakowska 48*

🕐 *Sun 9am–7pm*

ℹ *services: Mon–Fri 6.30am, Sat 8am, Sun 9.30am, 11.30am, 1.15pm (Tridentine Mass), 6.30pm*

The Baroque-style Pauline Basilica on Skałka Hill is a popular pilgrimage destination.

★ 4 Pauline Basilica on Skałka Hill

Like Wawel and Jasna Góra hills, Skałka is a major place of worship in Poland. It is here that King Boleslaus the Bold reportedly murdered Stanislaus of Szczepanów, the Bishop of Cracow and the future patron saint of Poland.

The veneration of St Stanislaus is an on-going phenomenon in Cracow. Every year, the holy relics are carried in procession from Wawel Cathedral to Skałka Basilica. This is one of the city's most important traditions, cultivated ever since the 13th century (see: St Stanislaus Procession ➤ 228).

The Pauline Fathers came to Cracow from the Jasna Góra Sanctuary in Częstochowa: chronicler Jan Długosz brought the monks over in 1472. Since then, the basilica has been in the hands of the white-habited Paulines.

The Basilica on Skałka Hill is a fine example of Baroque architecture. However, the first church built on the site was constructed much earlier, probably in the first part of the 13th century; some historians claim it was as early as the 10th century. An indisputable fact

is that a Gothic church commissioned by King Casimir the Great (♔ 1333–1370) had existed for a long time before it was replaced with the present edifice in the 18th century.

As you enter the church, take a look at the engravings on the granite steps. These are the names of the generous benefactors whose donations financed the grand entrance stairs in 1892. In St Stanislaus Chapel (Kaplica św. Stanisława), visitors can see the steps on which the bishop is said to have been slain; he was killed while he was celebrating Mass (see: Wawel Cathedral ➤ 46). Yet another noteworthy item is a silent witness of the martyrdom: the stump reportedly used to cut the bishop's corpse into pieces.

The crypt is a national pantheon, the final resting place of those Poles

Water from the stream by the Skałka Basilica is said to have healing properties.

who made an important contribution to the country's cultural heritage. The first person to be buried here was Jan Długosz (1415–1480), whose remains were interred in the crypt in 1880. Other eminent Poles included artists Stanisław Wyspiański (1869–1907), Jacek Malczewski (1854–1929), Adam Asnyk (1838–1897) and Józef Ignacy Kraszewski (1812–1887). Poet Czesław Miłosz (1911–2004), a Nobel Prize winner, was entombed here in 2004.

Water from the garden pond near the church entrance is said to be good in treating eye and skin ailments. Legend links it to the martyrdom of St Stanislaus: the king was cutting up the bishop's body so vehemently that one of the fingers shot out into the river, which then acquired healing properties. ∎

Pauline Basilica of SS Michael and Stanislaus (Bazylika Paulinów p.w. św. św. Michała Archanioła iStanisława, Biskupa i Męczennika)

✉ *ul. Skałeczna 15*

@ *www.skalka.paulini.pl*

🕐 *basilica: 9am–6pm daily; crypt: Apr–Oct 9am–5pm, Nov–Mar only upon request (ask at the monastery gate)*

5 Church of St Catherine of Alexandria

This monumental Gothic building is one of the oldest churches in Kazimierz. Built by the town's founder, it has survived fires, pillaging by enemy troops, floods, and even earthquakes.

The dominant feature of the interior decoration is the grand high altar. Its painting depicts the mystic marriage of St Catherine. The arch between the nave and an austere white chancel is adorned with a 17th-century crucifix, surrounded by a host of angels that were sculpted during WWII. Remember to see the cloisters that date back to the times of King Casimir the Great, displaying Gothic and Renaissance paintings.

The construction of the church did not go as planned. It was built in stages, and works most probably started in the 14th century. The chancel was the first

to be erected, even though construction had to be stopped because of a fire. The central nave was completed only later; it was supposed to be longer by about 12 m. So much can be gathered from the foundation remnants. There may have been plans to extend the church, which would explain the lack of an ornamental facade. Instead, there is just a plain wall, the temporary character of which is further manifested by the lack of entrance doors (one can enter only from the sides). However, even if the extension plans were a fact, they eventually came to nothing. The church

The 17th-century statue of St Rita in St Catherine's Church is an object of ardent veneration.

was not enlarged. A chapel of St John the Baptist, now dedicated to St Monica and called the Hungarian Chapel (Kaplica Węgierska), was added to the facade in the 15th century.

The chapel is open to the public only once a year (on April 26, the Feast of Our Lady of Good Counsel, portrayed in the chapel). On all other days, it is an enclosed place of prayer for the Augustinian nuns. Their convent is located in ul. Skałeczna, opposite the church and the adjoining gardens. For daily services, the nuns arrive through a covered gallery that connects the convent with the church.

Down through the centuries, the church has been haunted by almost all disasters possible. It burnt down several times, and the fire of 1556 resulted in the collapse of the apse's ceiling. In 1534, the church was flooded, and it served as a storehouse and a hospital during the enemy invasion called the Swedish Deluge (1655–1660). The church was also damaged by earthquakes. The first one took place in 1443 and must have

been very severe since it brought down the vault of the chancel. The second one came in 1786 and was a bit milder. However, the structure was gravely damaged, which was one of the reasons why the Austrian authorities closed down the church ten years later.

The building was also falling into ruin because the Austrians used it as a storehouse. Due to disrepair, the Senate of the Free City of Cracow ordered its demolition in 1827. The church escaped this fate thanks to the appeals of the Augustinian friars and the support of the Bishop of Cracow. The church was renovated and then consecrated again in 1864. ∎

Church of St Catherine of Alexandria (Kościół św. Katarzyny Aleksandryjskiej)

✉ *ul. Augustiańska 7*

🕐 *visiting: Mon–Fri 10am–4pm, Sat 11am–2pm, before or after services on Sun*

ℹ *services: Mon–Sat 7am, 8am (apart from July and Aug), 6pm; Sun 7am, 9am (apart from July and Aug), 11am, 12.15pm, 6pm*

Podgórze

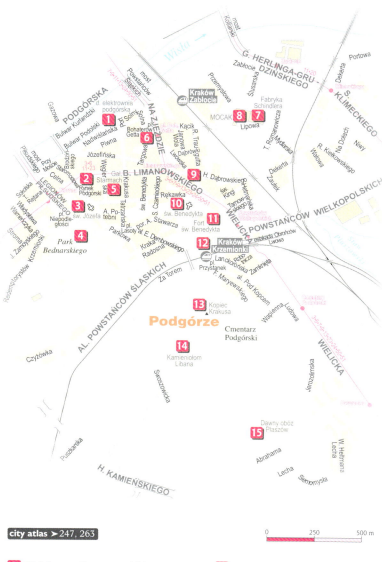

city atlas ➤ 247, 263

0   250   500 m

On the Right Bank of the Vistula

The past of Podgórze, once an industrial town, is scarred by the Holocaust. But it would be wrong to view the district only through this lens. There is so much more to Podgórze, which is full of interesting places with intriguing stories.

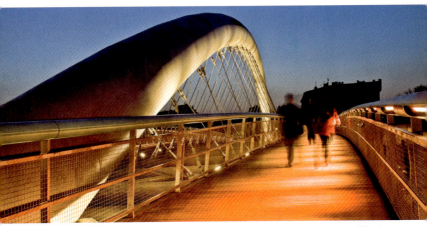

You can get from **Kazimierz** (➤ 68, ➤ 88) **to Podgórze by a footbridge that spans the Vistula.**

Podgórze consistently fights against the label of a dull post-industrial district with hardly anything to offer visitors. It is getting better at proving that unfair description wrong every year. One can even notice a budding fashion for exploring Podgórze. The district seems to be heading for success similar to that enjoyed by Kazimierz (➤ 68). The district was certainly made more tourist-accessible by the Father Bernatek Footbridge over the Vistula, constructed in 2010 with pedestrians and bikers in mind. The important thing is that the bridge gives access to the most interesting places in Podgórze, such as the trendy Drukarnia jazz club, which moved here from Kazimierz.

The oldest part of Podgórze has a low, planned architecture. Two-storey houses stretch in even rows. The area is an example of spatial order and a well-thought-out architectural plan, especially around the Podgórze Main Square (➤ 102). Those who set off to wander around the streets of the district will

A "Heart-bridge"

The Father Bernatek Foot-bridge (Kładka ojca Bernatka) is a particular favourite with young couples, who profess their love in a singular way.

Walking down the bridge, note the many padlocks locked on railings and bars. Some have names and initials engraved on them. Lovers leave padlocks here to seal their love, and throw the keys into the Vistula to make it eternal. Sometimes, you will see not only padlocks, but couples locked – in a kiss.

often come across runs of stairs – yet another characteristic feature of Podgórze.

The area was first inhabited as early as the Paleolithic Age. The 7th century saw the arrival of the Slavs, who are believed to have created the Krakus Mound (➤ 113). Some say that the Celts could have ventured here as well. Medieval documents are the first to mention villages on the site of the later town of Podgórze. These villages were the granary of Kazimierz, situated over the Vistula.

The Krakus Mound (➤113) affords a panoramic view of the Old Town (➤50).

A watershed point in the history of Podgórze came in 1784, when Emperor Joseph II granted it municipal rights (Podgórze had been in Austrian hands since the First Partition of Poland in 1772). In order to encourage people to settle in the new town, Joseph II granted the inhabitants a number of privileges, such as religious liberties. In addition, a bold economic policy was followed: industrialists were relieved of taxes for 30 years, and those who wanted to erect new buildings were given land lots for free. The Emperor wanted thus to establish a large centre able to challenge the neighbouring Cracow (outside Austrian control) as soon as possible.

The 19th century saw a rapid growth of the town on the wave of the Industrial Revolution. The development was driven in part by the lack of space for industrial investments in downtown Cracow, but also by a deliberate plan on the part of Podgórze. Cement and chemical works were constructed here, building stone was extracted, and bricks were made. Even a power station (➤101) was opened here, and this was several years before the existence of its counterpart in the much larger and older Cracow. The growing population numbers speak for themselves: in the early 19th century, Podgórze was inhabited by 2,000 people, in 1890 by over 12,000, and in 1910 by nearly 24,000.

Over the years, Podgórze repeatedly lost and regained its independence from the neighbouring Cracow. In 1809, both cities were included in the Duchy of Warsaw, a Polish state established by Napoleon. The following year, Podgórze became one of Cracow's districts for the first time. It took only five years before Podgórze was given back its municipal status. The town came under Austrian control again, as did Cracow after a failed uprising in 1846. The cities stayed separate entities, but they were linked by a network of forts constructed by the Austrian authorities. Its remnants can be seen today, also in Podgórze (see: St Benedict's Fort ➤111). The fortifications were together called the Cracow Fortress (Twierdza Kraków).

WWII was a truly tragic episode in the history of Podgórze. Nazi occupiers turned it into a ghetto, where Jews were jammed on a relatively small area (see: Ghetto Wall Remnant ➤110). The ghetto had a Polish-run "Under the Eagle" Pharmacy (➤107) and the seat of the Jewish council, the *Judenrat* (see: Podgórze Main Square ➤102).

When the Cracow ghetto was brutally liquidated (see: Plac Bohaterów Getta ➤106), the surviving Jews were deported to the Płaszów Camp (➤116). However, the neighbourhood had some brighter moments even during WWII: Podgórze was the location of the famous Schindler Factory (➤107), where the lives of over 1,000 Jews were saved. ■

A walking tour of Podgórze takes about 4–5 hours. Add one hour minimum for a visit to the Schindler Factory (➤107). Remember to wear comfortable shoes, as parts of the route are not paved. The grounds of the Płaszów Camp (➤116) are extensive and grassy, while the Liban Quarry (➤115) is genuinely perilous and difficult to walk: you enter at your own risk.

An eatery in pl. Bohaterów Getta (➤106) is located approximately halfway through the itinerary. There is a lot of walking ahead, so consider grabbing a bite. Once you pass St Benedict's Church (➤111), you will not find even one shop to buy anything to eat.

Access by public transport:

1 6 9
Ⓣ *7, 9, 11, 13, 24, 50, 51 (Plac Bohaterów Getta)*

2–5
Ⓑ *304, 522, 614, 904 (Korona)*
Ⓣ *3, 6, 8, 10, 11, 23, 40 (Korona)*

7–8
Ⓣ *11, 20 (Zabłocie), 7, 9, 11, 13, 24, 50, 51 (Plac Bohaterów Getta)*

10–14
Ⓑ *108, 127, 158, 163, 174, 178, 463, 522, 614, 904 (Powstańców Wielkopolskich)*
Ⓣ *3, 6, 7, 9, 13, 23, 24, 50, 51 (Powstańców Wielkopolskich)*

15
Ⓑ *108, 127, 158, 163, 174, 178, 463, 522, 614, 904 (Powstańców Wielkopolskich); 107, 143, 174, 243, 301, 463, 522, 614, 904 (Dworcowa); 144, 173, 179, 184, 304, 610 (Kamieńskiego)*
Ⓣ *3, 6, 7, 9, 13, 23, 24, 50, 51 (Powstańców Wielkopolskich or Dworcowa)*

1 Old Power Station

This public utility power station was the pride of Podgórze. One of the first ones in the whole Galicia area, it was opened almost five years before the one in Cracow.

The old power station is one of the most characteristic post-industrial buildings in Podgórze. Only 100 years ago, streets and houses were illuminated solely by gas and kerosene lamps. A local power station was thus a significant step towards the electrification of Podgórze and Cracow. On March 1, 1900, the current was transmitted through copper wires to the lanterns of Podgórze Main Square (➤102). Their glow eclipsed for a moment even the twinkling of stars, as reported by delighted residents.

The power station did not operate for long. Although it worked for some time even after the merger with Cracow's power plant in 1915, it eventually closed down in 1926. All the furnishings were removed, and the desolate building became home to baths and a night shelter for the home-

less. Then, it housed a clinic of dermatology and venereology, and – after WWII – an emergency ambulance service.

Today, the building of the old power station is undergoing a conversion into the Museum of Tadeusz Kantor, a distinguished theatre director. It will be the main seat of the Cricoteka – the Centre for the Documentation of the Art of Tadeusz Kantor. The projected works include the construction of another building, designed especially to constitute a harmonious whole with the preserved power station. The museum will probably be inaugurated in December 2012. ■

Old Power Station in Podgórze
(Dawna elektrownia podgórska)
✉ *ul. Nadwiślańska 4*
🕐 *closed to visitors*

2 Podgórze Main Square

Though seemingly triangular in shape, the Main Square actually has the form of a trapezium. It marked the very centre of the town and served as a marketplace and a tram terminus. The former Town Hall building has a rich history.

The corner of the house at No.12 is ornamented with a bizarre stag.

The layout of the Main Square is not a product of chance. The square tapers towards the church (➤ 103) to make it look more impressive; the square itself appears to be longer than it really is. The effect would probably be more noticeable if it was not for the trees, planted in the communist era.

The large building at the corner of the Main Square at No. 1 was once used as the Town Hall. It was constructed in the mid-19th century, and has been altered a few times since then. Prominent features include a monumental neo-Baroque facade with the coat of arms of Podgórze. Under the communist regime, it was replaced with the logo of the communist party, and then after 1989 with the crowned white eagle – the emblem of the independent Poland. The coat of arms of Podgórze was returned to its place only in the mid-1990's; this

is one of the unique cases where the national emblem has been knocked off the wall to be supplanted with the coat of arms of a town. The eyes are attracted to the tall round-arched windows on the second floor. Behind them, there is a hall where the town council once assembled. It is considered to be one of the finest rooms of that type in Cracow. Sadly, the building is not open to visitors, since it now houses a branch of Cracow's Municipal Council.

Under the Nazi occupation, the Town Hall was the seat of the *Judenrat* – a Nazi-appointed Jewish Council, expected to make sure that the occupier's orders were met quickly and efficiently. The first *Judenrat* head was Marek Biberstein, who tried to prevent deportations. He was arrested and moved from one camp to another. His last stop was the Płaszów Camp (➤ 116), where he was killed. The Nazis found his successor, Dr Artur Rosenzweig, not "effective" enough at rounding up ghetto inhabitants for deportation from pl. Zgody (now pl. Bohaterów Getta ➤ 106), so he was dismissed and sent on a transport to the Bełżec Camp on June 1, 1942. The successive *Judenrat* head, Dawid Gutter, was killed in the Płaszów Camp.

The Main Square has a number of interesting landmarks. The corner of No. 12 features two stags with one head, topped with wide antlers. The adjoining building is called the House of the Black Eagle (Dom Pod Czarnym Orłem). It used to accommodate an inn and a wine bar. In the 1970's, the word for "black" was knocked off the facade and the eagle was painted white to resemble the national emblem. The house was once used as a town hall as well. ■

The soaring, richly ornamented St Joseph's Church is a gem of neo-Gothic architecture.

Podgórze Main Square (Rynek podgórski)
🍴 *restaurants: Cesare Ristorante, Rynek Podgórski 9* 🔴🔴 €); *Makaroniarnia,*

ul. Brodzińskiego 3 🔴 €) €); *Cafe Rękawka, ul. Brodzińskiego 4b* 🔴🔴 €)

3 St Joseph's Church

The Main Square's architecture is dominated by the central parish church of Podgórze. It may seem to be centuries' old, but appearances are deceptive. A fine example of the neo-Gothic style, it is barely 100 years old.

Before St Joseph's Church was built, Roman Catholic inhabitants of Podgórze celebrated Mass in an old uniform storehouse. The room adapted as a chapel welcomed the believers for almost 15 years before the first parish church was constructed. The latter, however, did not exist for long. It was consecrated in 1832, but soon turned out to have a number of serious faults, done in the construction process. The structure was in danger of collapsing, and was demolished at the beginning of the 20th century.

The present church building, consecrated in 1909, is one of the finest examples of neo-Gothic architecture in Poland. Particularly prominent are its majestic facade and the tower's cupola, reminiscent of one of those atop St Mary's Basilica (➤23). The lofty interior of the three-nave basilica church (especially the vaulted ceiling and stylised altarpieces) is Gothic in style. The church boasts as many as 67 representations of saints: statues and paintings adorn the facade and the interior walls. The stone figure of St Joseph holding

Baby Jesus can be seen in the centre of the high altar.

The organ that can be heard here was made for a church in Bak (Caucasus) by a Warsaw company before the outbreak of WWI. Various difficulties, including financial ones, made it impossible to complete the deal even after the war, and the brand-new instrument stayed in Warsaw. At that time, the exchange rate was very unstable – not to say unpredictable – so instrument workshops did not accept long-term orders. That is why the parish priest and the parishioners of St Joseph's Church opted for buying a ready-made organ. Installed in 1922, it has served to this day.

The residence of the parish priest is much older than the church itself. Parts of the building date back to about 300 years ago. The presbytery was once an inn, and the basement was used to store items needed to run such an establishment. For the decades that followed, the basement lay abandoned, and the damp made it deteriorate gradually. The basement emerged from a major renovation in the 1980's as the so-called Quarry of John Paul II (Kamieniołom im. Jana Pawła II), a meeting place for democratic opposition activists. It now holds family meetings, premarital courses, exhibitions and small concerts. ■

St Joseph's Church (Kościół św. Józefa)
✉ *ul. Zamoyskiego 2*
@ *www.jozef.diecezja.pl*
🕑 *7am–6pm daily*
ℹ️ *services: Mon–Sat at 7am, 8am, 6.30pm; Sun at 7.30am, 9am, 10.30am, noon, 6.30pm, 8pm*

4 Bednarski Park

The green oasis of Podgórze is one of the most picturesque public parks in Cracow. An example of a successful recultivation of former industrial grounds, the park was founded at the end of the 19th century on the site of a disused quarry.

Bednarski Park has a playground, a sandpit, and a football pitch. Those who come here for a walk can wander around looking for calcareous rocks and a bizarre tree that grows horizontally – a real favourite with young visitors.

The park is located on the site of an old quarry, opened in the Middle Ages. The idea to reclaim the excavation grounds came from Wojciech Bednarski, a local teacher and a true friend of Podgórze. It was thanks to his persistence and financial contributions that the park was inaugurated in 1896. This enterprise may well be seen as one of the pioneering recultivation projects of former industrial grounds in Poland. Works were comprehensive in nature, synchronised with the extension of the town itself – the soil dug up during the construction of new houses was used to roughly level the surface area of the park. A wide flight

Master Twardowski

Every Polish child knows the legend of Master Twardowski, a sorcerer and an alchemist. His laboratory was allegedly situated in Podgórze, in the part of the quarry that is preserved to this day.

To obtain magical powers, Master Twardowski made a pact with the devil. He was to hand over his soul in Rome; no wonder, then, he steered clear of the city. One day, he entered a tavern without noticing that its name was "Rome"; the devil materialised at once, seized Twardowski and carried him away. The scared man started praying. This proved too much for the devil, who dropped Twardowski. The man landed on the moon, where he allegedly can still be seen on clear nights.

The picturesque grounds of Bednarski Park once held a quarry.

of steps was added in the 1960's. Today, the park is considered to be one of the most scenic in Cracow. It consists of two parts: an old neoclassical sector, and a more recent one, modernist in style. ■

Bednarski Park (Park Bednarskiego)
🕑 *open to the public 24/7*
ℹ️ *entrance from ul. Parkowa (main gate) and from pl. Niepodległości*

5 Starmach Gallery

This privately-owned gallery presents mainly Polish contemporary art. It has seen exhibitions by artists Tadeusz Kantor, Jerzy Nowosielski and Magdalena Abakanowicz.

The building of the Starmach gallery vaguely reminds one of Jewish architecture. This association is correct: the place was once a house of prayer for Jews, built in the years 1879–1881 and in operation until WWII. After the war, the building was used as a factory and a storehouse. The gallery was founded in 1989 by a couple of art historians, Teresa and Andrzej Starmach. It was first located in the House of Angels (Dom Pod Aniołami) at No. 45 in Podgórze Main Square. When the gallery was moved to the old Jewish house of prayer, it gained a truly intriguing exhibition space.

The focus of the gallery is Polish art, in particular connected with Cracow. However, there are also exhibitions of works by international artists, such as Andy Warhol and Nobuyoshi Araki. The gallery offers commercial services as well. The building is home to the Nowosielski Foundation (Fundacja Nowosielskich), headed by Andrzej Starmach. The foundation awards prizes to young Polish artists and is considered to be one of the most prestigious art organisations in Poland. ■

Starmach Gallery (Galeria Starmach)
✉️ *ul. Węgierska 5*
☎️ *+48 12 6564915*
@ *www.starmach.com.pl*
🕑 *Mon–Fri 11am–6pm*
€ *free*

105

The chair installation in pl. Bohaterów Getta commemorates the Jews who were killed here during WWII.

6 Plac Bohaterów Getta

Under the Nazi occupation, today's Ghetto Heroes Square witnessed the brutal killing of the inhabitants of Cracow ghetto. 2005 saw the installation of 70 metal chairs to commemorate these tragic events.

During WWII, this was the central square of the Jewish ghetto (called pl. Zgody back then). It was usually very crowded. People came here to take a breath of fresh air, leaving the overpopulated flats they were forced to live in; the cramped conditions inside stuffy rooms were truly unbearable. Every day, the square looked to be overtaken by a big rally. From the perspective of what we now know about the fate of the ghetto, it was as if the community had assembled together in premonition of danger.

March 14, 1943 – the second day of the ghetto liquidation – was warm and sunny. The inhabitants of the ghetto's Part B (for those unable to work) were driven to the square and then systematically killed in the neighbouring streets and gates. The ground was soaked with blood. The screams of the murdered and machine gun shots echoed off the walls. To save on ammunition, the Nazis lined children up one behind another, and babies were piled in prams – one bullet was enough to take many lives. Those who survived the carnage were deported to death camps, the Płaszów Camp (➤ 116) and Auschwitz (➤ 176), among others.

The name of the Ghetto Heroes was given to the square after the war to pay tribute to the victims. Life went on, and the square came to hold a coach station, as it had before the war. It was only in 2005 that the site was thoroughly redesigned to pay full respect to the Nazi victims. It has become one of the most poignant places in Cracow. There are about 70 metal chairs arranged all over the square, illuminated at night. The architects were inspired by an excerpt from the memoirs of Tadeusz Pankiewicz, *The Cracow Ghetto Pharmacy*: a description

"Under the Eagle" Pharmacy

It was the only pharmacy in Cracow's ghetto. Founded in 1909, it continued to operate until the very liquidation of the Jewish sector. It offered not only medication, but also help and shelter.

The pharmacy owner, Tadeusz Pankiewicz (1908–1993), was the only Pole to have stayed here when the Jewish ghetto was set up. He did not only sell medication: sometimes medicaments were distributed for free among those most in need. The pharmacy was the meeting place for the Jewish *intelligentsia*, and the hiding place for people threatened with deportation. It also served as a "window on the world" and a contact point, since Polish employees transmitted messages out of the ghetto, and brought in food. It should be noted here that Poland was the only country under Nazi occupation where any help given to Jews was automatically punishable by death, and the penalty was usually executed on the spot.

Pankiewicz was named a Righteous among the Nations. After the war, he resigned from running the pharmacy. His recollections of Cracow's ghetto bear testimony to the truth of the Nazi genocide of Jews.

The pharmacy is now home to a museum. A part of the building is a reconstruction of the old pharmacy interior. Exhibitions are dedicated to everyday life in a ghetto, in a concentration camp and Nazi-occupied Cracow. Sunday shows present a documentary that tells the story of Bernard Offen, a Holocaust survivor who lived through Cracow ghetto and five concentration camps.

"Under the Eagle" Pharmacy
(Apteka pod Orłem)

✉ *pl. Bohaterów Getta 18*

☎ *+48 12 6565625*

🕐 *Nov–Mar: Mon 10am–2pm, Tue 9am–4pm (closed on the 1st Tue of the month), Wed–Thu 9am–4pm, Fri 10am–5pm, Sat 9am–4pm; Apr–Oct: Mon 10am–2pm, Tue–Sun 9.30am–5pm*

€ *PLN 6 (PLN 5), free on Mon; guided tours in English: PLN 100 per group*

ℹ *free film shows: Sat and Sun at 11am*

of cases, clothes and chairs scattered around after the ghetto liquidation. On the anniversary, the March of the Living (➤ 227) departs from here. ∎

Ghetto Heroes Square
(Plac Bohaterów Getta)

🍴 *Wczoraj i dziś eatery, pl. Bohaterów Getta 10* 🔴 €) €)

★ 🟥7️⃣ Schindler Factory

In Cracow, Oskar Schindler underwent a dramatic transformation. As a member of the Nazi Party, he came to make a fortune using forced labour. Eventually, he saved over 1,000 Jews and was named a Righteous among the Nations.

An enamelware factory called Rekord was founded in 1937 by three men of Jewish descent. The factory did not bring the profit they expected, and was declared bankrupt after two years of operation. When the German troops entered Cracow, the property was taken over by Oskar Schindler. The industrialist, born in 1908 in Moravia (Austria-Hungary), was a member of the Nazi Party and came to Poland to capitalise on the German invasion. He extended the factory and renamed it *Deutsche Emailwarenfabrik* (German Enamelware Factory). DEF soon started to make products for the German army.

The factory employed mainly Jewish workers. Their number increased from 100 in 1940 to over 1,000 in 1944. At first, Schindler tried to ensure relatively good conditions solely for pragmatic reasons: well-fed and healthy workers were simply more efficient. With time, however, his attitude towards

Oskar Schindler's factory is situated on the Cracow Industrial Heritage Route. The wartime refuge of Jews now houses a museum on the German occupation of Poland.

his subordinates changed diametrically. The turning point was the liquidation of the ghetto in Podgórze and the action of moving its inhabitants to the Płaszów Camp (➤ 116). The brutal handling of people and inhumane conditions of living in the camp made Schindler determined to protect "his" Jewish workers.

The industrialist commissioned living barracks for more than 1,000 Jewish workers to be built close to the factory. The official rationale was that he wanted to economise on the time it took the workers to arrive. Schindler's powers of persuasion, vast social relations (and bribes, most probably) at last won over Amon Goeth, the commandant of the camp, to this plan. In secret from other Germans, Schindler increased food rations and provided his workers with health care. When Płaszów was turned into a concentration camp, "Schindler's Jews" were officially placed under the control of the SS. Afraid of unexpected inspections and their unthinkable consequences, Schindler spent nights in his study in case he would have to intervene.

Schindler made the impossible happen. When the Red Army drew near,

it became evident that the Germans would not be able to hold the city. The decision to complete the "Final Solution of the Jewish question" in Cracow was taken: every camp inhabitant was to be exterminated. Schindler managed to obtain permission to move the factory to Moravia, and to take with him all the Jewish workers (about 1,200 people in total). If it had not been for his commitment as well as huge financial outlays on food and medication for workers on the one hand and bribes for Nazi officials on the other, "Schindler's Jews" would have been killed in gas chambers like their brothers from the Płaszów Camp.

Schindler's dedication and bravery were recognised by Holocaust survivors. Yad Vashem, the Israeli Holocaust Martyrs' and Heroes' Remembrance Authority, awarded him with a medal and the title of the Righteous among the Nations (given to Gentiles who risked their lives saving Jews during WWII). The inscription on the medal and on the plaque set in a factory wall is a quote from the Talmud: "To save a life is to save the world."

The building now accommodates a museum dedicated to the time of Nazi occupation. The rooms hold exhibitions on the realities of Nazi-ruled Cracow, on the tragic fate of Jews, their life in the ghetto and the camp. Multimedia items enhance genuine wartime exhibits. You can see here the original raree show that operated in pl. Szczepański, go over the ghetto wall, or visit a reconstruction of a barber's shop. A great interior design heightens the impression up to the point of feeling transported back in time into the centre of events. Visitors are not separated from the exhibits by any bars or glass screens, which makes the tragic past more immediate. The museum also shows documentaries shot during the war; watching the screenings is a disturbing experience. All this makes for a fascinating as well as a deeply moving visit. ◼

Emalia – Oskar Schindler's Factory (Fabryka Emalia Oskara Schindlera)

✉ *ul. Lipowa 4*

☎ *+48 12 2571017, +48 12 2570095, +48 12 2570096*

🕐 *Nov–Mar: Mon 10am–2pm, Tue–Sun 10am–6pm; Apr–Oct: Mon 10am–4pm (until 2pm on the 1st Mon of the month), Tue–Sun 10am–8pm*

€ *PLN 17 (PLN 14), free on Mon*

ℹ *last admission: 90 minutes before closing time; ticket reservation by phone or on the website of the Historical Museum of the City of Cracow (www.bilety.mhk.pl); on Mon, you need to collect a free entrance ticket from the ticket office – their number is limited*

8 Museum of Contemporary Art

This museum proves that Cracow does not limit itself to the cultivation of its past and the promotion of its historic monuments. The city follows the newest art trends as well.

The museum displays works by artists of the last 20 years. The collection comprises dozens of works and is growing every year. The big names include Robert Kuśmirowski, Dick Higgins, Wilhelm Sasnal, Krzysztof Wodiczko and Mirosław Bałka. There are also many temporary exhibitions.

The museum is situated on the grounds of the old Schindler Factory. Its exhibition rooms have a total surface area of over 4,000 square metres. The interior is modern and ascetic in style. ◼

Museum of Contemporary Art in Cracow (MOCAK Muzeum Sztuki Współczesnej w Krakowie)

✉ *ul. Lipowa 4*

☎ *+48 12 2634000*

@ *www.mocak.com.pl*

🕐 *Tue–Sun 11am–7pm*

€ *PLN 10 (PLN 5), free on Tue*

🚊 *3, 6, 23 (Limanowskiego), 7, 9, 11, 13, 24, 50, 51 (Plac Bohaterów Getta), 11, 20 (Zabłocie)*

The Museum of Contemporary Art was designed by Claudio Nardi.

109

9 Ghetto Wall Remnant

Walking along ul. Lwowska, you come across a remaining section of the ghetto wall. It is topped with round arches that are characteristic of Jewish architecture, and looks like a row of lined up *matzevot* (Jewish tombstones).

The ghetto wall separated Jews from other Cracovian communities between 1941 and 1943.

There were more than **68,000 Jews inhabiting Cracow in November 1939.** Soon, the Nazis started forced deportations in which thousands of people were transported out of the city. More humiliations and persecutions followed: Jews were made to wear Star of David badges, allowed to use only marked off sections on trams, banned from walking in the Planty (➤ 53) and from moving around the city at night. But it was going to get much worse.

The Nazis avoided the "ghetto" term, speaking of the "Jewish residential area" instead. Such inscriptions were put on all the four gates through which the ghetto could be entered after it was walled in March 1941. Depending on the source, between 16,000 and 20,000 Jews are estimated to have been jammed into 320 houses inhabited by only 3,500 people before the ghetto was established. This means that there were only 2 square metres of living space per individual Jew. The ghetto had one hospital, a pharmacy and a bathhouse.

Food rations were steadily diminishing. An adult Jew was given 100 grams of bread a day. There was also a small monthly ration of sugar and fat. Hence, food prices in the ghetto increased manifold in a short period of time, and famine became widespread across the population. The Nazis then started deporting Jews to death camps. The first mass transportations took place in June and October 1942. In total, between several and twenty thousand people were deported, under the supervision of the Jewish policing service.

Those who stayed were divided into two groups. People able to work had to settle in Part A of the ghetto, while the elderly, the weak and children were placed in Part B. In March 1943, the ghetto was liquidated. Workers were moved to the Płaszów Camp (➤ 116); others were killed on site or deported to death camps such as Auschwitz-Birkenau (see: Auschwitz ➤ 176).

The other remnant of the ghetto wall can be seen by the school in ul. Limanowskiego at Nos. 60-62, close to the intersection of ul. Wielicka and al. Powstańców Śląskich (entry through the gate to the left of the building). ■

Ghetto Wall Remnant
(Fragment muru getta)
✉ ul. Lwowska 27
🍴 Jadłodajnia, ul. Lwowska 11 ● ◎ ◎

🔟 St Benedict's Church

Lasota Hill boasts the city's smallest church. It is open to the public only once a year, on the occasion of the traditional Podgórze parish fair.

A small shingled church looks its best in the soft autumn sunlight, among multi-coloured leaves. The plain interior can be seen only on the first Tuesday after Easter. The dominant feature is a Baroque-style altarpiece, placed at the end of a small chancel that is a bit narrower than the nave: a typical layout of small Romanesque churches. The present appearance dates from the 16th century.

The story of this little gray church is much longer than one would expect. It was built probably in the 13th century on the site of a pre-Romanesque rotunda. Some historians say that it could have been a seat of Benedictine monks before they settled down in Tyniec (➤ 167).

This theory would certainly account for its choice of patron saint. ■

St Benedict's Church
(Kościół św. Benedykta)
✉ Lasota Hill
🕐 open on the 1st Tue after Easter; services at noon, 4pm and 6.30pm
ℹ Starting from the intersection of ul. Wielicka and al. Powstańców Śląskich, follow the path past an old cemetery (on the left). If you want to reach the footbridge towards Krakus Mound (➤ 113), which affords a view of the Silva Rerum Mural (➤ 112), walk down the path by the school fence (the gymnasium visible from the meadow should be to your right). Exit into ul. Dembowskiego. The footbridge is in view to the left. Lasota Hill can also be reached from the direction of Bednarski Park (➤ 104).

🔢 St Benedict's Fort

The extensive meadow on Lasota Hill features a squat red-brick building. It is one of the most interesting structures of the former Cracow Fortress – fortifications that were constructed by Austrian occupiers in the 19th century.

St Benedict's Fort was part of a fortified defence complex, known as the Podgórze bridgehead. The main building was the (no longer existing) Krakus Fort, situated close to Krakus Mound (➤ 113). Nearby, there were two Maxi-

milian towers. One of them is St Benedict's Fort. The other one, Krzemionki fort, was demolished and replaced with the Cracow TV Studio, which can be seen from the Lasota Hill.

111

The fort was built on the plan of a hexadecagon. The structure is 38 m in diameter, while the inner courtyard is only 8 m in diameter. The building served as a barracks and an artillery post. It was surrounded with a moat.

After Poland regained independence in 1918, the fort was converted into living space. It was intermittently inhabited until 1984, when the last occupants moved out. The many ideas for the redevelopment of the landmark have come to nothing. Today, the fort is locked up tight and slowly falls into ruin. It is in dire need of revitalisation. ■

St Benedict's Fort – Fort No. 31
(Fort św. Benedykta – Fort nr 31)
✉ *Lasota Hill*
ℹ *inaccessible to visitors*

The Rękawka Festival

On the first Tuesday after Easter, Podgórze celebrates the Rękawka folk festival. Lasota Hill is the site of a church *fête*. Festivities are also held at the foot of Krakus Mound, featuring a knight village reconstruction.

The name "Rękawka" probably derives from the Serbian *raka* (tomb) or the Czech *rakew* (coffin). Legend has it that, when Krakus died, his subjects built him a mound, fetching soil in their sleeves (in Polish: *rękaw*). The annual festival was thus a tribute to the ruler, and a sort of a pagan All Souls' Day. The custom was then adopted by Christians, who gave it a new dimension. The Catholic All Souls' Day is celebrated on November 2, but the inhabitants of Podgórze continue to cultivate the ancient springtime tradition as well.

Originally, Rękawka was held at the foot of Krakus Mound. When the nearby fort was constructed, celebrations moved to Lasota Hill. St Benedict's Church now hosts a *fête* with rainbow-coloured stands, and Krakus Mound overlooks even more festivities.

12 *Silva Rerum* Mural

Podgórze commemorated the 750th anniversary of Cracow's foundation in an unconventional way: the city's history was represented in an enormous, almost 100-metre-long *Silva Rerum* graffiti painting.

Created in 2007, the *Silva Rerum* mural is one of the largest paintings of its type in the world. It is hard not to notice this multi-coloured graffiti, 5 metres' high and 90 metres' long. You can admire it as you walk along al. Powstańców Śląskich from the footbridge that leads to Krakus Mound (➤ 113), or even from the window of a bus that runs past the wall. The sheer length of the painting promises quite a "slideshow"; ample opportunity for a more detailed scrutiny is provided by traffic jams, very common here.

The graffiti presents the history of Cracow from ancient times to the present day. It depicts the foundation of the city, the Prussian homage to the Polish king, and more recent events, such as the construction of Nowa Huta. The portrayed figures are connected with Cracow and include kings, saints, and 20th-century personages such as Piotr Skrzynecki, the founder of the Piwnica pod Baranami (➤ 207), and Pope John Paul II.

The Latin term of *Silva Rerum* ("forest of things") stands for a home chronicle, once very popular among the Polish nobility. This special book contained the family history, economic records, cooking recipes, amateur poetry attempts, etc. In most cases, the sheer number of documents and materials made it necessary to use whole coffers for storing these family treasures.

The 100-metre-long graffiti entitled *Silva Rerum* depicts the history of Cracow.

Such chronicles were often chaotic, like a literary collage. The mural seems to be inspired by such a form: the depicted people and events, arranged chronologically, appear to make up a colourful mosaic, a great "graffiti patchwork." The choice of location for the painting was not random. It stresses the special ambience of the district and the fact that it is increasingly popular among artists, also those outside of the mainstream art movements. ■

Silva Rerum Mural (Mural Silva Rerum)

✉ *al. Powstańców Śląskich*

ℹ️ *Walk along al. Powstańców Śląskich towards Łagiewniki (c. 2 minutes from the intersection with ul. Wielicka), or go to the footbridge which is the extension of ul. Dembowskiego.*

★ 🔢 Krakus Mound

Despite the on-going historical research, the origin and the precise time of building the mound remain unknown. The many hypotheses, both mythical and scientific, only add to the aura of mystery that surrounds it.

A sunrise view from Krakus Mound is a memorable experience. The mist-covered Old Town (➤ 50) bristling with church towers, or even the chimneys of a heat and power station lit up by daybreak sunlight – all this makes for a unique romantic scenery on a crisp chilly morning.

But the place is worth visiting not only at dawn. Late risers will not be disappointed either. The mound affords a wide panoramic view over the city: Wawel Hill (➤ 40), St Mary's Basilica (➤ 23), churches in Kazimierz (➤ 88) and Podgórze. You will also see the industrial Cracow (Podgórze TV tower, Łęg power station). The city's two skyscrapers are the glazed blue tower, affectionately dubbed "błękitek" (which could be loosely translated as the "blue thingy"), and the "Skeletor" by the Cracow University of Economics, an incomplete structure that has offended the eyes of Cracovians for dozens of years.

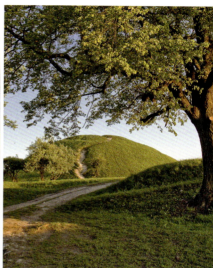

The best time to go up Krakus Mound is early in the morning or at sunset.

The landmark is said to be the resting place of Krakus, the legendary founder of Cracow. After he died, the town inhabitants allegedly built his burial mound with soil fetched in their sleeves. Some see this little detail to be the origin of the Rękawka Festival (➤112).

The theory of the inhabitants' undertaking was proved unlikely in the 1930's. Archaeologists bored a narrowing tunnel from the top of the mound to its base. No human remains were found. This does not mean that the tomb hypothesis is totally wrong: the ruler could have been cremated. However, an even more interesting discovery was made. The core of the mound is a horizontally-placed wooden pole, attached to large wicker containers filled with earth. This elaborate, ingenious framework ensures that the mound is stable and durable.

Yet another hypothesis, stating that the mound used to be a pagan cult site, appeared when the tangled tree roots of an over 300-year-old oak were found at the top. Hence, historians estimate that the mound could have been created in the 7th century, and that the sacred tree was cut down after the state converted to Christianity under Duke Mieszko I. Others link the mound to the Celtic colonisation in the Polish territories (verified by archaeological finds). On May 1 – a Celtic holiday – the sun as observed from Krakus Mound rises directly above Wanda Mound (➤138), built roughly at the same time.

Also the Austrian authorities found the mound well-suited to their needs when constructing the fortifications around the city (the so-called Cracow Fortress). They built a fort here. The fort was demolished after WWII, and the bricks were used to reconstruct Cracow's dwelling houses. The old fort was accessed by a long winding alley; a considerable stretch has been preserved to this day. One can also discern vestiges of the foundations, and – with a bit of practice – a general outline of the fort. ■

**Krakus Mound/ Krak Mound
(Kopiec Krakusa/ Kopiec Kraka)**

ℹ *When climbing the mound, keep to the designated path winding up to the top; going straight up by one of the wild paths causes devastation.*

The old labour camp of the Liban Quarry can be seen from Krakus Mound.

14 Liban Quarry

Steven Spielberg chose the Liban Quarry to film the scenes set in the Płaszów Camp (situated nearby). The quarry was indeed the site of a Nazi camp of forced labour.

The name may sound exotic, but it actually comes from Bernard Liban, a co-owner of the Liban & Ehrenpreis company (founded in 1873). The field of activity was extracting stone and processing it into lime. Huge furnaces and a hall were built, and a railway line was extended to reach the site. After WWII, the quarry was nationalised into a state-owned enterprise, which changed names many times. Extraction and lime production lasted until the end of the 1980's. Today, the bottom of the abandoned excavation site reveals rusting furnaces and some largely unidentifiable metal machinery parts.

During WWII, the quarry was worked by forced labour: it was the penal camp of the so-called *Baudienst* – the Nazi-created construction service, consisting of young Polish men. Those who tried to flee were sent to the Liban Quarry camp, which could accommodate about 800 prisoners. The gruelling burden of work was made even worse by particularly dire living conditions.

Steven Spielberg's Oscar-winning *Schindler's List* was shot on location here. The gloomy quarry made such an impression on the director that he decided to use it to film the scenes set in the Płaszów Camp (➤ 116); in reality, Płaszów was situated in the nearby extensive meadows. Half a million dollars' worth of scenery pieces were built. These included over 30 barracks, watchtowers, barbed wire fencing and an access road made of *matzevot* replicas. Some scenery elements, e.g. fence posts and road fragments, can still be seen today. Covered in mist, they look so authentic that they send shivers down one's spine.

Walking the quarry is dangerous for its steep slopes and scattered parts of old equipment. One enters at one's own risk. But you do not need to go down to the bottom of the quarry to see the remains of furnaces, buildings and Spielberg's film set. For a good view from above, it is enough to walk along the path running from Krakus Mound (➤ 113) that lines the precipice.

One of the quarry walls is a favourite with rock climbers. In the Polish climbing community, it is known as El Pułkownik (El Colonel), so called in reference to the famous El Capitan in the Yosemite National Park. El Pułkownik is situated by the quarry entrance from the side of ul. Za Torem. Gravity challengers will find well-prepared climbing paths with rings and rappel stances (climbing grades vary between VI+ and VI.5). ■

Liban Quarry (Kamieniołom Libana)
ⓘ *careful: a dangerous and remote area*

🔟5 Płaszów Camp

The site of the camp barracks is now swept by wind. No barbed wire fencing or watchtowers have been preserved; grass is growing where Jews and Poles were killed. But the memory of what happened here has not been lost.

The crack in the Monument to the Nazi Victims symbolises mass murder.

The camp was established on the site of two Jewish cemeteries. In the Jewish tradition, a cemetery is inviolable as well as ritually impure. The choice of this location, as well as using *matzevot* to build camp roads, was aimed at humiliating Jews, violating the principles of their religion and desecrating the remains of their ancestors. One of the camp prisoners recollected for the Jewish Historical Institute how the Nazis had excavated the tombs for barrack foundations: "When facing the skull, Bagermeister Jews had to remove gold teeth and bridges. (…) He once told me cynically: you see, the ground is paved with gold, all you have to do is pick it up."

Historians estimate that the Płaszów Camp held a total of up to 150,000 prisoners, of whom over 80,000 did not survive the war. It was a forced labour camp for Jews; then Poles were sent there as well. The camp was gradually expanded until it covered an area of 180 ha. Prisoners were further deported to death camps, e.g. Auschwitz (➤ 176). In 1943, Płaszów was turned into a concentration camp; the construction of gas chambers and crematoria started, but was not completed because the Eastern front drew closer. Faced with an inevitable defeat, the Nazis liquidated the camp in 1945. The last transport to Auschwitz-Birkenau left Płaszów a few days before the Red Army entered Cracow.

Płaszów was an industrial slave labour camp. Prisoners made uniforms for the German army, and worked in joiner's and locksmith's shops. Much harder tasks were assigned in the nearby Liban Quarry and in transporting the excavated stone. The main aim of this work, as well as some deliberately pointless activities (such as boring a "potato cave" in solid rock) was to work prisoners to death. The fact that the barracks were jammed and sanitary conditions were very poor made the situation worse. Even in the summer, people were sometimes allowed to use the bathhouse only once in several weeks. The death toll was increased even further by the ubiquitous famine. A physical labourer should consume about 4,500 calories a day. The official food ration for camp prisoners was half that amount, while in practice it often did not exceed even 1,000 calories.

Many people were killed in mass executions. The camp grounds used to hold several mass graves; during the camp liquidation, the Nazis tried to cover up all traces of their atrocities by forcing prisoners to exhume and cremate the corpses. Mass shootings took place on the so-called H-hill (Hujowa Górka, dubbed after Unterscharführer Albert Hujar who ordered executions; the name is also a play on a Polish obscenity). The hill now features a tall wooden cross with a thorn crown.

Not much is left of the camp. The *matzevah* of Chaim Abrahamer is probably the only one to have been left intact; there are but a few pieces of other tombstones. The Grey House at the intersection of Jerozolimska and Abrahama streets, a pre-war seat of a Jewish Funeral Association, was adapted by the Nazis to hold seclusion and torture cells. The adjacent commemorative stone is dedicated to the first Poles executed here,

The cross topped with a crown of thorns marks a former execution site.

and the *matzevah* monument at the back commemorates Jews. To the right of the Grey House, opposite new residential blocks, are the ruins of a pre-funeral house. The villa once inhabited by Amon Goeth (the camp commandant) is situated in ul. Heltmana at No. 22. The balcony from which he was shooting at prisoners overlooks the garden.

The main Płaszów monument is dedicated to the Nazi victims of all nationalities. The best view is from the direction of ul. Kamieńskiego. The crack that runs through the lined-up bodies is a symbol of mass extermination. The Polish text inscribed on a nearby monument to murdered Jews puts it succinctly: "Human language has no words to define the atrocity of this crime"... ■

Old Płaszów Camp (Dawny obóz Płaszów)

🛈 *extensive and partly overgrown terrain, hard to navigate; access from Krakus Mound along the Liban Quarry; the main monument is best reached from the Kamieńskiego and Makowa stops, the Grey House and Goeth's villa from the Dworcowa stop*

117

Nowa Huta

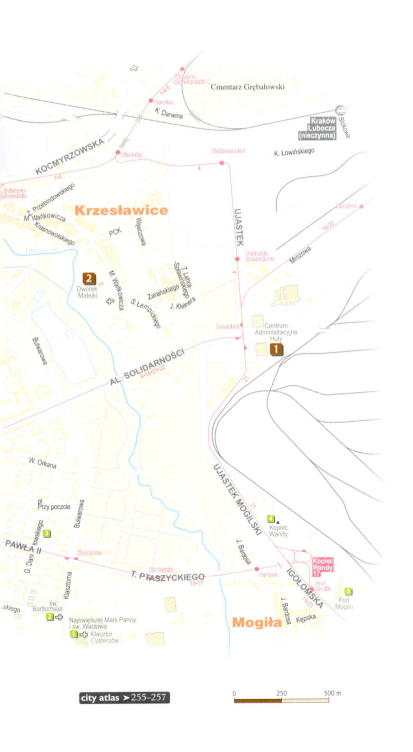

Cmentarz Grębałowski

Kraków
Lubocza
(nieczynna)

KOCMYRZOWSKA

K. Darwina

K. Łowińskiego

Elektrownataś

UJASTEK

Krzesławice

Z. Przebindowskiego

M. Wańkowicza

Krasnowolskiego

PCK

Wąwozowa

Mrozowa

Dworek
Matejki

M. Wańkowicza

T. Lehra-
Spławińskiego

Zarańskiego

S. Łempickiego

J. Klenera

Centrum
Administracyjne
Huty

Bulwarowa

AL. SOLIDARNOŚCI

W. Orkana

pl.
Przy poczcie

Bulwarowa

G. Daniłowskiego

PAWŁA II

Klasztorna

Klasztorna

UJASTEK MOGILSKI

Kopiec
Wandy

**Kopiec
Wandy
17**

J. Bartosza

T. PTASZYCKIEGO

Bardosa

IGOŁOMSKA

Fort
Mogiła

Fort
Mogiła

św.
Bartłomieja

Najświętszej Marii Panny
i św. Wacława

Klasztor
Cystersów

Mogiła

J. Bartosza

Kępska

0   250   500 m

A Model Socialist Town

Nowa Huta was meant to be a working-class "town without God," a counterpoise to the intellectual Cracow. The Socialist-Realist layout impresses with its grand-scale, thorough planning. Despite its name ("New Steelworks") and the nearby metallurgical conglomerate, it is a very green district.

A tank situated close to the People's Theatre (➤130) **is an icon of Nowa Huta.**

In the Socialist-Realist style, buildings were to be "national" in form and "socialist" in content. In communist newspeak, these expressions meant no less than that architecture was to represent the power of a people's democratic state through its plainness and monumentality, as well as some details characteristic of a given country. The Renaissance was chosen as the "national" style of Poland, hence so many Renaissance elements in the architecture of the 1950's (when the Socialist-Realist style was prevalent).

It seems unjust to dismiss Socialist Realism as a boring and unimaginative style. You will learn as much by walking in pl. Centralny (➤126) and al. Róż (➤127), and stopping by the gate of the steelworks: the Steel-

works Administrative Centre (➤122) is a showpiece of the Polish Socialist-Realist style. Nowa Huta's street design is also worth a note. Residential blocks are usually separated from the street with a green strip and a wide pavement. Thanks to this solution, windows do not give directly onto busy streets, which is a constant nuisance in downtown Cracow. A good example is the monumental al. Solidarności, resembling a bit Karl-Marx-Allee in Berlin. The squares between the blocks are planted with trees. There are also parks with alleys (e.g. Ratusz Park) and a reservoir close to the Matejko Manor (➤123).

The decision to build a new town in the vicinity of Cracow was taken in 1947. The first block was constructed in the Wanda housing estate, as noted

"Pass a Brick!"

Andrzej Wajda's film Man of Marble (1976) – the first part of the famous Man of Iron (1981) – tells the story of a Nowa Huta bricklayer. A model for the main character was Piotr Ożański, a Hero of Socialist Labour.

In July 1950, Ożański's team laid over 33,000 bricks during one shift; that amounted to 525 percent of the workload standard. In October, the team decided to break the record they had set. The goal: 50,000 bricks! All went well until the incident depicted by Wajda. Ożański, who worked without protective gloves, was passed a burning-hot brick. Some said it was by accident. Others – including official propaganda – claimed that it was an act of sabotage to delay the completion of Nowa Huta. In reality, it is not even certain if the bricklayer grasped the brick or managed to move his hand away at the last moment. Whatever actually happened, the team is reported to have accomplished their plan, laying 66,000 bricks in just 8 hours.

The life of Nowa Huta centres around the Socialist-style pl. Centralny.

on a plaque in ul. Mierzwy at No. 14. In 1951, the town was incorporated into Cracow, which did not stop the construction from progressing as planned. In line with the twisted logic of communism, a large part of the district was built on the most fertile type of soil, the black earth.

Nowa Huta was supposed to be thoroughly secular, but inhabitants themselves fought for the Nowa Huta Cross (➤129) and the district's first church, the so-called Lord's Ark (➤131). The Church of Our Lady of Częstochowa (➤125), run by the Cistercians, is modern and interesting in form.

The area has been connected with metallurgy for centuries. In Krzesławice, archaeologists have unearthed 2nd-century bloomeries (furnaces used for smelting iron) and some metal tools. A copper smelter, probably visible from Wawel Hill (➤40), was already in operation in the 15th century.

The story of Nowa Huta (not just in the 20th century) is presented in a branch of the Historical Museum of the City of Cracow, dedicated to Nowa Huta (os. Słoneczne 16). ∎

A walking tour around Nowa Huta should take about 3–4 hours. Not long ago, the area was considered dangerous. The crime rate is now not higher than in other Cracow districts, but venturing among the buildings on your own after dusk is not a good idea. Most landmarks here are not illuminated, and there is hardly any reason to visit Nowa Huta by night.

Nowa Huta is not a very tourist-oriented district, so the culinary offerings are rather poor. There are, however, many groceries where you can buy something to eat. A nice place for shopping (especially as far as fruit and vegetables are concerned) is pl. Bieńczycki; you can visit it on your way to the nearby Lord's Ark (➤131).

The quickest way to reach Nowa Huta from the centre of Cracow is by bus lines Nos. 501, 502, 522. These are express lines that skip a lot of bus stops, which means that the journey takes less time than on regular lines.

In the 1970's, the steelworks employed 40,000 people. It was named after Lenin until 1990.

Access by public transport:

1–2

Ⓑ *117, 132, 138, 139, 142, 149, 163, 172, 174, 211, 242, 463, 501, 601, 604, 609 (Kombinat)*

Ⓣ *4, 16, 21, 22 (Kombinat)*

3–4

Ⓑ *113, 123, 132, 139, 142, 153, 163, 172, 463, 501, 601 (Struga)*

Ⓣ *4, 16, 21, 22 (Struga)*

5–7

Ⓑ *121, 163, 174, 463, 501, 502, 522, 601, 608, 609 (Plac Centralny)*

Ⓣ *4, 15, 16, 17, 21, 22 (Plac Centralny)*

8–10

Ⓑ *110, 122, 123, 139, 149, 153, 169, 202, 212, 222, 232, 604, 608 (Teatr Ludowy)*

Ⓣ *1, 5 (Teatr Ludowy)*

1 Steelworks Administrative Centre

The steelworks' administrative buildings were erected in the 1950's. The plant, then named after Lenin, used to be called the "Doge's Palace." With a bit of goodwill, one can indeed discern some Italian influence in the socialist structures.

The entrance to the steelworks is guarded by two parallel buildings. They are used for administrative purposes (one is the seat of the board). The inhabitants of Nowa Huta have dubbed the buildings the "Doge's Palace" for their many architectural references to the Renaissance. Even though the edifices are quite wide apart, they were connected by an underground passage. It was used during the Solidarity strikes, when other evacuation routes were cut off by the regime's ZOMO paramilitaries.

The buildings are crowned with intricate attics. Take some steps back to see their small turrets. The finials atop are modelled on the lantern above the dome of St Peter's Basilica in Rome. Window frames are said to resemble those in Wawel Castle (➤43). The interiors are equally monumental with their partly preserved coffer ceilings and the original furniture from the 1950's. Sadly, they are inaccessible to tourists.

The steelworks was named after Lenin for over 35 years, from 1954

The gate of the Steelworks is flanked by two squat administrative buildings.

(the 30th anniversary of the death of the Russian revolutionary). That year saw the official inauguration of the steelworks; even though it had been in operation before that time, it was during this opening that pig iron was poured out of the huge furnace for the first time.

After the fall of communism, the name was changed to the Tadeusz Sendzimir Steelworks. Tadeusz Sendzimir, awarded an honorary doctorate by Cracow's University of Science and Technology (AGH), had rendered great service to the Polish steel industry. The present owner of the steelworks is Arcelor Mittal, a global steel company.

The plant was renamed ArcelorMittal Poland, but Cracovians still speak of the Administrative Centre of the Tadeusz Sendzimir Steelworks. ■

Steelworks Administrative Centre (Centrum Administracyjne Huty)

✉ ul. Ujastek 1

ℹ *The grounds of the steelworks can be entered only by organised tourist groups by prior appointment at the steelworks branch of the Polish Tourist and Sightseeing Society (Hutniczy Oddział PTTK), Osiedle Stalowe 16/2, phone Nos. +48 12 6804820 and +48 12 6804821, www.pttkhts.hg.pl.*

2 Matejko Manor

Jan Matejko's one-storey shingled manor in Krzesławice (once a village, now a city neighbourhood) was his refuge from the hustle and bustle of the 19th-century Cracow. The artist spent a lot of time here, resting and painting.

This was the resting and working place of Jan Matejko (1838–1893) – one of the most eminent Polish painters and a former head of the Academy of Fine Arts in Cracow. He gained fame as the author of historical paintings that depicted Poland's most important figures and events. The building is equipped with the period's original furniture, the easel, and the artist's

123

The bust of painter Jan Matejko stands in front of his favourite manor house.

drawings. Among the most treasured exhibits is a gallery of 44 portraits of Polish kings, painted by Matejko's students on the basis of his sketches (these remain the best-known royal representations in Poland). Yet another highlight is a meticulous study of a horse head by Matejko. However, for a larger collection of the master's works visit the Sukiennice Gallery (➤29) and Jan Matejko Museum (see: Ulica Floriańska ➤22).

Jan Matejko was not the first distinguished personage to own this manor house. The building was earlier inhabited by Hugo Kołłątaj, a Polish Roman Catholic priest and political thinker who co-authored the world's second constitution (after the American one). One of the museum rooms is devoted to him.

The wooden porch of the manor house was designed by Jan Matejko himself. ■

In Pursuit of Inspiration

When Jan Matejko was working on a painting entitled *King Stephen Batory at Psków*, he allegedly had a problem with finding a suitable model for the monarch.

One day in St Mary's Basilica (➤23), Matejko reportedly saw a man who met his expectations. The painter watched the man intently and then followed him out of the church. The man was carrying a large sum of money on him, and took Matejko for a robber, so he started to run. When everything became clear, however, the man agreed to pose for Matejko. The only thing that is certain is that the money earned by selling *Batory at Psków* was enough to buy the manor.

Matejko Manor (Dworek Jana Matejki)
✉ *ul. Wańkowicza 25*
☎ *+48 12 6445674*
🕐 *Mon–Fri 10am–2pm, Sat–Sun on prior arrangement*
€ *PLN 5 (PLN 2)*

3 Church of Our Lady of Częstochowa

This is a true gem of modern sacral architecture. There is no conventional roof or windows. A huge structure of glass and metal allows natural light to penetrate the building. The church looks like a pile of stacked-up glazed cubes.

An intriguing roof of an irregular shape and a unique form is very impressive both from the outside and from the inside. Its appearance seems to allude to the fact that the building is situated in a housing estate called Szklane Domy (Glass Houses). The church is run by the Cistercians, who have a monastery and an age-old basilica in the nearby Mogiła (➤ 135).

The austere and ascetic décor of the interior is truly striking. It makes one think of Romanesque and Byzantine architecture. The round-arched, polychrome-covered recesses ornament the chancel wall. The church looks its best on sunny days, when sunlight comes in through the glazed roof. It warms up the cold walls and fills the interior with radiance.

Remember to take a look at the church from al. Solidarności. The glass structure atop and the small roof over the entrance make for a bizarre shape. With a bit of imagination, you may discern the form of a tree there.

The story of the church started with a free-standing cross. In the 1970's, it was the landmark by which inhabitants congregated. With time, they added a makeshift altar and a roofing, but had to wait for official permission to build a church. The construction started in 1982, and the consecration only took place in 1995. ∎

The Church of Our Lady of Częstochowa stands out for its extravagant roof.

Church of Our Lady of Częstochowa and Blessed Wincenty Kadłubek (Kościół Matki Boskiej Częstochowskiej i bł. Wincentego Kadłubka)

✉ os. Szklane Domy 7

@ www.parafia-szklanedomy.pl

🕐 6.30am–6pm

€ *free*

🍴 *Banolli Pizzeria, os. Centrum B 8 (at the intersection of al. Solidarności and Przyjaźni)* ● € €

ℹ️ *services: Mon–Sat at 6.30am, 7am, 8am, 6pm, Sun at 6.30am, 8am, 9.30am, 11am, 12.30pm, 2.30pm, 5pm, 7pm, 8.30pm*

Pl. Centralny is a representative example of the Socialist-Realist "Polish national style": not very refined, but modelled on the Italian Renaissance (arcades, attics).

★ 4 Plac Centralny

Although situated a bit out of the way, the square is not called "Central" for nothing. As the most iconic place of the district, pl. Centralny is one of the first associations with Nowa Huta that comes to a Cracovian's mind.

The oldest housing estates are situated between the five streets that radiate from the Central Square. The layout is best admired from a bird's eye perspective. On the map or an air photo, the district resembles a symmetrical maze. It makes one think of a dexterity game, in which a small metal ball is to be manoeuvred through a network of passages to the focal point – pl. Centralny.

It was not a child's toy, however, that served as the inspiration for the architects of the square. They seem to have modelled their design on Renaissance and Baroque architecture. Note the arcades of the massive buildings, the loggia-like balconies, the wide roads with a lot of traffic… The grand scale of the architectural plan for Nowa Huta becomes particularly evident here.

Although the square appears to constitute a consistent whole, the actual plan has never been fully realised. Viewed from al. Róż (➤ 127), the layout seems a bit incomplete. On one side, pl. Centralny branches off into five streets, while extensive meadows stretch in the background on the other. This "wasteland" was not part of the original plan. Architects intended to have a theatre building erected here, but after the opening of the People's Theatre (➤ 130, ➤ 202) enthusiasm for the idea (not to mention the funding) waned considerably.

A few years ago, the name of the square became a bone of contention. It was to be renamed after Ronald Reagan, but the locals protested, as they had grown attached to the old name. A compromise was reached, and the square is now officially called the Ronald Reagan Central Square (pl. Centralny im. Ronalda Reagana).

In the past, al. Róż was adorned with flowers only in red – communism's No. 1 colour. This changed after 1989, much to the advantage of the street.

For a flavour of the old ambience, visit the shops under the arcades. The grocery, the bookshop and the Cepelia store have kept their furnishings, the arrangement of shelves, ceilings and chandeliers since the socialist heyday. ∎

★ 5 Aleja Róż

The central place in the wide, flower-decorated Rose Avenue used to be occupied by an enormous Lenin Statue. For years, the inhabitants of Nowa Huta tried to remove it. They only succeeded in 1989.

The name of the Rose Avenue comes from the type of flowers that were planted here to add some colour to the dreary Socialist-Realist architecture. Apart from the aesthetic value, these roses carried an additional meaning: they were red, which was communism's favourite colour. A large part of the avenue is a pedestrian precinct. The most representative stretch connects pl. Centralny (➤ 126) with Ratusz Park (➤ 128); both sides are lined with squat several-storey apartment blocks, placed wide apart. The precinct is broad, which further enhances the monumental character of the layout.

Between 1973 and 1989, a huge Lenin Statue marked the centre of the avenue. The author was Cracovian sculptor Marian Konieczny, who also reconstructed the Grunwald Monument (see: Plac Matejki ➤ 17).

Al. Róż is home to Stylowa restaurant, the décor of which harmonises with the architectural style of the district. In the summer, take a seat at a table outside to observe pl. Centralny and Ratusz Park. ∎

Rose Avenue (Aleja Róż)

🍴 *Stylowa restaurant, os. Centrum C 3 (by al. Róż)* 🔴🔴 €

127

The sculpture in Ratusz Park remains open to interpretation.

Lenin of Nowa Huta

The revolutionary leader was depicted walking deep in thought, his long coat rippling in the wind. The seven-ton statue was disliked by the district's inhabitants, who tried to have it removed at any cost.

There were several attempts to knock down the statue in al. Róż. Once, a local placed a bike and a pair of shoes in front of Lenin together with a note which could be roughly translated as: "Get your shoes and your gear, cycle the f... out of here." People also tried to blow

the monument up. In 1979, Andrzej Szewczuwianiec planted two 6-kilogram explosives. One of them fell off the pedestal and the blast smashed the windows in the nearby buildings, leaving Lenin unscathed. The other explosive took away one of the figure's feet. This event inspired the inhabitants of Nowa Huta to give the square the informal name of Vlad the Foot-loose. Other attempts followed. Paint was hurled and fire was set to the statue. Eventually, the monument was knocked down in 1989, after the political transformation.

6 Ratusz Park

Nowa Huta was supposed to have its own town hall. There were architectural projects, funds were raised, but in the end the construction was not even started. The projected site for the building is now one of the city's public parks.

Al. Róż (➤ 127) leads to the place that was once the heart of Nowa Huta, the projected location of a representative town hall and some modern-style buildings. The plans were not abandoned even when Nowa Huta was incorporated into Cracow in 1951. The build-

ing was to be the showpiece of Socialist Realism, and the spire was designed to be higher than the taller tower of St Mary's Basilica (➤ 23).

Stalin died in March 1953. The demise of the despot who had placed so much emphasis on Nowa Huta, and a deepening crisis in Poland and the USSR, put an end to the project.

Park Ratuszowy ("the park of the town hall") takes up roughly half the area of the once projected main square. Some call the site "Piccadilly," alluding to the well-known Piccadilly Circus of London. It is a popular meeting place, and a venue for spontaneous chess games. The park looks its best in the spring and in the summer, when the green is most verdant, and roses in flower beds come into bloom.

A bizarre statue that can be seen in the park invites everyone to give free rein to their creative imagination. The significance of the monument is far from clear; it is hard to say what this mysterious piece of art is supposed to represent. The largely indefinable white sculpture is commonly known as a "Fish," though this might be not in line with the creator's intentions. ◼

Ratusz Park (Park Ratuszowy)
🕐 accessible 24/7

7 Nowa Huta Cross

The communist authorities did not envisage a church in Nowa Huta. It soon turned out, however, that the town's working-class inhabitants did want one – and demanded it loud and clear. Riots broke out, and the authorities used force.

In the latter 1950's, the communist administration seemed to give in to the popular demand and gave permission to build a church. The chosen construction site (at the junction of the then Marx and Mayakovsky streets) was consecrated and marked with a cross in 1957. However, the communists did not keep their word. They withdrew permission only two years later, and decided to have a school constructed there. It was part of a propaganda campaign which aimed to build 1,000 schools to celebrate the anniversary of 1,000 years of the Polish statehood in 1966.

On April 27, 1960, the cross became an integral part of the city's history. The authorities of the district commissioned its removal, and the heavy equipment took over the site previously allotted to the church. This change of plans was met with strong opposition of the inhabitants, who clashed with the militia. The situation was getting worse, so anti-riot squads called ZOMO (Motorized Reserves of the Citizens' Militia) were brought from neighbouring towns. The paramilitaries used tear gas, water cannons, and even live ammunition.

The inhabitants of Nowa Huta fought hard to keep the cross in the public space.

129

The People's Theatre is much more than a relic of the communist past.

Due to evening power cuts, the town was plunged into darkness. The clashes lasted for two days. Nearly 500 people were arrested, 100 of whom were sentenced to as many as five years in prison.

The school was eventually constructed, but the cross stayed where the locals had put it. Old crucifixes, decaying over time, were replaced with the new ones. The remnants of the original cross were placed in the Lord's Ark (➤ 131) and then taken to Rome by Karol Wojtyła shortly before he be-

came Pope John Paul II. The site where the cross was put up over 50 years ago is now marked with a monument, a cast bronze cross with handprints that symbolise its defenders. Right behind stands the Church of the Holiest Heart of Jesus from the 1990's. ■

Monument to the Nowa Huta Cross (Pomnik Krzyża Nowohuckiego)
✉ *ul. Ludźmierska 2 (os. Teatralne), in front of the Church of the Holiest Heart of Jesus*

8 People's Theatre

One of the youngest theatres in Cracow, it has produced experimental and *avantgarde* performances, as well as working-class drama in line with the Party's programme. The stage has seen skinheads and punk rockers acting side by side.

The performance that inaugurated the theatre in 1955 was entitled *Krakowiacy i Górale* (*Cracovians and Highlanders*); this is why the neighbouring estates are called Krakowiaków and Górali. It was a highly acclaimed premiere, praised by Sławomir Mrożek – one of the best-known Polish writers

who worked in a Cracow daily back then.

In 1989, the new head of the theatre, artist and politician Jerzy Fedorowicz, introduced art therapy workshops for young people. The idea was to animate the youth of Nowa Huta, to fight aggression and addiction. Particularly memorable was the production of Shakespeare's *Romeo and Juliet*, in which the houses of Capulet and Montague were played by representatives of two subcultures at war with each other: punks and skinheads. There were also shows staged by rehabilitating drug addicts and the residents of a local children's home, who acted out a poignant adaptation of *The Little Prince*.

By the theatre building, in ul. Mościckiego (os. Górali 23), you will find a tank – a Nowa Huta icon. This is no dummy: the tank was used by the Polish People's Army formed on the Soviet soil during WWII. It is said to have destroyed one German anti-aircraft gun and three armoured vehicles. ■

People's Theatre (Teatr Ludowy)

✉ os. Teatralne 34

☎ box office: +48 12 6802111; customer service: +48 12 6802112

@ www.ludowy.pl

🕐 box office: Tue–Fri 1pm–6pm, Sat 3pm–6pm, Sun – two hours before the show

€ tickets: PLN 18–42

9 Lord's Ark

The Church of the Blessed Virgin Mary Queen of Poland, also known as the Lord's Ark, is the first church to have been built in Nowa Huta. Its treasures include a Moon rock, a poignant figure of Christ, and a picture of Our Lady the Armoured on a molten shrapnel base.

The popular name of the "Lord's Ark" derives from the unusual shape of the church. The wooden roof resembles a boat drifting on a "wave" set with 2 million river pebbles. Some say that the walls themselves look like the sides of a ship. The name alludes to the biblical story of the Flood: as Noah's ark was a refuge from the waters flooding the Earth, so the church seemed to be a shelter from the communist reality of Nowa Huta.

The interior is dominated by a dramatic figure. The 8-metre-tall sculpture depicts the crucified Christ, resurrected from the cross. His tensely arched body is full of expression, attached to the wall not by nails but metal tubes. The creator is sculptor Bronisław Chromy.

The bronze tabernacle represents the birth of the universe; the tabernacle doors feature a Moon stone, brought by the Apollo 11 crew. The altar is made of one single piece of marble and looks like an open hand. Below the altar is located the so-called grotto: a chapel with a figure of Our Lady of Fatima, coronated with a gold crown on papal orders. Thus, the Lord's Ark is also St Mary's Sanctuary. The Eucharistic adoration takes place in the chapel.

The vault holds the Reconciliation Chapel (Kaplica Pojednania). It displays several wooden *pietàs* that commemorate the most painful events in the history of Poland. Here, you can see a unique picture of Our Lady the Armoured on the base of molten shrapnel and bullets removed from the wounds of the Polish soldiers who had fought in the Battle of Monte Cassino (1944). ■

Lord's Ark – the Church of the Blessed Virgin Mary Queen of Poland (Arka Pana – Kościół Matki Bożej Królowej Polski)

✉ ul. Obrońców Krzyża 1

@ www.arkapana.pl

🕐 6am–6pm daily

€ free

ℹ services: Mon–Sat at 6am, 6.30am, 7am, 7.30am, 8am, 11am, 6pm (8am and 11am in the Fatima Chapel); Sun at 6.30am, 8am, 9.30am, 11am, 12.30pm, 2pm, 4pm, 5.30pm, 7pm (Sept–June an additional service at 10am in the Reconciliation Chapel)

Mogiła

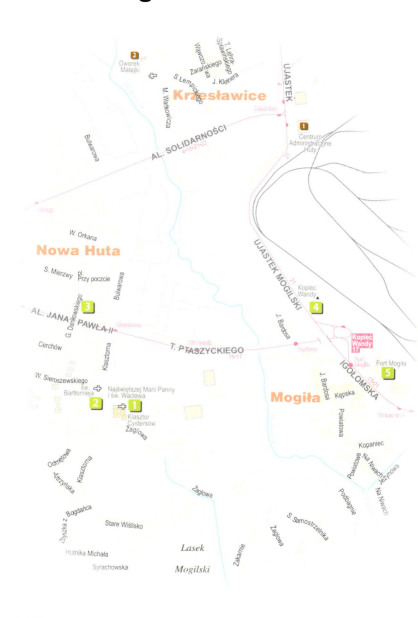

0   250   500 m

city atlas ➤256–257

The Cistercian Estate

The city's neighbourhood of Mogiła has been linked to the Cistercians for almost 800 years. The growth of the sanctuary was hindered neither by the pagan name of the former village nor by the construction of the communist Nowa Huta.

The high altar of the Cistercian Church (➤135) features a 15th-century pentaptych.

The name of Mogiła – an old Polish word for a "grave" – comes as a surprise to most Polish-speaking tourists. However, the inhabitants of today's Cracow neighbourhood, just like their predecessors from the time when the place was still a village, do not even notice the ambiguity that lurks in phrases such as "I live in Mogiła" or "I'm heading for Mogiła." Strangers to the region may grin, but the name has been in local use since at least 1291, when it was first mentioned in written records. It probably derives from Wanda Mound (➤138), believed to be the grave of Wanda, a daughter to Krakus – the legendary founder of Cracow.

The Cistercians came to Mogiła in the 13th century. They built an abbey (➤135) and an adjoining church, very impressive in size. It was originally meant for the Order exclusively. Lay people could enter the church only on special occasions; their place of daily worship was the much smaller wooden St Bartholomew's Church (➤136).

The Cistercians greatly contributed to the development of the village. They introduced new farming techniques and had local rivers regulated. The 15th-century Mogiła already had a watermill on the Dłubnia River, and a paper mill that soon came into the hands of the Order and became known for high quality handmade paper.

133

The spacious square by the Cistercian church features a John Paul II statue.

In the 20th century, the grounds of Mogiła were taken over for the construction of a new town called **Nowa Huta** (➤118) – now one of Cracow's districts. It incorporated the Mogiła village in 1951. The Cistercian Abbey and the local parish were a spiritual oasis for the builders and inhabitants of the communist model town, where there was no place for religious worship. This deadlock lasted until 1977, the year that the Lord's Ark (➤131) was consecrated.

It is not a well-known fact, but the construction of Nowa Huta made it possible to conduct thorough excavations of the area. A wealth of prehistoric finds came as a surprise even to archaeologists, who studied the future construction sites of Nowa Huta in great detail. The impressive collection of prehistoric items and vestiges of the first settlement has been so far presented only in parts. Recently, an idea has been raised to display the totality of the finds in the Mogiła Fort (➤139). The decision has not been taken yet.

Some of the old village ambience has been preserved in ul. Klasztorna. The street architecture consists of single-family housing, so very different from the nearby concrete block estates. The origins of the place are documented in the few surviving wooden buildings and the above-mentioned wooden church. ■

For touring Mogiła off-season (Nov–Apr) it is best to choose a Sunday, even though the Abbey Church (➤135) holds a lot of Sunday Masses, when visiting is not allowed. However, the interior of St Bartholomew's Church (➤136) can be seen only right before or after the Sunday Mass; and it is well worth seeing. A tour of the abbey and the wooden church takes about one hour. If you plan it right, you will be able to see both churches during the breaks between services. At the height of the season (May–Oct), it is better to come on a Friday or Saturday – St Bartholomew's Church is then open to visitors, and Masses in the Abbey Church are held less often.

There are no eating places along the route, apart from the baker's shop at ul. Klasztorna 2a (c. 250 m from St Bartholomew's Church as you walk towards the cemetery). However, it is closed on Sunday, so you should take a packed lunch with you – especially if you plan to go up Wanda Mound (➤138) and visit the Mogiła Fort (➤139). If that is the case, remember to allocate another 2 hours.

The distance between the Cistercian estate (landmarks 1–3) and Wanda Mound (➤138) and the Mogiła Fort (➤139) is not interesting to walk, so it is better to take a tram. The suggested order of 4–5 given below (first the fort, then the mound) is not a must. If you want to start with the mound, take tram No. 17 from the Klasztorna tram stop and get off at the Kopiec Wandy stop. If you want to start with the fort, in turn, take tram No. 15 from the Klasztorna tram stop and get off at the Fort Mogiła stop. The distance between the mound and the fort is covered on foot.

Access by public transport:

1–2
- 153, 174, 609 (Klasztorna), 113, 123 (Klasztor Cystersów)
- 15, 17 (Klasztorna)

3
- 153, 174, 609 (Klasztorna)
- 15, 17 (Klasztorna)

4
- 17, 21 (Kopiec Wandy)

5
- 221 (Fort Mogiła)
- 15, 21 (Fort Mogiła)

★ 🔢 Cistercian Abbey in Mogiła

The Cistercians have been present in Cracow since 1222. Their abbey soon became a pilgrimage destination. The miraculous figure of the crucified Christ and the Holy Cross relics still attract one million pilgrims every year.

A Holy Relic

A special reliquary in the Cistercian Abbey holds a piece of the Holy Cross, on which Christ is believed to have died.

The holy relic was ceremonially brought to Cracow before WWII. However, the document that attested to the relic's authenticity must have been lost in war turmoil. In the 1960's, the Cistercian abbot made an appeal to the Pope, asking for another relic the authenticity of which would be officially confirmed by the Catholic Church. The request was successful, and the Cistercians obtained another part of the Holy Cross, transferred from the Basilica di Santa Croce in Rome. It can be seen during the church fair on September 14, and at the end (4am–5am) of an all-night vigil held every first Friday of the month.

The Cistercian church enchants with its 18th-century polychromies.

The Cistercian church was consecrated in 1266. The austere Romanesque-Gothic building was constructed in line with the general recommendations of the Cistercian monastic rule. The church was modest, and the ascetic brick and stone walls were whitewashed in the 16th century. The characteristic chancel with a plain closing wall has survived to this day.

Inside, the church is ornamented with wall paintings; the dominant colours are green, yellow and gold. The interior was redecorated in the Baroque style in the 18th century after a great fire, and it was also then that the modest facade was added. The building also boasts older historic features. Particularly impressive is the high altar: a 15th-century pentaptych with a figure of Mary, surrounded with three stained glass windows. The scene of the Annun-ciation is also worth a look. The creator of the fresco was Stanislaus Samostrzelnik, a Cistercian monk who lived at the turn of the 16th century. He is considered to be one of the most outstanding painters of the Polish Renaissance. Another one of his paintings, located in the cloister, depicts the crucified Christ.

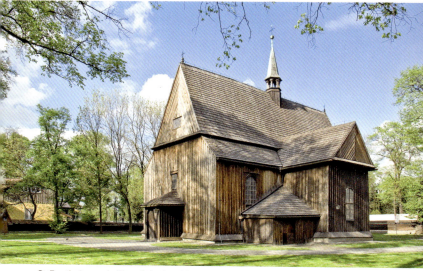

St Bartholomew's Church is the oldest wooden three-nave temple in Poland.

The Chapel of the Miraculous Christ (Kaplica Cudownego Pana Jezusa) is a special pilgrimage destination. The cross it holds probably dates from the 14th century. A fervent worship of the crucifix started in 1447, when the church was struck by lightning and burnt to the ground. It was only the crucifix that escaped the flames almost unharmed: the burnt hair was replaced with a real-hair wig. The many miracles worked by the Christ figure are testified to by the abbey chronicles and votive offerings (there would have been even more if it had not been for the turbulent history of the region). ■

Cistercian Abbey in Mogiła
(Opactwo Cystersów w Mogile)
- ✉ ul. Klasztorna 11
- @ www.mogila.cystersi.pl
- ⌚ 6.30am–6pm daily
- ℹ services: Mon–Sat at 6am, 7am, 7.30am, 8.30am, 6pm, on the 1st Fri of the month also at 9.30am, 4pm, 5pm, 8pm and midnight, Sun at 6.30am, 8am, 9.30am, 11am, 12.30pm, 2pm, 4.30pm, 6pm

★ 2 St Bartholomew's Church

The sight of a small village church so close to Nowa Huta's concrete housing blocks may come as a surprise – all the more so as the building is one of the very few wooden churches within the city limits of Cracow.

The church and the adjoining old cemetery are surrounded by a wooden fence. The only entrance is through the bell tower. It is like a magic gate into the ancient world, mainly because of the indefinable, yet unmistakable smell of old wood, which makes one think of some vague mysteries of the past. As you pass through the bell tower, just take a deep breath and close your eyes for a moment.

The church is one of the most treasured monuments of wooden ar-

chitecture in Poland. The first written mention of the structure comes from the 13th century. The present building was erected in 1466 after a major fire. So much can be gathered from an inscription left on the portal of the porch by its builder, Maciej Mączka. The landmark is Poland's oldest three-nave hall church built in wood that has kept its Gothic shape to this day. Originally, the shingled roof reached down to the underpinning. It was then made shorter; the present form dates from 1740, as does the boarding.

On the inside, the walls are decorated with 18th-century polychromies. The painting on the ceiling of the chapel on the right depicts St Bartholomew and two angels holding a bloody knife, which is a reference to the Apostle's martyrdom by flaying.

The interior is in semi-darkness, just like so many other small village churches. The air is filled with the characteristic scent of a sacred place. Standing inside the larch-plank structure, it is hard to believe that an enormous steelworks and a busy city are not that far away. ■

St Bartholomew's Church
(Kościół św. Bartłomieja Apostoła)
✉ ul. Klasztorna 11
🕐 Jan–Apr, Nov–Dec: before or after the Sunday Mass; May–Oct: Fri noon–4pm, Sat 10am–2pm, Sun noon–4pm
ℹ services: Sun at 11.30am, Oct–June also at 9am and 10.15am

3 Mogiła Cemetery

The cemetery is much older than the adjacent 1950's blocks of the Wanda housing estate – the first to be built in Nowa Huta. The parish burial ground dates from the 18th century and remains in the care of the Cistercians.

The place makes one think of the inevitability of passing, and the ageless relevance of the Latin phrase *memento mori* (not least for the bustling residential blocks that show behind the silent crosses). This cemetery is certainly worth a visit, even though it lacks the magnificent tombs of the Rakowice Cemetery (➤ 25). The old burial ground in Mogiła belongs to the parish of St Bartholomew (➤ 136) and was founded after the Third Partition of Poland (1795). It holds about 2,000 graves, the oldest of which was put up in the mid-19th century. The common tomb of the Cistercian Fathers can be found in the main alley of the cemetery.

As a result of the growth of Nowa Huta, the cemetery was closed down. The town's builders and inhabitants had been buried here, but a new, larger cemetery in Grębałów was founded. The residents of Nowa Huta have been buried there since 1964, and the old cemetery

The Mogiła Cemetery is hemmed in by the housing blocks of a Nowa Huta estate.

in Mogiła is no longer used for burials. Exceptions are made only for interments in family graves, but this does not happen very often. ■

Mogiła Cemetery (Cmentarz w Mogile)
✉ ul. Jana Pawła II and ul. Daniłowskiego

4 Wanda Mound

The lowest of Cracow's mounds lies very close to the steelworks grounds. It is a popular walking destination, and used to be a source of inspiration for artists. There is a legend that explains its beginnings, but the original purpose of the mound remains a mystery.

The landmark is said to be the final resting place of a daughter to Krakus, the mythical founder of Cracow. Legend has it that Wanda rejected the proposal of a German ruler. In order to prevent retaliation and a raid on the city, she decided to take her own life, and threw herself into the waters of the Vistula. Her body was buried near the place where it had been recovered from the river, now about 2 km away. It is difficult to assess the credibility of the story, but the legend of Wanda who did not want a German for a husband ranks among the best-known in Poland. Back in the communist era, people joked that the candidate for a husband must have apparently come from East, not West Germany.

Some sources describe Wanda as exceptionally beautiful. Jan Długosz, a 15th-century chronicler, wrote that nature had endowed her with good looks "not only generously but prodigally." The chronicle recounts the legend, but with an ending quite different to the popular version: it is the rejected German ruler that kills himself, and Wanda lives on to govern her country.

The exact time when the mound came into existence has not been determined. There are several hypotheses, the most popular of which propounds the 7th or the 8th century. Yet another theory says that the landmark was built by the Celts, just like Krakus Mound (➤ 113). The proof quoted in support

of this idea is the astronomical interrelationship of the two sites. For instance, visitors standing at the top of Wanda Mound on November 4 or February 6 (around the time of the old Celtic holidays) will see the sun setting directly above Krakus Mound.

The site was often visited by artists and writers. Among others, the mound was climbed by Jan Matejko, who went on walks around the neighbourhood during his frequent stays in his out-of-town house (see: Matejko Manor ➤ 123). He designed the monument that stands atop the embankment (now renovated). A visit to the mound inspired Cyprian Norwid to write a play entitled *Wanda*. It draws on the Romantic concept of Poland as the "Christ of the nations," popular in the period's literature, and makes the pagan protagonist die in 33 AD, the year that Christ is believed to have been crucified.

Largely forgotten in the last decades, the mound is now being rediscovered by the city inhabitants. The area has been tidied up, video surveillance and lighting has been installed. However, it is not the best of places to watch a sunset, since this out-of-the-way site might be dangerous after dusk. ■

Wanda Mound (Kopiec Wandy)
✉ ul. Ujastek

The Eagle Monument atop Wanda Mound was designed by painter Jan Matejko.

5 Mogiła Fort

This is one of the many forts built by the Austrian occupiers. The infantry stationed here were to guard the strategic route that ran along the Vistula. The fort is now a peculiar tourist landmark which starts the Cracow Fortress trail.

The structure is of a totally different character than St Benedict's Fort (➤ 111) **in Podgórze:** it is not a dignified tall building, but a one-storey infantry bunker, going deep underground. The fort was constructed between 1895 and 1896. When Austrian troops left the town, it was used for a variety of functions, and then completely abandoned. During WWI, it served military purposes; in WWII, it came to hold a German barracks. When the war ended, the fort was home to the builders of Nowa Huta. It then fell into disuse, and has been gradually deteriorating ever since.

Today, the fort is difficult to access and overgrown with thickets. It holds the most interest for militaria enthusiasts and urban explorers. The main entrance features a large inscription in white that says "Keep out," to which some joker added "Mogiła": it is a play on words, since the name of the neighbourhood also means a "grave" in Polish, thus reading "Keep out of your grave." This mock piece of advice is not as absurd as it appears – exploring the nooks and crannies of the fort may prove quite perilous. Metal screens have been mostly stolen, and holes in the pavements have not been secured. There have been some plans for the renovation and adaptation of the building for different purposes, but none of them has gone past the initial stages. ■

Mogiła Fort (Fort Mogiła)
🕐 *not accessible to visitors*
ℹ *dangerous area, difficult to navigate*

From Zwierzyniec to Piasek

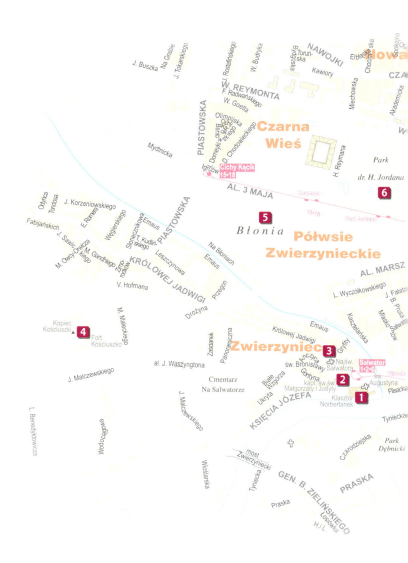

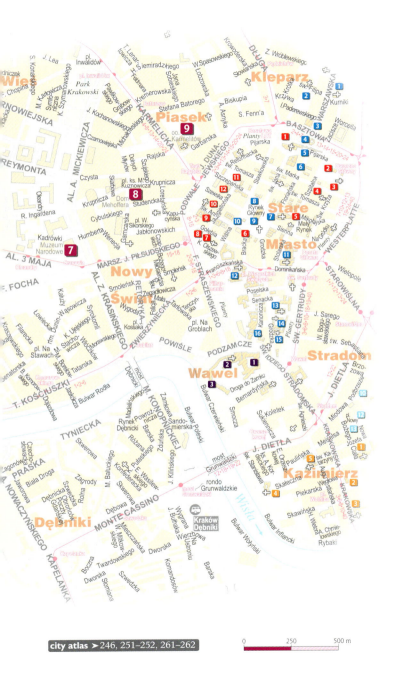

0   250   500 m

The Diversity of the Old Suburbs

Zwierzyniec is the greenest part of Cracow, featuring Kościuszko Mound, an age-old Premonstratensian Convent and the Romanesque Church of the Holiest Saviour. With its dense housing and street network, Piasek is the very opposite.

Cracovians come to the Błonia (➤149) to get away from the hectic city life.

In the prehistoric era, today's Zwierzyniec witnessed mammoth huntings. The hill of Blessed Bronisława, which holds Kościuszko Mound (➤148), has preserved vestiges of an early hunting culture of 28,000–18,000 BC. Archaeologists have also found the bones of 86 mammoths, which makes it the largest mammoth excavation site in Poland. The impressive number of bones in such a small area and the fact that they were mostly dismembered and carefully cleaned of meat remains has led the archaeologists to propose a hypothesis that the place was a sort of a mammoth meat cutting point. The theory was borne out when approx. 500 stone tools were unearthed. It is also possible that the bones, left behind by people, were gnawed on by wild animals: cave hyenas and wolves left their teeth marks on them.

Zwierzyniec was first mentioned as a village in 1224. However, a Vistulan settlement existed here as early as the turn of the 10th century. The growth of the village in the subsequent centuries was stimulated by the Premonstratensian Abbey, founded in 1162. Yet another major place of worship for the locals was one of Cracow's oldest churches, dedicated to the Holiest Saviour (➤146). Its construction preceded the establishment of the Premonstratensian Convent (➤144); some Romanesque elements survive to this day. Zwierzyniec stayed in the hands of the Premonstratensian nuns until 1910, when it was incorporated into Cracow. It had its own manor farms, mills, blacksmith's shops and brickyards; even royal estates were located here. In the local gardens, Queen Bona Sforza (1494–1557, wife to Sigismund the Old) got some rest, and King Henry of

Valois (👑 1573–1574) was claimed to abandon himself to disreputable passions.

Enemy raids, epidemics, and natural disasters did not spare Zwierzyniec. It was plagued by marching troops. The convent and neighbouring buildings were ravaged by frequent fires. In 1587, Zwierzyniec was invaded by the future Archduke Maximilian of Austria, a pretendent to the Polish throne. It also suffered damage in the Swedish Deluge of 1655. On both occasions, Zwierzyniec was devastated when the suburbs were burnt down to clear the ground for fighting. But fire was not the only destructive element that threatened Zwierzyniec: floodings of the Vistula and the now unsubstantial Rudawa River (regulated in 1903) took away possessions and demolished local houses. Flood waters carried away not only things but people as well. The most damage was done to the convent in the 1813 flood, when the level of water in the church reached the altars. Only 200 years ago, the flooding area of the Rudawa encompassed the Błonia (➤149), now a perfect place for walking, celebrations and open-air events.

Today, Zwierzyniec is one of Cracow's districts. It has a much larger area than the former village, since it incorporates other historic places as well. Zwierzyniec is the greenest part of Cracow, with the highest percentage of recreation grounds. And, even though there are more and more new housing estates, you will still find here the peace and quiet of one-family architecture – e.g., when walking from the Chapel of SS Margaret and Judith (➤146) towards Kościuszko Mound (➤148).

The name of Piasek became established only in the 19th century. At first, it was used only for the grounds of the Carmelite Church. The Polish word *piasek* is also a reference to one of Cracovian legends (see: Carmelite Church in Piasek ➤152). With time, the name stuck to the entire area of the city's old outskirts, previously called Gar-

bary. Garbary was the only independent settlement under the jurisdiction of Cracow which had its own town hall. It was housed in the 18th-century building at ul. Karmelicka 12. This part of the city is much closer to the Main Square (➤26) than Zwierzyniec. It is characterised by much denser architecture, which can be seen on the way to the Mehoffer House (➤152). ∎

The route takes about 3–4 hours. Add to this one hour for going up Kościuszko Mound (➤148), and for a visit to each of the museums. There is a car park by the mound.

The best walking trail up Kościuszko Mound runs along al. Waszyngtona (the extension of ul. bł. Bronisławy, the street that is home to the Chapel of SS Margaret and Judith ➤146 and the Church of the Holiest Saviour ➤146). Going down the mound, you can take the Zaścianek path down at the Diabelski Most intersection (marked with a plaque on a tree). In the Błonia (➤149), at the Józef Piłsudski obelisk in the alley along al. Focha, you will get a view over the towers of the Old Town (➤50), Wawel Hill (➤40) and Kościuszko Mound. Following the alley, you will get close to the entrance of Jordan Park (➤150).

Eating places and shops are located at the end of the suggested route, beyond the Błonia and Jordan Park.

Access by public transport:

1–3
🚌 100, 109, 209, 229, 239, 249, 259, 269, 409 (Salwator)
🚊 1, 2, 6 (Salwator)

4
🚌 100 (Kopiec Kościuszki) – from Salwator, 101 (Kopiec Kościuszki) – from Most Grunwaldzki

5
🚌 134, 152, 192, 292, 902 (Przegon, Instytut Reumatologii)
🚊 15, 18 (Park Jordana, on demand)

6
🚊 15, 18 (Park Jordana, on demand)

7
🚌 109, 114, 124, 134, 144, 164, 169, 173, 179, 192, 194, 292, 409, 502, 608, 610, 618 (Cracovia)
🚊 15, 18 (Cracovia)

8–9
🚌 124, 152, 304, 424, 502, 522, 601, 608, 618, 902 (Teatr Bagatela)
🚊 2, 3, 4, 8, 13, 14, 15, 20, 24 (Teatr Bagatela)

★ **1** Premonstratensian Convent

The story of this extensive fortified complex goes back to the 12th century. The Vistula and the Rudawa Rivers surround the convent, which ranks it among the city's most scenic places. The courtyard is the starting point for the figure of Lajkonik on his traditional march to the Main Square.

The Premonstratensian Convent was often besieged, hence the thick wall around it.

Lajkonik

Every year, the first Thursday after Corpus Christi Day sees the well-known emblematic figure of Lajkonik departing from the convent courtyard to frolic about on his progress to the city centre.

Lajkonik looks like a medieval Tatar, wearing colourful attire and a pointed cap. An inseparable element of the costume is a hobbyhorse. Lajkonik wields a ceremonial baton, with which he deals blows to those walking around the Main Square (➤ 26); no one gets offended, as this is a good-luck charm. The tradition dates back to the 18th century. It draws on an old legend about an army unit of Zwierzyniec rafters who defeated the Tatars when they tried to seize the convent. The Polish commander put the khan outfit on and ceremoniously entered Cracow with his soldiers, announcing the victory over the Tatars.

The history of the convent dates back to 1162. One of the few vestiges of the Romanesque period is a fragment of the 13th-century portal located under the tower. The convent, about 1.5 km away from the medieval town of Cracow, was an easy target for attackers and pillagers. It was repeatedly burnt down and plun-

dered by the Tatars. The greatest damage was sustained during the invasion commanded by the Archduke Maximilian of Austria in the latter 16th century. A thorough conversion took place at the turn of the 17th century, and the present form of the building dates from that time.

During the Swedish Deluge, between 1655 and 1657, the church was used as a stable. The invaders burnt the convent down and planned to raze the damaged walls to the ground. They even brought over some workers from Wieliczka (➤ 172) especially to have the building pulled down, but the miners delayed starting the demolition, which saved the church. When the danger was over, the church was renovated.

The best view of the Premonstratensian Convent is afforded from the other side of the Vistula.

The interior was decorated mostly in the 18th century in white and golden colours. The painted ceiling attracts the gaze. Take a look at the Blessed Bronisława altar on the left, between the nave and the chancel: it holds the remains of the 13th-century Premonstratensian nun. For the best view of the fortified convent buildings, walk over to the other side of the Vistula (only for keen walkers – the nearest bridge is situated about 800 metres away). ■

Premonstratensian Convent (Klasztor Norbertanek)

✉ *ul. Kościuszki 88*

@ *www.norbertanki.w.krakow.pl*

🕐 *visiting only before services*

🍴 *Cafe Zwierzyniec, ul. Królowej Jadwigi 4*
€€ €

ℹ *services: Mon–Sat at 6.30am, 7.15am (apart from July–Aug), 8am, 6pm (only on the 1st Fri of the month), 7pm; on Sun at 6.30am, 7.30am, 9am, 10.30am, noon, 1.15pm, 3pm (on the 1st Sun of the month), 7pm*

The *Emaus* Church Fair

Each Easter Monday sees a veritable siege of pilgrims and tourists who want to take part in one of Cracow's best-known church *fêtes*.

The name derives from the biblical town of Emmaus, where two of Christ's disciples headed after his death. When the resurrected Jesus appeared before them, they did not recognise him.

The tradition of visiting the Premonstratensian church, located outside the city, was started in the Middle Ages. Cracow has grown since then, and the church is now within the city limits, but the old custom survives as a combination of a religious holiday with a festival. Stalls and stands are covered with rainbow-coloured sweets and lollipops, toys and trinkets; children have fun on the roundabouts and jump castles. Ul. Kościuszki is hard to navigate. Walks to the nearby Kościuszko Mound (➤ 148) and Wolski Forest (➤ 154) are part of an unwritten tradition.

2 Chapel of SS Margaret and Judith

This is one of the few Polish examples of the wooden sacral architecture based on a central plan. Hence, even though the chapel is usually closed, its interesting structure is worth seeing – if only from the outside.

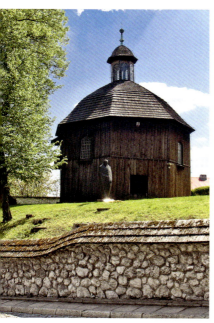

The octagonal Chapel of SS Margaret and Judith is a rare historic building.

The chapel was built on a plan of a regular octagon in the years 1689–1690. It was commissioned by the Premonstratensian nuns to replace two chapels that had burnt down. The chapel is constructed entirely in wood and has a shingled roof; despite repeated renovations, it has preserved its original form. The 17th-century Baroque altar was moved here from the nearby Church of the Holiest Saviour.

In the 17th century, the area around the chapel became the burial ground for epidemic victims. Bodies were interred in deep pits, covered with quicklime and planks. The remains were later moved to the cemetery by the Church of the Holiest Saviour. ■

Chapel of SS Margaret and Judith (Kaplica św. św. Małgorzaty i Judyty)
✉ *ul. bł. Bronisławy 8*
🕑 *visiting only before or after services*
ℹ *services: May–Oct on the 1st and the 3rd Sun of the month at 11.15am*

★ 3 Church of the Holiest Saviour

The origin of the church probably goes back to the 10th century; some Romanesque elements survive to this day. The church is surrounded by stone tombstones, and there is an intriguing wooden cabin nearby.

The church interior amazes with its diversity of architectural styles. The windows of the nave are Gothic; the Baroque décor contrasts with the austerity of the Romanesque chancel, covered with Renaissance frescoes. The chancel itself is certainly the most interesting part of the building. It preserves some remains of the 12th-century stone blocks. The highlight is a small round-arch window – a textbook example of Romanesque architecture. The feel of the past is also attributable to the frescoes, which are not that old – they date

A Shoe for a Fiddler

The altarpiece painting to the left of the nave shows an unusual representation of the crucified Christ. It was inspired by a legend.

The Crucifixion is a common motif in Christian art, but the way it is depicted in the Church of the Holiest Saviour stands out for its originality. Jesus is wearing a long gilded robe and a royal crown. Even more surprisingly, he shakes an ornamented shoe off his foot for a folk musician who stands below.

The painting is based on an old legend about the crucifix that was brought here from Moravia after Duke Mieszko I adopted Christianity for the Polish state in 966. As a fervent worshipper of Christ, Mieszko I financed the lavish dress and shoes for the figure. A poor fiddler came regularly to pray under the crucifix, playing religious tunes. Jesus was touched by the plight of the poor man and decided to relieve his misery, dropping one of his costly shoes straight into the fiddler's hands.

The Church of the Holiest Saviour is one of the oldest in Cracow.

from the 16th century. The back wall of the chancel should be seen from the outside. Its bare exposed surface is a singular chronicle of alterations made to the building.

The Church of the Holiest Saviour is one of the oldest Christian places of worship in Cracow. Source documents confirm that it was consecrated in 1048; some claim that the first building on the site was probably constructed one century earlier. The question remains open to discussion. The story that should be ruled out, however, is the legend of St Adalbert (c. 956–997) – the first Slavic Catholic saint and the patron saint of Poland – preaching from the stone pulpit outside the church. The major snag in the tale is that the pulpit dates from the 17th century.

Whatever the timing, the choice of the Holiest Saviour for patron saint testifies to the fact that this church was a major one in the region. Built on the former pagan cult site, it must have played a key role in Christianising the locals. The church stands among the tombstones of a small cemetery. It used to be the burial ground of the parishioners and Premonstratensian nuns. Take a look around for a 19th-century wooden house, adjoining the stone wall. Its former purpose remains a mystery, but it is popularly known as a "gravedigger's hut." ■

Church of the Holiest Saviour (Kościół Najświętszego Salwatora)
- ✉ *ul. św. Bronisławy 9*
- ⏱ *visiting only before or after services*
- ℹ *service: Sun at 11.15 (May–Oct on the 2nd and the 4th Sunday of the month)*

147

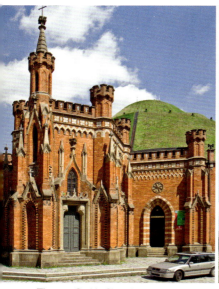

The neo-Gothic Chapel of Blessed Bronisława is the entrance gate to Kościuszko Mound.

★ 4 Kościuszko Mound

One of the city's icons, the mound that overlooks Cracow makes a great walking destination and viewing point. It is surrounded by a well-preserved fort built by Austrian occupiers, now home to a popular radio station.

The construction started three years after the death of Tadeusz Kościuszko (1746-1817), a Polish independence leader. The funds came from voluntary contributions. The main works took place between 1820 and 1823. Cracovians joined in spontaneously; Poles across social classes combined forces to build this monument.

Kościuszko Mound is encircled by fortifications built by the Austrians in the mid-19th century as part of the so-called Cracow Fortress. A large part is now occupied by the RMF radio station. The structure also holds a museum with an exhibition entitled "Kościuszko's Insurrection and Traditions in Cracow," and an exhibition of wax figures called "The Polish People's Roads to Liberty."

The entrance is through the Chapel of Blessed Bronisława (Kaplica bł. Bronisławy). The 13th-century Premonstratensian nun prayed on the site, and was said to appear here after her death. The chapel was built in the 18th century, but it was soon destroyed by Austrian troops during the construction of the fortress. This was met with protests from Poles, whose voice was heard by the Emperor himself. He ordered the reconstruction of the chapel; the result can be seen to this day. ∎

Kościuszko Mound (Kopiec Kościuszki)

☎ *Kościuszko exhibition: +48 12 4251116; wax figure exhibition: +48 12 6253560*

@ *www.kopieckosciuszki.pl*

🕑 *Mound: from 9am until dusk (May–Sept Fri–Sun until 11pm); exhibitions: Jan–Feb 9.30am–4pm, Mar 9.30am–5pm, Apr 9.30am–6pm, May–Sept 9.30am–7pm, Oct 9.30am–6pm, Nov 9.30am–4pm, Dec 9.30am–3pm*

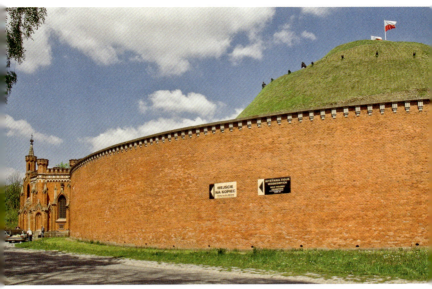

The Mound is encircled by the fortifications of the so-called Cracow Fortress.

€ *PLN 11 (PLN 9)*

¶¶ *Pod Kopcem restaurant* 😊😊😊*, grill on the terrace (open seasonally)* 😊😊€

ℹ *exhibitions are located by Kościuszko Mound in Fort no. 2 Kościuszko, bastion V*

5 Błonia

Poland's largest meadow in the city centre is a perfect place for walking. The first Polish plane took off from here. The area has been the venue of Papal Masses that gathered thousands of believers, and of many other cultural events.

The extensive area served as pasture grounds for a long time. The locals were granted the right to graze cattle as early as the Middle Ages. It has never been officially withdrawn, thus even in the 20th century cows were chewing on grass in the Błonia public park. Likewise, it is hard to believe that not so long ago – in the 19th century – the grounds were marshy and often flooded by the nearby Rudawa River. Just 15 minutes' walking distance from downtown Cracow, the Błonia is a favourite park with walkers and rollerbladers (especially al. 3 Maja).

The park looks particularly beautiful in the autumn, when the leaves of lined-up trees turn gold and red. Walkers can enjoy great views of Kościuszko Mound (➤148), the Old Town (➤50) and Wawel Castle (➤43). Consider coming here at dawn, especially if it promises to be a sunny day and the morning is hazy. In good weather, the view of church towers bathed in the morning sun, rising majestically over the mist-covered meadows, is gratification enough for an early rising.

The site has seen unusual events and momentous celebrations. In 1910, it hosted the festivities on the 500th anniversary of the Polish victory over the Teutonic Knights in the Battle of Grunwald. 23 years later, Marshal Józef Piłsudski took the salute on the 250th

149

anniversary of the Polish defeat of the Ottomans in the Battle of Vienna (the event is commemorated by an obelisk). There were also Masses celebrated by Popes John Paul II and Benedict XVI. They filled the park full of believers (up to 2.5 million in 2002).

The Błonia has witnessed tragic events as well. During the cholera outbreak in 1707, infected people were brought and left here so as to prevent the epidemic from spreading. They were looked after in a field hospital run by nuns of the Order of the Holy Spirit. In 1901, the park was the scene of Michał Bałucki's suicide. The playwright took his own life most probably as a result of his deepening mental illness and negative critical feedback on his dramatic works. ■

Błonia in Cracow (Błonia krakowskie)
Any Time restaurant, ul. Emaus 28b

Jordan Park was founded to inculcate patriotism and sports values in young Poles.

6 Jordan Park

The park's pitches, courts and gymnastic equipment served to improve the health and physical condition of children and young people. With time, the park infrastructure has changed considerably, but the mission remains the same.

It is Poland's first recreational park that was established especially with children and youth in mind. The originator and founder of the project was physician Henryk Jordan (1842–1907). He was a true pioneer of physical education, and his ideas were revolutionary at that time. Towards the end of the 19th century, physical culture was not yet an issue, and recreation was not valued as highly as it is now. Public parks that are named Jordan's Garden (*ogródek jordanowski*, after Henryk Jordan) can be found all around Poland.

Jordan's concept was to combine physical activities with patriotism. Hence, the park held not only team sports fields and gymnastic equipment, but also busts of eminent Poles. The latter were taken down by the Nazis during WWII, but are now being gradually restored (36 of the original 45 have already been put back).

The once untended park is now slowly regaining its past glory. There are new playgrounds and up-to-date basketball and football pitches. The artificial lake can be traversed in a hired kayak, and the toboggan

hill is very popular with kids in the winter. The park features even some ramps for roller bladers. It also welcomes those who want to take a walk in peace and quiet, escaping the hustle and bustle of Cracow. ■

Jordan Park (Park im. Henryka Jordana)
🕐 Apr–Oct: 6am–10pm; Nov–Mar: 6am–8pm
€ free

7 National Museum

The Main Building of Poland's oldest National Museum boasts an impressive Gallery of 20th-Century Polish Art. Visitors can also trace the over-millennium-old military history of Poland, and admire fine works of decorative art.

The National Museum was founded in 1879. It was first housed in the Sukiennice. The construction of today's Main Building started in 1934 and was completed in 1989. The museum has nine other departments, e.g. the Mehoffer House (➤152), the Sukiennice (➤28), the Matejko House (➤23) and the Princes Czartoryski Museum (ul. św. Jana 19), where you can see the famous *Lady with an Ermine* by Leonardo da Vinci.

The museum holds a large collection of works by Polish 20th-century artists, such as Leon Wyczółkowski, Jacek Malczewski, Olga Boznańska, Stanisław Ignacy Witkiewicz, Jerzy Nowosielski and Wilhelm Sasnal. The exhibition entitled "Arms and Uniforms in Poland" is also worth a look. It presents armour and military items in use from the Middle Ages to the 20th century. The collection consists of 1,600 exhibits, including the belongings of Polish military leaders: Tadeusz Kościuszko's homespun peasant coat, and Józef Piłsudski's service dress tunic.

The third permanent exhibition in the Main Building is the Gallery of Decorative Art. The highlight of this collection is the so-called Włocławek

Goblet, a 10th-century silver vessel. Other valuable exhibits include period dresses, chasubles and silk *kontusz* sashes, as well as ceramics and porcelain. Truly unique are individual pieces of the coffee service set designed in 1910 by Josef Hoffmann, an architect from Vienna. There are also clocks, musical instruments, and *judaica*.

The Museum holds popular temporary exhibitions. Over 100,000 art lovers came to see works by Jan Matejko, Józef Mehoffer and Stanisław Wyspiański. Foreign art has been represented by Marc Chagall, Andy Warhol and French Impressionists. ■

**National Museum – Main Building
(Muzeum Narodowe – Gmach Główny)**
✉ al. 3 Maja 1
☎ +48 12 2955500
@ www.muzeum.krakow.pl
🕐 Tue–Sat 10am–6pm, Sun 10am–4pm
€ permanent exhibitions: PLN 10 (PLN 5); permanent and temporary exhibitions: PLN 18 (PLN 9); free on Sun (permanent exhibitions)
🍴 Tribeca café on site ●●●
ℹ the ticket at PLN 18, valid for 14 days, entitles the bearer to a single visit to each of the Main Building exhibitions; audioguides to the three permanent galleries (English, German, French etc.) – PLN 5

8 Mehoffer House

Józef Mehoffer (1869–1946) was a leading artist of the Young Poland movement, famous for his paintings and designs of stained glass windows and gardens. You can now visit his old house with reconstructed dining, living and private rooms.

Józef Mehoffer's works are representative of the Polish modernist movement, the so-called Young Poland (Młoda Polska, c. 1891–1918). He studied under Jan Matejko at Cracow's Academy of Fine Arts (see: Plac Matejki ➤ 17) and became famous for his paintings and stained glass windows. He also took part in decorating St Mary's Basilica (➤ 23) and the Crown Treasury at Wawel Castle (➤ 43).

Józef Mehoffer bought the house in 1932. After the artist's death, first his son, and then a grandson tried to found a museum here. The plan succeeded only in 1996, after the building, Mehoffer's paintings and personal possessions had come into the hands of the National Museum (➤ 151).

On display are paintings, drawings and design projects, as well as everyday items that belonged to the artist. The most valuable works include landscapes *The Red Umbrella* (*Czerwona parasolka*) and *The Vistula Near Niepołomice* (*Wisła pod Niepołomicami*), as well as the "Florentine" portrait (*portret florencki*) of his wife, and *The Rose of Saron* (*Róża Saaronu*). Mehoffer's family spared no effort to have the interiors refurbished so as to faithfully reconstruct the living room as well as the private chambers upstairs.

The garden at the back was founded by Mehoffer. It now holds Cafe Ważka that serves tea, coffee, desserts and simple hot dishes, e.g. dumplings. ■

Józef Mehoffer House
(Dom Józefa Mehoffera)
✉ ul. Krupnicza 26
☎ box office: +48 12 3708186, reception desk: +48 12 3708188
🕐 Wed–Sun 10am–4pm
€ PLN 8 (PLN 4), free on Sun
🍴 Cafe Ważka ●€€; Vega vegetarian bar ➤ 191, ul. Krupnicza 22 ●€€

9 Carmelite Church in Piasek

The church in the bustling ul. Karmelicka is a very special place. Legend shrouds not only its origins and its greatest pride – a miraculous painting of the Virgin Mary, but also an alleged footprint on the facade of the building.

Historians claim that the church was built at the end of the 14th century, but a well-known legend gives a much earlier date. It says that Duke Vladislaus Herman (1043–1102) constructed the church as a votive offering after he recovered from scurvy. When the duke was ill, the Virgin Mary appeared to him in a dream. She told him to dig a hole where violets were blooming, take handfuls of sand and rub his face with it. Vladislaus did so, the illness subsided, and the grateful duke commissioned a church on the site where the violets had grown.

The building was repeatedly destroyed in the many wars that passed through Cracow. It burnt down for the first time at the end of the 16th century, and suffered great damage during the Swedish Deluge in 1655, and the Bar Confederation against Russians (1768–1772). As a result, the building has been reconstructed and altered many times. The present form

The facade of the Carmelite Church in Piasek is a fine example of the Baroque style.

A Queen's Footprint

The external church wall at the intersection of ul. Karmelicka and ul. Garbarska features a latticed stone. It bears an extraordinary impression.

Legend has it that this is a footprint of Queen Jadwiga (♛ 1384–1399). Allegedly, one of the masons who worked on the construction site had a sick daughter, but he could not afford to treat her. During her visit, Jadwiga noticed that the man was upset. When he revealed what the problem was, she decided to help him. She placed one foot on a stone, tore a gold buckle off the shoe and gave it to the mason. When she left, the man noticed her foot had left a mark in the stone. He decided to set it in the wall of the church, where it can be seen to this day.

dates from the 17th century. The church facade is modelled on Il Gesù Church in Rome – a showpiece of Baroque architecture. Inside, the central place is occupied by a monumental altar from the early 18th century. Also interesting are the long wooden stalls of the chancel, decorated with paintings and gildings. A noteworthy item in the left nave is an altarpiece that depicts Jude the Apostle – the patron saint of lost causes.

Do not miss the miraculous painting of Our Lady of Piasek (**Matka Boska Piaskowa**), a fresco from c. 1500 on a side wall. It has survived all the fires and raids, which was regarded to be a miracle. As a cult item, the fresco was encased in a chapel. Miraculous healings and other blessings ascribed to the intercession of Our Lady of Piasek fill volumes. In 1883, the painting was decorated with Papal crowns. John III Sobieski (♛ 1674–1696) prayed in front of it before he set off to the Battle of Vienna, and painter Jan Matejko got married here. ■

Carmelite Church of the Visitation of the Blessed Virgin Mary in Piasek (Kościół Nawiedzenia Najświętszej Maryi Panny oo. Karmelitów na Piasku)

✉ ul. Karmelicka 19

@ www.krakow.karmelici.pl

🕑 6am–7pm daily

🍴 restaurants: Mamma Mia ➤ 189, ul. Karmelicka 14 ●●€; C.K. Browar ➤ 181, ul. Podwale 6-7 ●●€

ℹ services: Mon–Fri at 6am, 6.30am (apart from July–Aug), 7am, 7.30am (apart from July–Aug), 8am, 9am, 4.30pm, 7pm; Sun at 6am, 7am, 8am, 9am, 10am, 11am, noon, 1pm, 4.30pm, 7pm

Wolski Forest

Olszanica

B. Leśniana
K. Wyżgi
Jagiełła
I. Kosmowskiej
RZEPICHY
Za Skłonem
CHEŁMSKA
Przyszłości
Zakamycze
Junacka

Głogowiec
RZEPICHY
Zakamycze

4 Kopiec Piłsudskiego

al. Do Kopca

Pod Sowińcem

RZEPICHY
Do Obserwatorium
ORLA
Astronomów
Astronomów
Astronomów
al. Wędrowników
al. Pustelnika
al. Żubrowa
al. Do Kopca

Ogród Zoologiczn
5

L a s

Rędzina

marsz. M. Wolskiego

al. Konarowa

6 Klasztor Kamedułów

W. Oszustowskiego
Bagatela
Cz. Niemena
ORLA
Zaszkolna
Zaogrodzie
Pod Janem
KSIĘCIA JÓZEFA
Orla
Dalekia
Bażancia
al. Wędrowników
Krucza

Bielany
Sępia
Skalna
Przepiórcza
Zakręt

city atlas ➤ 249–250, 259

0   250   500 m

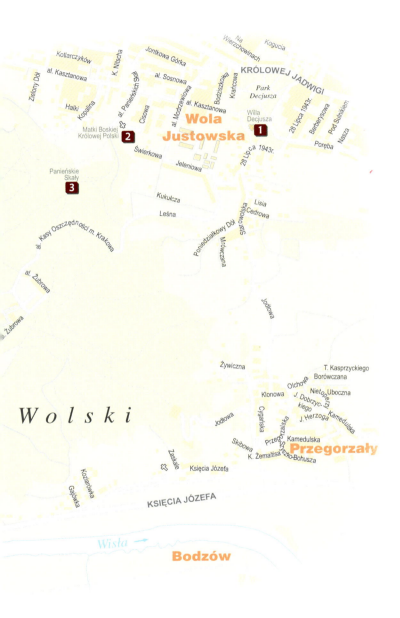

The Green Lungs of Cracow

The city's largest forest complex covers an area of over 400 hectares. It is a perfect recreational and tourist place, home to a zoological garden and a monastery with a strict monastic rule. A Renaissance palace is situated nearby.

The park grounds around the Decius Villa display sculptures by Bronisław Chromy.

Wolski Forest (Las Wolski) has a very varied landscape. It features deep ravines, extensive meadows and, most prominently, the hills of Srebrna Góra (326 m a.s.l.), Pustelnik (352 m a.s.l.) and Sowiniec (358 m a.s.l.) with Piłsudski Mound (➤ 161). They all tower over Cracow. The forest contains three nature reserves and interesting rock formations, including the legend-shrouded Panieńskie Skały (➤ 160). Located almost at the very heart is a zoo (➤ 161); on the outskirts, there is a Camaldolese Monastery (➤ 162). All these tourist attractions make Wolski Forest a popular walking and cycling destination. Tourist trails make it easier to move around the area.

The forest is home to many interesting species of plants and animals. With a bit of luck, you will spot a roe deer, a fox or a hare stealing amid the beeches, oaks and birches that dominate local broadleaved woods.

The grounds of Wolski Forest boast some landmarks of particular interest. Among them is the city's largest mound, named after Marshal Józef Piłsudski to commemorate the regaining of independence by Poland in 1918. Nearby, there is the Tadeusz Mazowiecki Liberty Oak Alley (Al. Dębów Wolności im. Tadeusza Mazowieckiego). 1999 saw the planting of 10 saplings to mark a decade of freedom after the fall of communism in Poland; a new tree is added every year. Tadeusz Mazowiecki, after whom the alley is named, was the Prime Minister of the first democratically elected government after WWII.

The forest has a beautifully situated zoological garden. The view over Wolski

Forest (e.g., from the Cracow–Katowice motorway) is incomplete without the white towers of the Camaldolese Monastery. Though usually closed to women, it is very popular among Cracovians and tourists alike. ■

Walking the route should take about 4 hours. Remember to wear comfortable shoes: there are a lot of steep stretches which can be slippery (especially after the rain). The route's only restaurant can be found in the Decius Villa (below).

There is a car park by the Decius Villa. On working days, you can also use a car park by the zoo (PLN 6 for a passenger car).

Access by public transport:

1
Ⓑ *102, 152, 192, 292, 902 (Park Decjusza)*

2–3
Ⓑ *102, 192, 292, 902 (Kopalina)*

4–5
Ⓑ *134 (Zoo)*

6
Ⓑ *109, 209, 229, 239, 269 (Bielany Klasztor)*

1 Decius Villa and Park

The villa was one of Poland's finest Renaissance residences and a place of philosophical debate. Devastated after WWII, it has regained its past glory. The park grounds are an open-air gallery of sculptures by Bronisław Chromy.

Justus Ludovicus Decius was a secretary to King Sigismund the Old (♔ **1506–1548**) and a true educated man of the world. In 1528, he commissioned a Renaissance villa near Cracow. The house was a meeting place of different cultures for the exchange of views and experiences. After Decius' death, the tradition was upheld by his son, and the villa became the main Polish venue for Protestant encounters.

The story of the villa is full of ups and downs, times of great glory and almost complete devastation. Extended at the end of the 16th century, it changed hands many times, gradually falling into ruin. The late 19th-century renovation resulted in its present form. WWII brought considerable damage. After 1945, the villa was adapted to house a tuberculosis hospital (among others), but lay in ruins from the 1970's. It was only in 1996 that the City of Cracow restored the building. The villa is now managed by the Villa Decius Association (Stowarzyszenie Willa Decjusza). The impressive facade features a three-storey arcaded loggia. Equally prominent are the representative stairs and two massive alcove towers on both sides of the loggia, covered with hip roofs.

The pride of the Decius Villa is a fine three-storey arcaded loggia.

The Bronisław Chromy Gallery contains portraits of celebrated Polish figures, such as writer Stanisław Wyspiański.

The villa is a venue for workshops, conferences and meetings, as well as wedding receptions. Newlyweds can choose between candlelit brick cellar rooms, and spacious white-decorated halls with small round tables. It is a very popular place with a fairy-tale ambience that attracts a lot of future married couples. An additional asset is a park around the villa, a perfect setting for wedding photos.

The Renaissance-style park that surrounds the villa holds a private gallery of Cracovian artist Bronisław Chromy. The sculptor is known mainly for the dramatic representation of the crucified Christ in the Lord's Ark (➤131) of Nowa Huta, and for the statue of the Wawel dragon in front of the Dragon's Den (➤48). Chromy's gallery is housed in a former band shell, but his works line the walking alleys as well. Particularly noteworthy are the *Cyclists* and a monument to the Piwnica pod Baranami (➤207). The latter has the form of an enormous crown set with pe-

culiar pearls: sculptures of the heads of artists and friends of the club, such as artistic director Piotr Skrzynecki, all-round artist Wiesław Dymny, and writer Czesław Miłosz.

The band shell itself is worth a visit. It dates from the 1960's and was re-adapted by Bronisław Chromy as a venue for exhibitions of sculpture, painting and ceramics. In the summer, chamber music concerts are held here. ∎

Decius Villa (Willa Decjusza)
✉ ul. 28 Lipca 17a
☎ visiting: +48 12 4253638 ext. 153
@ www.villa.org.pl
🕑 visiting only by prior appointment
🍴 restaurant on site ●●●

Bronisław Chromy Gallery
(Galeria Autorska Bronisława Chromego)
✉ ul. Krańcowa 4
☎ +48 663851167
@ www.chromy.art.pl
🕑 11am–7pm daily
€ free

The museum in Wola Justowska boasts an old granary and a chapel of Christ as the Man of Sorrows.

2 Open-Air Ethnographic Museum

Only two of the original three wooden museum buildings survive to this day; the church burnt down a few years ago. Since then, services for local parishioners are celebrated in the basement, which was saved from the flames.

In 1949, a decision was taken to found an open-air ethnographic museum in Cracow. Three wooden structures were brought over from different parts of Poland. The building of an old inn from the turn of the 19th century is now a presbytery. There is also an 18th-century granary. Unfortunately, the pride of the museum – a most treasured 16th-century church with four turrets atop the tower – is no longer in existence. In the past, the inn, the granary and the church seemed to have been there together for centuries. This fake village continued to exist until 1978, when the church was torched and burnt down completely. The locals decided to have it faithfully rebuilt, adding an under-ground lower church hall. The carefully reconstructed church was used only for 20 years. In 2002, the building went up in flames once again.

The lower church hall was roofed over with red metal sheeting, which makes it look like a large squat mushroom. Take a look inside to see sculptures by Bronisław Chromy. The reconstruction of the church is still under discussion. Apart from voices in favour of building a faithful replica of the wooden church, there are suggestions to construct a larger brick structure. The debate has been going on since 2002 and there is still no end in sight. However, it is clear that a brick church would compromise the atmosphere of this place. ■

The Panieńskie Skały reserve protects an old beech forest.

**Open-Air Ethnographic Museum
in Wola Justowska
(Skansen na Woli Justowskiej)**
✉ church: ul. Panieńskich Skał 18

🕐 *not accessible for visiting, the church
interior can be seen during services*
ℹ️ *services: Mon–Sat at 5pm (except July–
Aug), 6pm, Sun at 8am, 9.30am, 11am
(except July–Aug), 12.30pm, 6pm*

3 Panieńskie Skały

Interesting rock formations and an age-old forest are the main attractions of this small legend-shrouded nature reserve. It has an area of six hectares, and ranks among the most enchanting parts of Wolski Forest.

The area takes its name of the "Virgin Rocks" from a group of Premonstratensian nuns believed to have been hiding here. Legend has it that, during a Tatar raid, the nuns hastily left the nearby convent (➤ 144) and took to the forest. The invaders followed, and the nuns hid among rocks that mercifully closed around them, preventing a "fate worse than death." The women are said to be still praying together inside the hills that sometimes echo with religious song.

Some tourists even try to spot the figures of the nuns among the rocks, looking up from the bottom of the valley.

Calcareous rocks are set among an over-century-old beech forest. The steep slopes around a small valley and wide-stretching trees make for nice shade in the summer. The best time to visit, however, is the spring, when nature wakes up: the grass is strewn with blooming anemones and lilies of the valley. ■

4 Piłsudski Mound

The mound was built between 1934 and 1937. The city's most recent mound is also the largest: its diameter is 111 m at the base. It is named the "Grave of Graves," since it holds soil from battlefields and other places where Poles died.

Special urns contain soil from places where Polish soldiers fought in WWI. In the 1980's, Poles killed on WWII battlefields and sites of martyrdom, as well as victims of the subsequent communist oppression (1948–1989), were commemorated in the same way. The mound also came to hold soil from the plane crash site near Smolensk in Russia, where 96 people (including President Lech Kaczyński) lost their lives in 2010.

A one-metre-wide paved path leads up to the top, where you can admire a view over Wolski Forest and Cracow. The granite tablet features the cross of the Polish Legions – the armed forces created by Józef Piłsudski to fight in WWI. The monument is a replica of the original, removed in the 1950's by the communist authorities; the tank that was used partly damaged the mound. Yet another attempt by the authorities to lessen the significance of the landmark was the planting of trees in order to conceal it.

As a symbol of the Polish fight for independence, the mound was earlier doomed to leveling by the Nazi Governor-General Hans Frank. In the end, the order was not carried out. ■

5 Zoo

If you want to see what takins, aruis and Angola colobi look like, visit the zoological garden in Cracow. It is inhabited by many different species of animals from all over the world.

A strong asset of the zoo is its scenery: it is hard to imagine a better setting for animal pens than the verdant Wolski Forest. The 15-hectare garden is relatively small as compared against the four hectares of Cracow's Main Square (➤26), or the 120 hectares of the zoo in Gdańsk. This area, though limited in size, is home to many interesting animal species, from small basilisks (lizards) to huge elephants. The zoo is visited by as many as 250,000 people every year.

A true paradise for the youngest is the children's zoo (*minizoo*). Here, animals can be not only seen, but also fondled and even fed with the forage prepared by zoo staff. Children will get acquainted with (among others) goats, ponies, donkeys, llamas and Reeves' muntjacs – the world's smallest deer.

Many visitors come especially to see the zoo's frolicking monkeys. One can also take a look inside the brick building where they live. Other popular species include large predators, such as tigers, lions and jaguars. Remember to visit the pavilion of night animals. It is enveloped in darkness, but you can spot its inhabitants thanks to small lights. ■

Cracow Zoological Garden and Park (Miejski Park i Ogród Zoologiczny w Krakowie)

✉ ul. Kasy Oszczędności Miasta Krakowa 14
☎ +48 12 4253551, +48 12 4253552
@ www.zoo-krakow.pl
🕐 9am–7pm daily;
   children's zoo from 9.30am
💶 PLN 18 (PLN 10); children under 3 – free
🍴 a bar on site

The monastery entrance is adorned with a fresco of Saint Mary surrounded by monks.

★ 6 Camaldolese Monastery in Bielany

Life in silence, contemplation, physical labour and common prayer. For 400 years, Camaldolese hermits have adhered to a strict monastic rule, rejecting everything that does not lead to God. Women are rarely allowed behind these high walls.

The name of the Bielany neighbourhood derives from the Polish word for white, the colour of Camaldolese habits. Hermits came here at the beginning of the 17th century. At first, the isolated monastery was inhabited only by Italians, but increasing numbers of Poles turned to an ascetic monastic life.

White church towers overlook the treetops of Wolski Forest. The characteristic silhouette of the place of worship is visible even from the motorway and the ring road of Cracow. In the atmospheric interior, rich intricately-carved chapels contrast with an austere décor of the central nave, separated from the chancel by black railing. The lack of the organ and the pulpit is not accidental:

they are redundant in a place of quiet contemplation.

Male visitors may enter through the monastery gate and visit the church every day. Women are allowed in only twelve times a year, but even then the area that is subject to strict enclosure is inaccessible to them. Men can even consider going on an individual retreat. They are then allocated a cell to stay in for some time, leading a life of monastic discipline and daily routine.

The monastery comes alive on the occasion of the feast of Pentecost (Whit Sunday, the 50th day after Easter Sunday), when a church fair is held here. Colourful stalls groaning with sweets, souvenirs and toys set up all around

Generations of monks have been buried in the catacombs of the monastery in Bielany.

The Monastic Life

The monastery has a fixed daily routine. The bell awakes monks from their short sleep as early as 3.30am. Common prayers are followed by breakfast, eaten not together but individually.

The day is mostly devoted to praying, both common and in private cells. Contemplation is also enhanced by work, which is required by the order's rule. Silence is a must as well: talking is allowed only if necessary, always in a low voice, short and to the point. After the final vows, the Camaldolese monks usually renounce all contact with their families and friends, and may leave the monastery only up to five times a year for common outings. They never provide pastoral service, listen to the radio, watch TV or eat meat. All this to make sure that worldly affairs do not tear them away from personal closeness to God, achieved through prayers, contemplation and work.

the glade in front of the monastery are a great attraction for children. The place, usually an oasis of peace and quiet, turns into a bustling site teeming with people. Cracovians often combine the religious experience of visiting the monastery with a walk in Wolski Forest. ∎

Camaldolese Monastery in Bielany
(Klasztor Kamedułów na Bielanach)
✉ *al. Konarowa 1*
☎ *+48 12 4297610*

🕐 *male visitors: daily at 8am, 8.30am, 9am, 9.30am, 10am, 10.30am, 11am, 3pm, 3.30pm, 4pm;*

female visitors: on Easter Sunday, Easter Monday, May 3, Whit Sunday and Monday, the 1st Sunday after June 19, the 2nd and the 4th Sunday of July, the 1st Sunday of August, August 15, September 8, December 25

€ *free*

ℹ️ *services: at 11.30am daily*

Cracow Surroundings

Off the Beaten Track

Cracow is not all about the Main Square and Wawel Castle. There is also a number of interesting landmarks scattered around, closer to or further from the centre. Many historic monuments lure tourists out of the city limits.

The area around the Benedictine Abbey (➤ 167) is great for active leisure pursuits.

Cracow is the centre of the Lesser Poland Voivodeship (*województwo małopolskie*). The region has a varied landscape with mostly mountainous terrain, including the Tatras – the tallest Polish mountains on the border with Slovakia (the highest summit on the Polish territory is Rysy, 2499 m a.s.l.). The voivodeship contains six national parks, including the country's smallest, the Ojców National Park (➤ 168). On sunny weekends in the summer, crowds of Cracovians leave the city for the Polish Jurassic Highland, or for some corners of the region even further away.

The Lesser Poland keeps alive the old religious and family traditions. As in the past, the places famous for miracles attract pilgrims who come either on foot or (more and more often) by coach. These destinations come alive especially for church holi-days. For instance, the town of Kalwaria Zebrzydowska (➤ 174) is well-known all around Poland for the Passion play it stages every year from Holy Wednesday to Good Friday, attracting approx. 100,000 viewers. Recent years have seen an increase in the popularity of the Sanctuary in Łagiewniki after it was visited by Popes John Paul II and Benedict XVI. The basilica is worth seeing not just for spiritual experience: in good weather, the tower affords a view of the most important mountain ranges of the region, including the Tatras.

Among the main natural resources of the area is rock salt. In the Middle Ages, this mineral ranked among an assets in great demand, which made the towns of Bochnia and Wieliczka grow wealthy through their salt mines. The profit from sales also enriched the royal treasury. Already in the Renais-

165

The majestic Benedictine Abbey rises on rocks over the Vistula.

Sanctuary in Łagiewniki

Pilgrims come here to pray at the painting of the Divine Mercy, pictured after holy visions described by St Faustina. Her relics are also kept here.

The convent in Łagiewniki is connected with St Faustina Kowalska (1905–1938), known as the Apostle of Divine Mercy. St Faustina described her visions and conversations with Christ in her *Diary*. The convent's Chapel of St Joseph (Kaplica św. Józefa) holds the holy relics and the Image of the Divine Mercy with a Polish inscription that can be translated as "Jesus, I trust in you." It was painted by Adolf Hyła after St Faustina's death, in accordance with the suggestions she had made. The original painting was created in Vilnius under the saint's direction while she stayed there. The image can be seen in the city's Divine Mercy Sanctuary.

The basilica in Łagiewniki was built between 1999 and 2002 on an ellipsoidal plan. The central place is occupied by an altar with the Image of the Divine Mercy and a globe-shaped tabernacle. The lower church holds five chapels, including a Greek Catholic one with an iconostasis, and St Faustina's chapel. The 77-metre-high tower offers an impressive view over Cracow: Wawel Hill (➤ 40) and the Old Town (➤ 50). In good weather, you can see as far as the Tatra Mountains.

Sanctuary of Divine Mercy (Sanktuarium Bożego Miłosierdzia)

✉ *ul. św. Siostry Faustyny 3, Cracow*
@ *www.milosierdzie.pl*
🕐 *St Joseph's Chapel: 5.30am–9.30pm daily; basilica: 8am–7pm daily; tower: 9am–5pm daily*
Ⓣ *8, 19, 22, 23, 40 (Sanktuarium Bożego Miłosierdzia)*

sance, the salt mines were a magnet for adventurers, whom we might call the period's tourists. For centuries, the underground tunnels have remained as great an attraction, which is why they have been opened for visiting. The salt mine in Wieliczka (➤ 172) is one of Poland's most recognisable trademarks in Europe, and it has been listed as a UNESCO World Heritage Site.

The region has also witnessed WWII events that were tragic for Poles and Polish Jews. The Nazi Auschwitz-Birkenau Camp (➤ 176) has become an ultimate symbol of the Holocaust. ∎

★ 1 Benedictine Abbey in Tyniec

The grand Benedictine Abbey has been towering over the area for almost one millennium. Closed down in the 19th century for over 100 years, it has risen from the ruins since then. Today, like in the past, the building is inhabited by monks, and the church resounds with Gregorian chanting.

No other Benedictine Abbey could equal the one in Tyniec, as claimed by Henryk Sienkiewicz – a Polish Nobel Prize winning writer – in his historic novel *The Teutonic Knights* (1900). In one of the scenes, the enthralled characters look at the serrated walls and buildings stretching over the cliff in the light of the rising sun.

Many years have passed, but the description has lost none of its relevance. The abbey looks its best on a sunny day, when sunshine illuminates red roof tiles that contrast with the pastel-coloured walls of the church and adjacent buildings. The sight of dark rain clouds overhanging the abbey is also very impressive. Many visitors will be put into a pensive mood by this juxtaposition of the power of nature and the abbey that has endured for 1,000 years atop the steep calcareous rock over the Vistula.

The abbey is the oldest surviving monastery in Poland. The Benedictines have been present in Tyniec since the 11th century, and some historians quote the foundation date of 1044 after chronicler Jan Długosz. In 1124, the abbey already had an estate; this fact is confirmed by the oldest document in Tyniec, issued that year. It was probably then that the construction was completed and the church was consecrated.

Although situated a bit out of the way, Tyniec did not escape the turmoils of history. The abbey was plundered by the Tatars. In the 18th century, the Bar Confederates defended themselves here against the enemy troops (the walls along the road leading up to the complex date from that time). The place also suffered damage during the Napoleonic

wars. 1816 was a particularly important date in the history of the abbey. Tyniec was then under Austrian rule. Francis I, the Emperor of Austria, ordered the dissolution of the monastery. Monks came back here only one month before the outbreak of WWII; the restoration started after the war ended. Reconstruction works lasted until the beginning of the 21st century. The finishing touches to the inside were put in 2008.

SS Peter and Paul's Church (Kościół św. św. Piotra i Pawła) is a must-see. The highlight of the Baroque interior is an 18th-century black marble altar. Wooden choir stalls are also worth a look, not only when the Benedictine monks sit there during Masses. The choir features the scenes from the life of St Benedict. Yet another noteworthy item is the wooden crucifix made by artist Jerzy Nowosielski (1923–2011). The church has hosted an interesting meeting of cultures, the 2008 festival that brought together Gregorian chants, a whirling dervish and Sufi singing (Sufism is a mystical dimension of Islam).

The ground floor and the basement of the former library holds a museum. It displays the Neolithic tools found on the hill during excavation works, and Romanesque architectural details. Visitors are also introduced to the history of monasticism and the Benedictines through multimedia touch screens.

In addition, monks run the Benedictine Institute of Culture (Benedyktyński Instytut Kultury), which holds concerts, conferences and workshops for children. Visitors can stay for a few days in the Benedictine-run Abbey Guest House (Dom Gości). The Benedictines also manage a prolific "Tyniec" publishing house.

Remember to visit the shop with trademark Benedictine products. The most popular souvenirs include alcohol made in the abbey (many varieties of fruit wine, beer, mead, liqueur). There is a choice of fruit and mushroom preserves, natural medicaments and toiletries. You can also taste wholemeal pilgrim's bread with dried fruit and nuts (no preservatives added), prepared according to an old recipe used along the Santiago de Compostela route. A DVD (with English subtitles) records a day in the life of monks at Tyniec, affording a look into the abbey's library, chapels, and work places. ∎

Benedictine Abbey in Tyniec
(Opactwo oo. Benedyktynów w Tyńcu)
✉ *ul. Benedyktyńska 37, Cracow*
@ *www.tyniec.benedyktyni.pl*

🕐 *monastery grounds: 6.30am–7pm daily; museum: Mar 2–Nov 30: 10am–6pm; Dec 1–Mar 1: 10am–4pm; guided tours of the abbey (in Polish) Mar 2–Nov 30: Mon–Fri 9am–noon, 2pm–5pm, Sat 9am–2pm, 4pm–5pm, Sun 10am (church not included), noon–6pm; Dec–Feb: Mon–Fri 9am–noon, 2pm–3pm, Sat 9am–noon, 2pm, Sun 10am (church not included), noon–3pm – tours start on the hour; English guided tours only for organised groups by prior appointment*

💶 *monastery courtyard and praying in the church: free; museum: PLN 7 (PLN 5); guided tours of the abbey: PLN 6 (in English and other foreign languages: an extra charge of PLN 50); guided tours of the abbey and the museum: PLN 10 (PLN 8); audio guides in English: PLN 5*

🚌 *112 (Tyniec) – from Rondo Grunwaldzkie*

🍴 *Mnisze co nieco restaurant on site* 🔴🔴💶

ℹ️ *Abbey Guest House: Benedictine Institute of Culture, +48 12 6885452, +48 12 6885450, www.benedyktyni.eu*

★ 2 Ojców National Park

The Ojców National Park, though the smallest in Poland, is exceptionally varied. Here, you can see some interesting rock formations, visit two castles and a cave which was the hiding place of King Vladislaus the Short, and scoop up water from the so-called Spring of Love.

The village of Ojców boasts the picturesque ruins of a 14th-century fortress. The castle was built by King Casimir the Great. Among the surviving elements is the entrance gate, now one of the icons of the Ojców National Park. The other castle, fully restored, is situated in Pieskowa Skała, which is 7 km away. The characteristic white clock tower that adorns the Renaissance residence is visible from afar. Yet another impressive feature is an arcaded courtyard, resembling the better-known sight from Wawel Castle (➤43).

Tourists come to the national park to admire its interesting rock formations. The most interesting specimen is Hercules' Bludgeon (Maczuga Herkulesa), situated near the castle in Pieskowa Skała. The name comes from the bizarre shape of the calcareous monadnock. If you look carefully, you will see a metal cross at the top, which commemorates the first ascent of the landmark in 1933. Among the most popular walking areas are the surroundings of Cracow Gate (Brama Krakowska) – two rocks with a broad passage in between. In the past, the trade route leading to the Silesia region ran through the "gate."

The Spring of Love (Źródełko Miłości) is approx. 100 metres away from Cracow Gate. According to a legend, a young man and a woman were once walking past the site. Since the day was scorching hot, they drank some cold water from the spring. On tasting it, they immediately fell in love with each other. However, though wise men say there is a grain of truth in every legend, you had

The beautifully situated Castle in Pieskowa Skała looks like a dream scenery.

Łokietek Cave

The central figure of the legend that surrounds the cave is neither of the two kings involved, but… a spider.

Legend has it that the cave was a hiding place of Vladislaus the Short (♛ 1306–1333), called Władysław Łokietek in Polish. The king of Poland was fleeing from Wenceslaus II of Bohemia. When he got near Ojców, he hid himself in a cave, and a small spider immediately spun a thick cobweb over the entrance. The enemy soldiers thought that Vladislaus could not have entered without tearing the cobweb, and left. Hence, today's entrance grille resembles a cobweb.

The interior walls are blackened with smoke from burning torches that were used to light the way for visitors. At present, the 120,000 people that visit the cave every year follow the tourist trail by electric lighting.

**Łokietek Cave
(Jaskinia Łokietka, Grota Łokietka)**

☎ +48 12 4190801

@ www.grotalokietka.pl

⏱ Apr 14–Aug 9am–6.30pm;
Sept 9am–5.30pm; Oct 9am–4.30pm;
Nov 9am–3.30pm

€ PLN 7.5 (PLN 5.5)

better not rely too much on the spring in sorting out your love life. The effect of gulping the (by now) undrinkable water is likely to be different from expected.

The Ojców National Park is part of the Polish Jurassic Highland (Jura Krakowsko-Częstochowska). The region abounds in caves created in karst processes (the dissolution of soluble carbonate bedrock). One of the caves, called Łokietek Cave (Jaskinia Łokietka) allegedly served as the hiding place of King Vladislaus the Short. Another cavern, called the Dark Cave (Jaskinia Ciemna) was inhabited by people as early as 120,000–115,000 BC. Both caves are now accessible to visitors and prove to be a great tourist attraction.

169

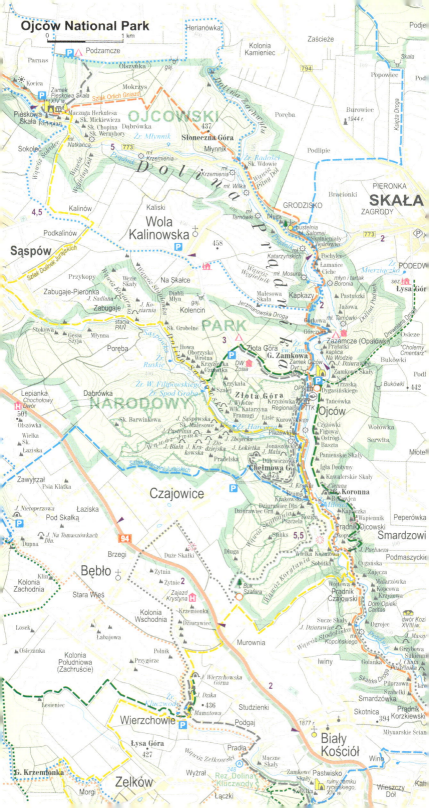

The Ojców National Park is a great example of karst topography.

You will also see the chapel "on the water." Reportedly, the reason behind this unconventional architectural solution was a decree by Tsar Nicholas II, prohibiting construction of sacral buildings "on Ojców soil." Cunning Polish builders kept to the literal sense of the decree, constructing a chapel over the Prądnik River. The unusual wooden structure was built in 1901 on the site of the former spa baths. With the river flowing beneath, the chapel looks quite startling. ■

Ojców National Park (Ojcowski Park Narodowy)
@ www.opn.most.org.pl
Ⓑ Unibus (Kraków–Ojców) from the car park in ul. Ogrodowa by Galeria Krakowska

Ruins of the Castle in Ojców (Ruiny zamku Kazimierza Wielkiego w Ojcowie)
🕐 daily, Apr–May: 10am–4.45pm; June–Aug: 10am–5.45pm, Sept: 10am–4.45pm, Oct: 10am–3.45pm; Sun and holidays: open for longer
€ PLN 2.5 (PLN 1.5)

Castle in Pieskowa Skała (Zamek w Pieskowej Skale)
☎ +48 12 3896004
@ www.pieskowaskala.pl
🕐 May–Sept: Tue–Thu 9am–5pm, Fri 9am–1pm, Sat–Sun 10am–6pm; Apr and Oct: Tue–Thu 10am–4pm, Fri 10am–1pm, Sat–Sun 10am–4pm; Nov–Mar: Tue–Fri (tours for groups of over 15 people, arranged at least one day in advance), Sat–Sun 10am–4pm (entry at 10am, 11am, 1pm, 2pm)
€ PLN 16 (PLN 9)
ⓘ non-stop unguarded car parks (PLN 6.50 for a passenger car): the main one at the intersection of access roads to Skała, Sułoszowa and Wielmoza, the other one on the side of Skała close to Hercules' Bludgeon in the river bend of Prądnik

Dark Cave (Jaskinia Ciemna)
☎ +48 12 3801011
🕐 Apr 28–Oct 7: 10am–5pm daily
€ PLN 6.50 (PLN 4.50)

St Joseph's Chapel "On the Water" (Kaplica św. Józefa Rzemieślnika „Na Wodzie")
🕐 Sun and holidays before and after services
ⓘ services: Fri at 4pm, Sun and hol. at 8am, 10am

St Kinga's Chapel in Wieliczka is almost entirely carved in salt.

★ 3 Wieliczka

The town of Wieliczka was well-known for salt extraction as early as the Middle Ages. The UNESCO-listed salt mine has one million visitors every year. See the Saltworks Castle, and on Easter Monday beware of the scary Siuda Baba.

Salt was obtained on the site of today's Wieliczka as early as 3,500 BC. The method used up to the 13th century consisted of water evaporation. Vast deposits of rock salt were probably discovered by accident. The subsequent salt mining lasted incessantly from the Middle Ages to the 20th century.

At a time when no one even dreamt of freezers, salt was used for food preservation. Other applications included leather tanning and gunpowder production. Salt often served as a means of payment as well.

A tour of the Wieliczka salt mine is like stepping into the underground world of tunnels and chambers. You will get to know medieval salt extraction techniques and grasp the specificity of working below the surface. Impressive features are not just corridors with their roofs supported by wooden beams, but also spacious halls. Among the finest chambers, one should cite St Kinga's Chapel (Kaplica św. Kingi). All the furnishings – sculptures, chandeliers, and even the floor – are carved in rock salt. Those who would like to see more of the underground passages may leave the main Tourist Route and go on a torchlit guided tour, wearing overalls and a safety helmet (provided on site). Who knows, maybe the chance of encountering the Kobold is greater then.

Tourists interested in the history of the town should visit the Saltworks Castle (Zamek Żupny). It was built in the 13th century for the administrator of Cracow's salt mines in Wieliczka and Bochnia. The visitor-accessible halls and cellars present the history of Polish settlement, a collection of bizarre salt shakers, remains of medieval walls and the oldest shaft in Wieliczka.

The small main square in the centre of the town features a parish

The Barącz Chamber (Komora Barącza) features a small brine lake, 9 m in depth.

church. Other noteworthy places of worship include a small 16th-century wooden Church of St Sebastian (ul. św. Sebastiana 23) and the Franciscan monastery (ul. br. Alojzego Kosiby 31) with the miraculous painting of Our Lady of Mercy. ∎

Wieliczka

Ⓑ *204, 244, 904 (Wieliczka), 304 (Wieliczka, Wieliczka Kopalnia Soli, Wieliczka Rynek), a PKS bus from the Local Coach Station (Regionalny Dworzec Autobusowy) or a train from the Central Railway Station (Dworzec Główny)*

Wieliczka Salt Mine (Kopalnia Soli „Wieliczka")

✉ *ul. Daniłowicza 10, Wieliczka*

☎ *+48 12 2787302, +48 12 2787366*

@ *www.kopalnia.pl*

🕐 *Apr–Oct: 7.30am–7.30pm daily; Nov–Mar: 8am–5pm daily; guided tours in English June–Sept 8.30am–6pm every 30 minutes, Oct–May 9am–5pm every hour (10am–1pm every 30 minutes)*

€ *guided tours in English, Italian, German, French, Russian and Spanish: PLN 68 (PLN 54)*

ℹ *a tour of the underground Tourist Route (approx. 2 km) and the Saltworks Museum (Muzeum Żup Krakowskich) takes approx. 3 hours; the temperature inside the salt mine is 14°C (57°F)*

The Siuda Baba Figure

On Easter Monday, the streets in Wieliczka are roamed by the mysterious, weird figure of Siuda Baba.

Despite a name that suggests a woman, Siuda Baba is in fact a man with a blackened face, wearing worn-out female clothing and a string of beads made from potatoes or chestnuts. The character is taken from a legend of a pagan temple on Lednica Hill near Wieliczka; Siuda Baba was a priestess looking after the holy fire there. She was never to leave the temple, hence her scruffy appearance and sooty face. Once a year, she went to town to catch a young woman: if she succeeded, the poor girl had to take her place at the temple.

Saltworks Castle (Zamek Żupny)

✉ *ul. Zamkowa 8, Wieliczka*

☎ *+48 12 2783266*

@ *www.muzeum.wieliczka.pl*

🕐 *May–Aug: Tue–Sun 9am–8pm; Sept–Dec: Tue–Sun 9am–3pm; Jan–Mar: Tue–Sun 9am–4.30pm; Apr Tue–Sun 9am–3pm*

€ *PLN 4 (PLN 3), free on Sat*

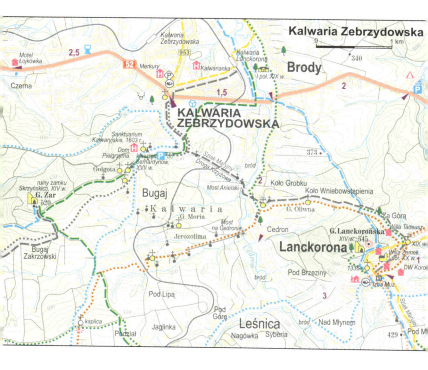

4 Kalwaria Zebrzydowska

The sanctuary in Kalwaria Zebrzydowska has been listed as a UNESCO World Heritage Site. It is called the Polish Jerusalem. Pilgrims walk the Devotional Path, and follow the traditional Way of the Cross on Good Friday.

Founded in 1600, it was the first Calvary in Poland. The construction of a little church dedicated to the Crucifixion of Christ (Kościół Ukrzyżowania Pana Jezusa) on Mount Żar, commissioned by the governor of Cracow Mikołaj Zebrzydowski, started the architectural complex. With time, other chapels and Stations of the Cross were added. Their names and spatial arrangement imitated the topography of Jerusalem. In this way, pilgrims could feel as if they were travelling in the Holy Land. Though not actually leaving Poland, they could climb Golgotha and the Mount of Olives (Góra Oliwna), as well as go across the stream of Kidron (Cedron).

Visitors may follow the paths of Christ (stopping at the Stations of the Cross) or St Mary's paths. There are 44 landmarks – mainly chapels and statues – on a total area of six square kilometres. The terrain is mountainous, so walking it demands physical effort.

Kalwaria Zebrzydowska is also home to a monastery complex run by the Friars Minor of the Observance. The central building is the Basilica of Saint Mary of the Angels (Bazylika Matki Bożej Anielskiej). The Mannerist church boasts a wealth of Baroque ornaments and nave ceiling paintings made by Włodzimierz Tetmajer, one of the leading artists of the Young Poland movement. The Zebrzydowski Chapel

(Kaplica Zebrzydowskich) that adjoins the basilica features a miraculous image of Our Lady of Calvary, revered since the 17th century. The Baroque-style chapel is itself worth seeing. Its dark walls, decorated with black marble, are illuminated by sunlight streaming through the dome lantern and high-placed windows.

For over 300 years, the town has staged the Lenten mystery play during Holy Week. The alumni of the local seminary and tourist guides act out Gospel scenes. They start with the triumphal entry of Christ on a donkey on Palm Sunday. The subsequent scenes are Judas' betrayal and the ensuing arrest of Christ. Thousands of pilgrims come on Good Friday to watch the Mystery of Christ's Passion. The *Via Dolorosa* procession heads for Golgotha. The mysteries in Kalwaria stand out for great attention to detail, such as period costumes. ■

The Basilica of Saint Mary of the Angels is the heart of Kalwaria Zebrzydowska.

Passion-Marian Sanctuary in Kalwaria Zebrzydowska (Sanktuarium Pasyjno--Maryjne w Kalwarii Zebrzydowskiej)

✉ *ul. Bernardyńska 46, Kalwaria Zebrzydowska*

@ *www.kalwaria.eu*

🕐 *6am–7pm daily*

€ *free*

Ⓑ *by bus from Cracow's Local Coach Station (Regionalny Dworzec Auto-busowy) or by train from the Central Railway Station (Dworzec Główny)*

5 Wadowice

It was in the city of Wadowice that Karol Wojtyła – the future Pope John Paul II – was born. Tourists can visit his family home, the church where he was baptised, and have a taste of the so-called *kremówka papieska*, a cream slice that was one of the Pope's favourite childhood cakes.

Karol Wojtyła was born in Wadowice on May 18, 1920. He lived with his parents at ul. Kościelna 7 until he moved to Cracow and started Polish studies. The house in Wadowice is now home to a museum dedicated to the late Pope. The collection includes archive photos, documents and belongings such as wooden skis with leather shoes. The museum is now closed for renovation; the reopening is scheduled for 2013. Part of the exhibition (e.g., a mockup of the Wojtyłas' home) is temporarily on display at the Catholic House (Dom Katolicki).

In the centre of Wadowice lies a small rectangular square, affording a great view of the white facade of the Baroque basilica church. The building was constructed between 1792 and 1798; the original wooden structure on the site dates back to the 14th century. The highlight is the font in which Karol Wojtyła was baptised.

When in Wadowice, you have to taste *kremówka* (puff pastry with a thick layer of vanilla cream or *blancmange*). The cake became particularly popular after the 1999 visit of John Paul II to Poland. At the

The Baroque Wadowice basilica is where the future John Paul II was baptised.

cakes to which they treated themselves after graduation exams at their secondary school. Since then, most Polish tourists do not leave Wadowice without savouring the city's speciality, now called Papal cream cake (*kremówka papieska*, ➤ 199). It is best to visit the city in May or June, during the Days of Wadowice, which start on May 18 to commemorate the anniversary of Karol Wojtyła's birth. ■

Wadowice

🚌 a PKS bus from Cracow's Local Coach Station (Regionalny Dworzec Autobusowy)

John Paul II Family Home Museum (Muzeum – Dom Rodzinny Jana Pawła II)

✉ ul. Kościelna 7, Wadowice
☎ +48 33 8232662
@ www.domrodzinnyjanapawla.pl
ℹ closed for renovation, the reopening is scheduled for 2013; part of the exhibition can be seen at the Catholic House

Catholic House (Dom Katolicki)

✉ pl. Jana Pawła II at No. I (left of the basilica), Wadowice
🕐 Oct–Apr: Tue–Sun 9am–4pm, May–Sept: 9am–6pm daily
💶 PLN 5 (PLN 3)

very end of the stay in his home town, the Pope reminisced about his childhood. He talked about the Wadowice of that time, his old friends, and the *kremówka*

★ 6 Auschwitz

People that perished here were of different nationalities, but nine out of ten victims were of Jewish origin. The Auschwitz-Birkenau concentration and extermination camp was set up by the German Nazis as part of the "final solution of the Jewish question." It is a chilling testimony to the Holocaust.

The Nazi camp in Oświęcim consisted of Auschwitz I, Birkenau (Auschwitz II), and numerous subcamps. All these sites witnessed one of the most atrocious crimes against humanity in world history. The number of victims speaks for itself. Between 1940 and 1945, up to 1–1.5 million people were killed here: approx. 1–1.35 million Jews, 150,000 Poles, and other nationalities. Extermination was carried out systematically, according to a prescribed procedure. Prisoners were spared to live as long as they could

work. Those who were assessed unfit for labour – as much as 70 percent – were sent straight to gas chambers, where they died in torment, stripped of their dignity. Listed as a UNESCO World Heritage Site, Auschwitz-Birkenau will remain forever a horrifying evidence of WWII genocide.

"Arbeit Macht Frei" (**"Work makes one free"**) – reads the sign above the main gate of Auschwitz. The cynicism is evident: the backbreaking labour of hungry prisoners, chilled to the marrow, consumed by diseases and whipped by

The infamous "Arbeit Macht Frei" sign over the gate is a replica of the original, which is displayed in the museum.

Nazi guards, was aimed at their ultimate exploitation and death.

The route runs past Block 11, where the first experimental killings with Zyklon B took place, and a crematorium where corpses were burnt. Visitors can see the starvation cell where Saint Maximilian Kolbe (1894–1941), a Polish Franciscan, died after volunteering to take the place of a stranger who had a family.

Auschwitz had facilities for human experimentation which included infecting prisoners with serious diseases, sterilisation and drug testing. One of the Nazi "physicians" was Josef Mengele, known as the Angel of Death. Piles of hair shaved from prisoners' heads, glasses and shoes taken from them, are a deeply distressing sight.

In the Auschwitz II-Birkenau camp, an area of 175 ha holds 300 wooden barracks surrounded by barbed wire entanglements. In 1944, they were inhabited by as many as 100,000 prisoners. Originally a labour camp, it was soon turned into an extermination site. A visit here is even more dejecting than in Auschwitz 1, if only for the ruins of the many crematoria blown up by the retreating Nazis. ■

Auschwitz Birkenau – German Nazi Concentration and Extermination Camp, 1940-1945 (Niemiecki nazistowski obóz koncentracyjny i zagłady (1940–1945) Auschwitz-Birkenau)

✉ *Auschwitz I, ul. Więźniów Oświęcimia 20*

☎ *+48 33 8448100; +48 33 8448099*

@ *www.auschwitz.org.pl*

🕐 *Dec–Feb: 9am–3pm; Mar, Nov: 8am–4pm; Apr, Oct: 8am–5pm; May, Sept: 8am–6pm; June–Aug: 8am–7pm; Auschwitz I: Apr–Oct 10am–3pm guided tours only; guided tours in English: Apr, Oct 10.30am–3.30pm every 60 minutes, May–Sept 9.30am–3.30pm every 30 minutes (Auschwitz II stays open)*

€ *free; guided tours in English, German, Spanish, French, Italian: PLN 40 (PLN 30), the price includes a tour of both camp parts, a shuttle bus ride, headphones, a documentary show*

🚌 *by bus from Cracow's Local Coach Station (Regionalny Dworzec Autobusowy) – some services stop by the Auschwitz entrance; by train from the Central Railway Station (Dworzec Główny) to the Oświęcim station, then bus lines Nos. 2, 3, 4, 5, 6, 9, 17, 23 (Auschwitz); Apr 15– Oct 31: free bus service every 30 minutes between Auschwitz and Birkenau*

ℹ *not recommended for children below 14 years of age; a tour of each part takes about 90 minutes, guided tours take approx. 4 hours*

Food and Drink

Cracow's eating establishments will please every palate and budget. They serve delicious food and excellent beverages (above, duck at Wierzynek and a pump room at ul. św. Jana 3).

The Flavours of Cracow

Varied offers of Cracow's many bars and restaurants are the proverbial cherry on the layer cake of the city's traditions. A historical cookbook of Cracow comprises Old Polish, Galician, and Jewish cuisines.

Cracow is the perfect place to try some traditional Polish dishes. Polish cuisine is considered to be stodgy and fatty. It is largely true, but you will not bother counting calories when given a chance to savour so many delicious dishes. When asked to name their national dish Poles will surely mention *bigos*: cabbage and sauerkraut stewed for several days with a variety of meats and mushrooms. A traditional Sunday dinner will usually include *schabowy* (pork chop fried in bread crumbs) with potatoes and a raw vegetable salad as a side dish. Another popular choice is *pierogi*, crescent-shaped Polish dumplings with meat, sauerkraut and dried mushrooms, cottage cheese, or blackberries. *Barszcz czerwony* (borscht, i.e. a clear beetroot soup) will go very well with sauerkraut *pierogi*. You should also try *żurek*, a sour soup cooked on a bread leaven base, usually served with hard-boiled eggs and white sausage.

The story of Cracow has left its mark on the local cuisine. A combination of Polish *bourgeois* and peasant traditions, it is enriched with Austrian influences due to the fact that part of the

A Ring-Shaped Snack

***Obwarzanek krakowski* (Cracow bagel) is the city's trademark product, a must-try snack if you want to have a "taste of Cracow." Baked ever since the 13th century, bagels are very popular among Cracovians. Hard-pressed students practically live on them.**

In 2010, *obwarzanek krakowski* became a Polish protected trade name in the EU. The first mention of the ring-shaped bread comes from 1257, when Boleslaus the Chaste granted bakers the right to sell it in the Main Square (➤ 26). The tradition survives to this day. Hawking bagel sellers and their handcarts can be found all around Cracow; it is estimated that 99 percent of bagels are sold this way.

Obwarzanki are best bought in the morning, when they are at their tastiest: freshly baked, aromatic, with a lightly browned, crispy crust and soft inside. You can choose between a number of varieties: garnished with salt, poppy or sesame seeds, recently also with cheese and hot spices. An additional advantage is their affordable price (approx. PLN 1.50 per piece).

Tasty, cheap and ring-shaped, Cracow bagels are the city's trademark snack.

Lesser Poland region – the so-called Galicia – was under Austrian rule from the late 18th century until 1918. Hence specialities such as *Wiener schnitzel*, Viennese cheesecake and Pischinger cake (crisp wafers with layers of chocolate cream).

Yet another important influence came from the Jewish community, present in Cracow since the 13th century. Most Jewish restaurants now centre around ul. Szeroka. Meat dishes are often served sweet, with raisins and almonds (e.g., in Klezmer Hois ➤ 185). The most characteristic dish is *cholent* – thick Shabbat stew of kosher meat, bean and groats, sometimes potatoes. It can be savoured in most Jewish restaurants: Klezmer Hois, Ariel (➤ 185), Ester (➤ 185). Other specialities include fish, especially the ever-popular carp, and kosher Israeli wine (in Ariel). The live klezmer music that often accompanies the meals is an integral element of the Jewish culture of Central Eastern Europe.

The No. 1 spice in the Cracow region is caraway. It is an important ingredient of a popular regional dish, Cracow's machanka (*maczanka*), thick pork stew eaten with a bread roll. Cracow also has its own way of serving tripe (*flaczki*): the dish does not contain meatballs and is thicker than in other regions of Poland. Yet another local dish is duck Cracow-style, served with buckwheat groats and mushrooms; you can taste it, for example, in Hawełka (➤ 181).

It is worthwhile making some effort to select a suitable eating establishment to try a particular dish. For huge *schabowy* chops, visit Polakowski (➤ 182); the best cooked roast pork knuckles are served with mustard, horseradish sauce and bread at C.K. Browar (➤ 181) and Kompania Kuflowa (➤ 182). Contrary to the name of *gołąbki*, which literally translates as "little pigeons," the dish is fortunately not made of the grey birds that can be seen in the Main Square (➤ 26). Instead, it consists of cabbage stuffed with minced meat (usually beef), rice or groats. The vegetarian version of *gołąbki* is offered by Vega (➤ 191). The best choice for homemade lunch meals is Jadłodajnia u Stasi (➤ 184), a family bar. ∎

€ € € **up to PLN 20**
€ € € **PLN 20–40**
€ € € **over PLN 40**

Each price bracket covers a main course and side dishes.

POLISH CUISINE

Bordo € € €

You would never believe that so many tables can be fit into small rooms like these. The place is nice and spruce, though packed with people at lunch time. The dish of the day is usually the best value-for-money offer in the Old Town (➤ 50). The menu includes a number of soups and main courses at an average price of PLN 14. Poultry cutlets, pork chops, roast meat and fish are served with chips, rice or potatoes (boiled or baked). You leave with a full stomach and a full wallet. ∎

✉ *ul. Gołębia 3*
☎ *+48 12 4211901*
@ *www.bordo-krakow.pl*
🕐 *8am–9pm*
🚋 *1, 3, 6, 8, 18 (Plac Wszystkich Świętych), 1, 7, 10, 12, 13, 19, 24, 40 (Poczta Główna)*

Chłopskie Jadło € € €

The "Countryside Cuisine" restaurants serve traditional Polish dishes in interiors styled on peasant rooms: walls are painted blue, furniture is made from wood, earthenware pots and rings of sausage and garlic complete the picture. Waitresses wear folk dresses. Food portions are large; meat and potatoes reign supreme. You can choose between pork and beef dishes, as well as the specialities of the Polish countryside: stuffed cabbage, *bigos*, spare ribs. For an appetiser, try a thick slice of leavened bread spread with seasoned lard. ■

✉ ul. św. Jana 3
☎ +48 12 4295157
@ www.chlopskiejadlo.pl
🕐 Mon–Thu, Sun noon–10pm, Fri–Sat noon–11pm
🚌 124, 152, 424, 502, 522, 601, 605, 608, 609, 610, 614, 618, 902, 904 (Dworzec Główny)
🚊 2, 4, 7, 10, 12, 13, 14, 15, 19, 20, 24, 40 (Dworzec Główny)

✉ ul. św. Agnieszki 1
☎ +48 12 4218520
🚌 128, 184, 609, 614, 904 (Stradom)
🚊 3, 6, 8, 10, 12, 18, 19, 22, 40 (Stradom)

✉ ul. Grodzka 9
☎ +48 12 4296187
🚊 1, 3, 6, 8, 18 (Pl. Wszystkich Świętych)

C.K. Browar €€€

The air-conditioned restaurant shares the entrance with the Mini Brewery & Pub; you should go down the stairs and past the cloakroom, then turn left. The noise from the bar next door is effectively muffled by sound-proof walls. Fish dishes are well worth trying, but the highlight of the menu is delicious meat; roast pork knuckle and a wooden platter with a choice of meats and baked potatoes is a classic. There is no shortage of garlic lard and pickles to whet the appetite, and the meal tastes best when accompanied with beer that is brewed right in the pub. ■

✉ ul. Podwale 6-7
☎ +48 12 4292505
@ www.ckbrowar.krakow.pl
🕐 noon–midnight, Fri–Sat noon–1am
🚌 124, 152, 304, 424, 502, 522, 601, 608, 618, 902 (Teatr Bagatela)
🚊 2, 3, 4, 8, 13, 14, 15, 20, 24 (Teatr Bagatela)

Hawełka €€€

The restaurant was founded in 1876. A long history translates into a tradi-tional approach: Hawełka serves mostly Polish cuisine, based on old tried-and-tested recipes. The specialities of the restaurant are mushroom soup served in a bread bowl, duck Cracovian-style, and the Antoni Hawełka *bliny* (a thick pan-cake made of yeast or leavened dough) with salmon and sour cream. The cheesecake is a must-try. Eminent guests have included Queen Elizabeth II, who dined here during her visit to Cracow. The restaurant interiors have a green colour scheme, which was popular back in the 19th century. Upstairs, guests can admire the paintings of Włodzimierz Przerwa-Tetmajer, a celebrated artist of the Young Poland movement. ■

✉ Rynek Główny 34
☎ +48 12 4220631
@ www.hawelka.pl
🕐 11am–11pm
🚌 124, 152, 304, 424, 502, 522, 601, 608, 618, 902 (Teatr Bagatela); 124, 152, 424, 502, 522, 601, 605, 608, 609, 610, 614, 618, 902, 904 (Dworzec Główny)
🚊 2, 3, 4, 8, 13, 14, 15, 20, 24 (Teatr Bagatela); 2, 4, 7, 10, 12, 13, 14, 15, 19, 20, 24, 40 (Dworzec Główny)

Jarema €€€

This is the best restaurant serving Eastern Polish cuisine in Cracow. The dishes on the menu are part of the Polish tradition, but they originate from the territory of to-day's Belarus and Lithuania. A visit here is a chance to taste the meals you will not find anywhere else in Cracow: creamed *pelmeni* (a type of meat dumplings), borscht with *kałduny* (dumplings filled with meat), potato sausage (*kiszka ziem-niaczana*). There is also a wide choice of meat meals: pork chops, veal steaks, even hare and quail dishes. The restau-rant is named after Prince Jeremi "Jarema" Wiśniowiecki (1612–1651), a famous Polish military commander associated with the historic Eastern Borderlands. ■

✉ *pl. Matejki 5*
☎ *+48 12 4293669*
@ *www.jarema.pl*
🕐 *noon–midnight*
Ⓞ *124, 152, 424, 601, 608, 610, 618, 902 (Basztowa LOT)*
Ⓣ *2, 3, 4, 7, 13, 14, 15, 20, 24 (Basztowa LOT)*

Kompania Kuflowa €€€

The "Beer Mug Company" restaurant at the foot of Wawel Hill (➤40) welcomes guests to its spacious halls. The impressive menu has been evidently designed with gourmands in mind. You will find here roast pork knuckles, potato pancakes filled with beef tenderloin and mushroom sauce, baked ducks, as well as king prawns and sautéed trout. All this accompanied with quality beer (served in beer mugs up to 1 litre in volume). ■

✉ *ul. św. Gertrudy 26-29*
☎ *+48 12 4212336*
@ *www.podwawelem.eu*
🕐 *6.30am–midnight*
Ⓞ *3, 6, 8, 10, 18, 19, 40 (Wawel)*
ℹ *a family room with playing space and slides for children*

Miód i wino €€€

The "Honey and Wine" restaurant, imitating the style of historic gentry and nobility classes, offers some Old Polish cuisine dishes, such as tenderloin stuffed with bacon and pickles (served with buckwheat and pork scratchings), and *bigos hultajski* – stewed cabbage, sauerkraut and a variety of finely chopped meat, in a bread bowl. You can also try the Cracow-style *maczanka*, yet another type of stewed meat. The average price per meal is approx. PLN 40, but some delicacies such as the flaming *shashlik* beef tenderloin, served on a sabre, costs almost three times as much. Oak tables and upholstered chairs invite tourists to sit down for long enjoyable feasting.

✉ *ul. Sławkowska 32*
☎ *+48 12 4227495*

@ *www.miodiwino.pl*
🕐 *11am–11pm*
Ⓞ *124, 152, 424, 601, 608, 610, 618, 902 (Basztowa LOT)*
Ⓣ *2, 3, 4, 7, 13, 14, 15, 20, 24 (Basztowa LOT)*

Miód Malina €€€

The "Land of Raspberry and Honey" (as the name can be loosely translated) is one of the best and most popular restaurants in Cracow. Set in a 14th-century burgher house, it is decorated with taste, and proves that a folk-style interior modelled on peasant cottages does not have to be gaudy and kitschy (as it is all too often the case). Light-coloured walls, modest wooden furniture, lace tablecloths, sideboards holding jars full of preserves: all this makes for an atmosphere of discreet elegance. The restaurant serves Polish specialities, tasty meat dishes (lamb cutlets, pork sirloin chops) and delicious desserts (*panna cotta* with raspberry mousse and fresh fruit, *tiramisù*, ice-cream). ■

✉ *ul. Grodzka 40*
☎ *+48 12 4227495*
@ *www.miodmalina.pl*
🕐 *noon–11pm*
Ⓞ *1, 3, 6, 8, 18 (Plac Wszystkich Świętych)*
ℹ *the menu is available also in Braille; a special menu for children*

Polakowski

This self-service restaurant serves traditional Polish food. The décor is quite original, if a bit kitschy, with vegetables and fruit arranged on shelves and white tablecloths. Nice brand-name tableware and friendly staff are real bonuses. The inconvenience of waiting in line is more than made up for by the taste of home-made meals at moderate prices. Check out the restaurant's large pork chop (*kotlet schabowy*) fried in lard. It usually covers the whole plate, and potatoes are placed on top for lack of space (you had better not order chips). It goes well with fried cabbage or grated beetroot.

Cracow offers not only traditional dumplings filled with meat, sauerkraut, or quark and potatoes, but also with some daintier stuffings such as liver and grated apple.

Schabowy is believed to be the most typical Polish dish you can get. Note: it is hard to eat the whole main course if you start with a bowlful of tasty soup. ■

- ✉ *pl. Wszystkich Świętych 10*
- ☎ *+48 12 4302156*
- @ *www.polakowski.com.pl*
- 🕐 *9am–10pm*
- Ⓣ *1, 3, 6, 8, 18 (Plac Wszystkich Świętych)*

- ✉ *ul. Miodowa 39*
- ☎ *+48 12 4212117*
- 🕐 *9am–10pm*
- Ⓣ *7, 9, 11, 13, 24, 50, 51 (Miodowa)*

U Babci Maliny

"Grandma Malina" will feed you well and to the top. The bar is located opposite the Juliusz Słowacki Theatre (➤ 54, ➤ 203). It is divided into two parts: a small but atmospheric self-service room with wooden benches (your order is given a number and you wait until it appears on an electronic display), and a restaurant with waiter service in the style of the 1930's (walk down the stairs on the right; prices are higher, but the menu is more extensive). You can choose between poultry, beef and pork dishes, Cracow-style cutlet stuffed with cabbage (the restaurant), and vegetarian meals. Also worth a try is sour rye soup in a bread bowl, potato cakes with goulash, and the ever-popular dumplings (baked or fried). ■

- ✉ *ul. Szpitalna 38*
- ☎ *+48 12 4214818, +48 12 4214819*
- @ *www.kuchniaubabcimaliny.pl*
- 🕐 *11am–11pm*
- Ⓑ *124, 152, 424, 502, 522, 601, 605, 608, 609, 610, 614, 618, 902, 904 (Dworzec Główny)*
- Ⓣ *2, 4, 7, 10, 12, 13, 14, 15, 19, 20, 24, 40 (Dworzec Główny)*

- ✉ *ul. Sławkowska 17*
- ☎ *+48 12 4227601*
- 🕐 *Mon–Fri 11am–9pm, Sat–Sun noon–9pm*
- Ⓑ *124, 152, 424, 902 (Basztowa LOT)*
- Ⓣ *2, 3, 4, 7, 13, 14, 15, 20, 24 (Basztowa LOT)*

U Stasi ⊖€€

"Stasia's Bar" (entrance from the building's annexe) has been serving traditional home dishes for years. Dumplings are a popular choice, washed down with sour milk or *kompot* (sweetened fruit infusion drink). Meat dishes and soups are also on offer. At lunch time, the place is packed with people, so no one has any qualms about joining strangers at the table. The regulars are an interesting mix, from students to businesspeople. It is better to come early: the number of portions prepared by the bar is not unlimited, and at the end of the day the offer is considerably reduced. You pay as you leave, declaring what you have eaten. ▪

✉ ul. Mikołajska 16
☎ +48 12 4215084
🕐 Mon–Fri noon–5pm
🚍 124, 152, 424, 502, 522, 902, 904 (Dworzec Główny)
🚋 I, 7, 10, 12, 13, 19, 24, 40 (Poczta Główna); 2, 4, 7, 10, 12, 13, 14, 15, 19, 20, 24, 40 (Dworzec Główny)

In traditional restaurants, such as Wierzynek, guests are treated like royalty.

Wesele ⊖€€

"The Wedding" restaurant takes its name from the title of Stanisław Wyspiański's play, a Polish 1901 classic on the celebrations of a marriage between a peasant girl and a representative of the Cracow *intelligentsia*. Light-painted walls contrast with cushions embroidered with red thread (up in the mezzanine) and the traditional wedding decoration of beads and bows. It is a cosy and stylish place. An additional attraction is a view onto the Main Square (➤ 26). The menu includes smartly served Polish dishes, as well as Italian cuisine delicacies such as golden ribs in plum sauce and plum vodka, or goose breast on a bed of pears roasted with honey and red wine. ▪

✉ Rynek Główny 10
☎ +48 12 4227460
@ www.weselerestauracja.pl
🕐 11am–11pm
🚍 609, 614, 904 (Poczta Główna); 124, 152, 424, 502, 522, 601, 605, 608, 609, 610, 614, 618, 902, 904 (Dworzec Główny)
🚋 I, 7, 10, 12, 13, 19, 24, 40 (Poczta Główna); 2, 4, 7, 10, 12, 13, 14, 15, 19, 20, 24, 40 (Dworzec Główny)

Wierzynek ⊖€€

This is probably the best-known restaurant in Poland. It is named after a wealthy merchant, Mikołaj Wierzynek, who held a magnificent feast in Cracow back in 1364. Eminent guests included King Casimir the Great and the greatest European monarchs of that time. It was such a sumptuous banquet that Polish hospitality and the power of the state won international renown. Some say that the feast was hosted in the very same house that now houses the restaurant. Everything is top-level here: the décor, the staff, food, and prices. The splendour of the interior is a feast for the eye, and a feast for the body is provided by a sophisticated menu offer with specialities such as rabbit in sour cream with home-made pasta and beetroots, and a composition of deer, roe deer and quail in pine wood sauce with millet groats mousse and broad bean. The restaurant has wined and dined a number of world-famous personages: Akihito, Emperor of Japan, former American President George H.W. Bush, former French President Charles de Gaulle, the late Nobel Peace Prize winner Yitzhak Rabin, director Steven Spielberg and actor Robert De Niro. ■

✉ Rynek Główny 15
☎ +48 12 4249600
@ www.wierzynek.pl
🕑 1pm–11pm
🚌 124, 152, 424, 502, 522, 601, 605, 608, 609, 610, 614, 618, 902, 904 (Dworzec Główny)
🚊 2, 4, 7, 10, 12, 13, 14, 15, 19, 20, 24, 40 (Dworzec Główny); 1, 3, 6, 8, 18 (Plac Wszystkich Świętych)

JEWISH CUISINE

Ariel

The restaurant is situated in the old Jewish quarter of Kazimierz (➤ 68). The name is taken from the Bible; archangel Ariel is one of the seven Angels of Presence. The restaurant specialises in Jewish cuisine. The interior décor resembles that of an old middle-class apartment. Walls are covered with a great number of paintings and *judaica*. One of the rooms holds evening concerts of Jewish music. You can try carp prepared the Sephardic way, Rachel's special (beef roulade served in golden-brown sauce), and a traditional Jewish stew called *cholent*. You can also check out the kosher wine from the Israeli Golan Heights. ■

✉ ul. Szeroka 17-18
☎ +48 12 4217920
@ www.ariel-krakow.pl
🕑 10am–midnight; concerts: daily at 8pm
€ concerts: PLN 25
🚊 7, 9, 11, 13, 24, 50, 51 (Miodowa)

Ester

The restaurant serves Polish and Jewish cuisines. The elegant décor is matched by a sophisticated menu offer. You can have a taste of veal stuffed with raisins, beef tenderloin steak with green pepper sauce, and traditional Jewish dishes: *cholent* and *latkes* (a sort of potato pancakes) with smoked salmon, a bell pepper composition and sauce. In the summer, take a seat in the restaurant's garden, affording a fine view over ul. Szeroka and the Old Synagogue (➤ 78). Evenings resound with live klezmer music, played by a band called Inejnem. ■

✉ ul. Szeroka 20
☎ +48 12 4337450
@ www.restauracjaester.pl
🕑 from 7am until the last guest leaves; concerts: Mon, Wed, Fri–Sun at 7.30pm
€ concerts: free, booking is recommended
🚊 7, 9, 11, 13, 24, 50, 51 (Miodowa)

Klezmer Hois

The 16th-century building was home to a *mikveh* (Jewish ritual bath house) until the outbreak of WWII. Today, it accommodates a hotel and a restaurant. The "Klezmer House" is much more than a name: concerts of klezmer music are held here every evening. Two atmospheric rooms look like a 1930's apartment. The menu comprises mostly Jewish dishes, often served sweet: duck with apples, turkey livers with almonds and raisins, *latkes* in apple sauce. An average meat meal costs over PLN 40. ■

✉ ul. Szeroka 6
☎ +48 12 4111245
@ www.klezmer.pl
🕑 9am–9.30pm; concerts: daily at 8pm
€ concerts: PLN 22
🚊 7, 9, 11, 13, 24, 50, 51 (Miodowa)

Endzior is no ordinary fast food bar: it is a local legend.

A QUICK BITE

Endzior Bar

Endzior is the best-known fast food bar in Kazimierz, one of the many outlets in Okrąglak (see: Plac Nowy ➤ 86). Its French bread pizzas are a classic. "Kazimierz – bread pizzas – Endzior" is an automatic string of associations in Cracow. As it is often the case with local cult places, the legend is greater than reality. However, the bread pizzas are genuinely worth trying, and so is another speciality of the bar: the "giant cutlet." ◼

✉ pl. Nowy 4b/14 (Okrąglak)
☎ +48 12 4293754
⏱ Mon–Sat 10am–2am
🚊 7, 9, 11, 13, 24, 50, 51 (Miodowa)

Fast Food in Cracow

The city has a "fast food tradition" of its own, encompassing French bread pizzas and grilled sausages – a particular favourite with party goers and nightlife enthusiasts. Check them out instead of going for a burger at a chain restaurant.

The most popular choice are bread pizzas with additions. True, most are ready-made cheese and mushroom rolls, but the added fresh ingredients can turn them into a real treat. The city's bread pizza paradise is the building of Okrąglak in Kazimierz (see also: Plac Nowy ➤ 86). Tiny food outlets located there are practically besieged by crowds of clients. You order at a small window and wait for your bread pizza, served straight from the oven. Most people line up at Endzior and Oko bars. The pride of the former are tasty cutlets, the latter is known for delicious potato cakes. At weekends (especially in the evening and late at night), you should expect long queues. The regulars of local drinking places often come here for a quick bite to build up energy for partying. Usually, there is also a grill set up in the vicinity of Okrąglak.

The city's offer of snacks includes grilled sausages, tasting like those roasted over a bonfire. The best sausages can be found in the evenings in front of the Hala Targowa building, close to the city centre. Night eaters crowding around a small table, having their meal standing up, is a sight that has already become an integral part of the city's landscape.

Oko Bar

Yet another bar in Okrąglak (see: Plac Nowy ➤ 86) that is worth a try. It does its best to escape from the shadow of Endzior, located nearby. There are several types of bread pizza to choose from. The basic one substantially fills the stomach, but extended variants are a richer culinary experience. Interesting options include highlander-style (with sausage and *oscypek* – smoked ewe's milk cheese), Hungarian-style (with chicken), vegetarian-style (with spinach) and Greek-style (with feta cheese). Additions include chives and sauces (especially garlic-flavoured). Equally popular are freshly prepared potato cakes. A large portion will be a challenge even to the most voracious customers. ∎

✉ *pl. Nowy 4b/12 (Okrąglak)*
🕐 *10am–midnight*
🚃 *7, 9, 11, 13, 24, 50, 51 (Miodowa)*

Sausages by Hala Targowa € € €

The place and the meal to give you an idea of Cracow's local colour. For almost twenty years, every evening (except for Sundays), white-coated sellers have been coming in a blue van and frying sausages on a large wood-fired grill. The sausages are the best in the city, made to order by a privately-run meat processing plant. You also get a large bread roll and mustard, and, if thirsty, orangeade made with mineral water. Try it once and all the kebabs of Cracow will lose their appeal. ∎

✉ *ul. Grzegórzecka, opposite the covered market (Hala Targowa, ul. Daszyńskiego 3)*
🕐 *Mon–Sat 8pm–3am*
🚌 *128, 184 (Hala Targowa)*
🚃 *1, 9, 11, 22, 50, 51 (Hala Targowa)*

The New Tastes of Cracow

The city's culinary horizons stretch much further than the old Galicia region. Cracow boasts some splendid Italian and Mediterranean restaurants. There are also places serving Georgian, Hungarian and Japanese cuisines.

Cracow has a lot of restaurants that specialise in the cuisine of a particular country. The Oriental offer is no longer limited to cheap Chinese food and kebab (which, incidentally, is better avoided – the disproportion between price and quality may be truly alarming). New smart restaurants are being established. The popularity of Italian cuisine never wanes; try, for instance, La Campana (➤188). There are also some really good pizzerias, such as Mamma Mia (➤189) and Trzy Papryczki (➤189), serving delicious thin-crust pizza with *boleti* or seafood. Cracow also loves Georgian dishes (Chaczapuri ➤190) and Hungarian meals (Balaton ➤189). Many restaurants' menus comprise specialities of various cuisines to please every palate. Szara Kazimierz (➤191), for example, is a perfect place not only for a dinner for two, but also for a business meeting.

Cracow boasts a few restaurants for lovers of *sushi* (rice, raw fish, and seafood). Connoisseurs say that the requisite of good quality *sushi* is the proper way of serving and eating – with chopsticks, naturally. The restaurants try to keep up with the customers' expectations, therefore they have the interiors designed and decorated especially so that they feel like Asian enclaves in the centre of Europe. Among the highly-recommended places one should mention Edo Sushi (➤188).

The international vogue for ecology and a healthy lifestyle brought vegetarian bars to Cracow. Green Way (➤191) is a bar chain that might not have that many outlets, but the dishes served there are usually very tasty and wholesome. Good locations and affordable prices make these vegetarian bars particularly popular with students. ∎

€ € € up to PLN 20
€ € € PLN 20–40
€ € € over PLN 40

Each price bracket covers a main course and side dishes.

CUISINES OF THE FAR EAST

Edo Sushi € € €

A visit here is a perfect way to be temporarily transported into the Land of the Rising Sun. The Japanese tradition is represented not only in a rich menu, but also the interior décor: austere, simple, and elegant. The most Japanese-style place to have dinner is one of the small *tatami* rooms, where guests sit on the floor at low wooden tables. The *sushi* served here ranks among the best in Cracow. It is made of original Japanese ingredients (except for the local water and salt, of course). The average cost of a meal for one person is PLN 40. ∎

✉ ul. Bożego Ciała 3
☎ +48 12 4222424
@ www.edosushi.pl
🕐 Mon–Wed, Sun noon–10pm,
   Thu–Sat noon–11pm
Ⓑ 128, 184, 609, 614, 904 (Stradom)
Ⓣ 3, 6, 8, 10, 12, 18, 19, 22, 40 (Stradom)

Genji Premium Sushi
€ € €

Opened in 2008, this Japanese–Korean restaurant has quickly gained considerable popularity. It is famous for high-quality *sushi*, soups, and lunch sets prepared by the chefs that come from the Far East: Mr Cho and Mr Oh. Guests are welcome to take a seat on the ground floor or in the basement, where tables are arranged in separate rooms. ∎

✉ ul. Dietla 55
☎ +48 12 4295959
@ www.genji.pl

🕐 Mon–Thu noon–10pm, Fri–Sat noon–
   11pm, Sun noon–9pm
Ⓑ 128, 184, 609, 614, 904 (Stradom)
Ⓣ 3, 6, 8, 10, 12, 18, 19, 22, 40 (Stradom)

MEDITERRANEAN CUISINE

La Campana € € €

The building that houses La Campana – the historic House Under Three Crowns (Dom Pod Trzema Koronami) – used to be a meeting place for the bell ringers of Wawel Cathedral (➤46). Today, it is dedicated to Italian cuisine, with a wide offer of pasta, meat and fish dishes, and original Italian *prosciutto* as an appetiser. You can choose between bright and cosy rooms, or a more austere décor of stone walls and a brick tunnel vault. ∎

✉ ul. Kanonicza 7
☎ +48 12 4302232
@ www.lacampana.pl
🕐 noon–11pm
Ⓣ 3, 6, 8, 10, 18, 19, 40 (Wawel)

La Fuente € € €

La Fuente – a charming eatery in a tiny place located close to the heart of Kazimierz (➤88) – serves Spanish-style meals and snacks. It has become famous for its freshly made *tapas* (appetisers), lunch meals, and *bocadillos* (hot crispy sandwiches, offered in a great variety: from salmon through chicken and *pesto* to grilled pork neck). *Tapas* can be served with canapés, stuffed vegetables, olives, or baked beans and bacon. ∎

✉ ul. Bożego Ciała 14
@ www.fuente.pl
🕐 Mon–Sat 11am–midnight,
   Sun 11am–11pm
Ⓑ 128, 184, 609, 614, 904 (Stradom)
Ⓣ 3, 6, 8, 10, 12, 18, 19, 22, 40 (Stradom)

Mamma Mia

The *trattoria*, situated in a courtyard off ul. Karmelicka, ranks among the best pizzerias in Cracow. It also serves other specialities of Italian cuisine, such as *risotto*, *spaghetti*, *gnocchi* (a type of dumpling), fish and seafood dishes. The pizza tastes heavenly thanks to its thin crust and delicious additions. The cosy interior is decorated in muted tones and illuminated with spot lighting. Tables are covered with white tablecloths, and the walls display photographs which make one think of the sunny Italy. ■

✉ *ul. Karmelicka 14*
☎ *+48 12 4300492*
@ *www.mammamia.net.pl*
🕐 *noon–11pm*
🚌 *124, 152, 304, 424, 502, 522, 601, 608, 618, 902 (Teatr Bagatela)*
🚊 *2, 3, 4, 8, 13, 14, 15, 20, 24 (Teatr Bagatela)*

Portofino

The restaurant is conveniently located near the city centre, close to the High Synagogue (➤80). In the summer, guests can take a seat in a pavement café; the district's narrow streets resemble a bit those in Italian towns. The menu includes meat, fish and seafood dishes, not to mention an obligatory offer of any Italian restaurant – a variety of pastas: with *finocchio* (fennel leaves), *capparis*, olives, sun-dried tomatoes, and chanterelles. Lunch is served between noon and 5pm; the price is approx. PLN 20. ■

✉ *ul. Wąska 2*
☎ *+48 12 4310537*
@ *www.portofino.pl*
🕐 *noon–11pm*
🚊 *7, 9, 11, 13, 24, 50, 51 (Miodowa)*

Sempre Bracka

The restaurant is housed on the first floor of a tenement by ul. Bracka (➤58); a separate room holds a lounge bar. The interior has a pastel colour scheme, illu-minated by chandeliers. The restaurant serves Mediterranean cuisine. At lunch time (noon–4pm), there is a special menu with a choice of dishes at prices that do not exceed PLN 20. ■

✉ *ul. Bracka 3-5*
☎ *+48 696858464*
@ *www.sempre.bracka.pl*
🕐 *noon–11pm*
🚊 *1, 3, 6, 8, 18 (Plac Wszystkich Świętych)*

Trzy Papryczki

In Cracow, everything has to be surrounded by a legend – even a pizzeria. The owners claim that its name comes from the ladies called the "Three Peppers" (*Trzy Papryczki*), who accompanied Queen Bona Sforza (1494–1557) from Italy to Cracow. They are believed to have founded Cracow's first pizzeria. This legend may be pure myth, but the fact is that the pizza served here is close to perfect. In particular, check out the *boleti* or seafood variants. The place also offers a small number of pastas, and meat dishes: steaks (beef and pork), spare ribs, chicken breasts, chopped roast beef. It is a perfect place to have a meal, the interior decoration is warm, and the aroma from the wood-fired oven stimulates the appetite. ■

✉ *ul. Poselska 17*
☎ *+48 12 2925532*
@ *www.trzypapryczki.krakow.pl*
🕐 *11am–11pm*
🚊 *1, 3, 6, 8, 18 (Plac Wszystkich Świętych)*

INTERNATIONAL CUISINE

Balaton

Founded in 1969, the restaurant is an old-timer in Cracow's culinary market. The outside look is not very inviting, the old-style interior is not particularly impressive either, but the food is truly delicious. The chef's speciality is potato cakes with goulash (several varieties to choose from, including wild boar goulash) – allegedly invented to celebrate the traditional Polish-Hungarian friendship. Of course, the menu simply cannot lack chicken goulash and veal goulash. ■

✉ ul. Grodzka 37
☎ +48 12 4220469
@ www.balaton.krakow.pl
🕐 noon–10pm
🚋 1, 3, 6, 8, 18 (Plac Wszystkich Świętych)

Chaczapuri

This popular Georgian restaurant chain has taken over the Old Town (➤ 50) – it has now as many as five outlets. The great success of Chaczapuri is partly attributable to moderate prices: a main course costs PLN 30 maximum. The traditional Georgian plate consists of very finely chopped meat (too finely for some European palates); other choices include grilled neck of pork Caucasian style, and *shashliks*. The restaurant serves original Georgian wine. ■

✉ ul. Floriańska 26
☎ +48 12 4291131
@ www.chaczapuri.pl
🕐 noon–11pm, Fri–Sat noon–midnight
🚌 124, 152, 424, 502, 522, 601, 605, 608, 609, 610, 618, 902, 904 (Dworzec Główny)
🚋 2, 4, 7, 10, 12, 13, 14, 15, 19, 20, 24, 40 (Dworzec Główny)

✉ pl. Mariacki 8
☎ +48 12 4291166
🚌 609, 614, 904 (Poczta Główna); 124, 152, 424, 502, 522, 601, 605, 608, 609, 610, 614, 618, 902, 904 (Dworzec Główny)
🚋 1, 7, 10, 12, 13, 19, 24, 40 (Poczta Główna); 2, 4, 7, 10, 12, 13, 14, 15, 19, 20, 24, 40 (Dworzec Główny)

✉ ul. Sienna 4
☎ +48 12 4291166
🚌 609, 614, 904 (Poczta Główna)
🚋 1, 7, 10, 12, 13, 19, 24, 40 (Poczta Główna)

✉ ul. św. Anny 4
☎ +48 12 4226128

🕐 noon–11pm, Fri–Sat noon–midnight, Sun noon–10pm
🚌 124, 152, 304, 424, 502, 522, 601, 608, 618, 902 (Teatr Bagatela)
🚋 2, 3, 4, 8, 13, 14, 15, 20, 24 (Teatr Bagatela)

Nova Resto Bar

The restaurant offers breakfast and lunch at a set price (noon–4pm, PLN 19), as well as international dinner dishes: a choice of pastas, chicken fillet stuffed with spinach and *ricotta* cheese, duck breast with blackberry sauce and *gnocchi*, tiger prawns and steaks (of beef, pork, chicken, or salmon). There is also a bar with a wide selection of alcoholic drinks. Guests can take a seat in a spacious hall or in a large open-air terrace, turned into a heated indoor garden in the winter. ■

✉ ul. Estery 18
☎ +48 12 4214011
@ www.novarestobar.pl
🕐 9am–midnight
🚋 7, 9, 11, 13, 24, 50, 51 (Miodowa)

Szara

The "Grey" restaurant enjoys a very good reputation in Cracow, even though the clientele consists of tourists rather than locals. It is accommodated in a large historic house in the Main Square (➤ 26). Inside, eyes are pulled towards the Gothic cross ribbed vault, covered with polychromies. The restaurant serves a truly impressive number of international dishes. A classic beef *carpaccio, foie gras terrine* or reindeer tartare are perfect starters to the equally sophisticated main courses: fish soup *à la Bouillabaisse, plankstek* (beef sirloin served on an oak plank), a saddle of venison, and rabbit in Provençal herbs. A wide wine selection will make you giddy – and so will the bill. ■

✉ Rynek Główny 6
☎ +48 12 4216669
@ www.szara.pl
🕐 11am–11pm

Ⓑ *124, 152, 424, 502, 522, 601, 605, 608, 609, 610, 614, 618, 902, 904 (Dworzec Główny)*

Ⓣ *2, 4, 7, 10, 12, 13, 14, 15, 19, 20, 24, 40 (Dworzec Główny)*

Szara Kazimierz

International cuisine is served here. A great advantage is the restaurant's convenient location in ul. Szeroka (➤ 73), one of the most important streets in Kazimierz. Elegant interiors will be to the liking of those who prefer muted colours. The menu offer includes French fish soup *à la Bouillabaisse*, leg of lamb, pork loin, poultry dishes. The wine list comprises several types of white and red wine, as well as quality champagne. ■

✉ *ul. Szeroka 39*
☎ *+48 12 4216669*
@ *www.szarakazimierz.pl*
🕐 *11am–11pm*
Ⓣ *7, 9, 11, 13, 24, 50, 51 (Miodowa)*

VEGETARIAN CUISINE

Glonojad

The funny name of "Algae Eater" attracts the gaze of people crossing pl. Matejki. The interior of the vegetarian bar is simple, clean and bright, and the décor is nothing like the Hindu style (so popular in veggie eateries). On offer are vegetable *shashliks*, chickpea falafels, courgette and aubergine fingers, salads, freshly squeezed juice, wine, beer, etc. Healthy, tasty and cheap. ■

✉ *pl. Matejki 2*
☎ *+48 12 3461677*
🕐 *9am–10pm*
Ⓑ *124, 152, 424, 601, 608, 610, 618, 902 (Basztowa LOT)*
Ⓣ *2, 3, 4, 7, 13, 14, 15, 20, 24 (Basztowa LOT)*

Green Way

This popular vegetarian bar is part of an all-Poland Green Way chain. A good choice for a quick lunch during a break in an intensive sightseeing tour or between university classes, but not for savouring food or talking over the meal. The place is usually packed with people; tables are also arranged in the mezzanine. The offer encompasses the Hindu *kofta* (cheese chops in tomato sauce), a vegetable cake, and cabbage chops. A popular choice is wholemeal pancakes with fruit, and courgette dumplings – already a legend. You can wash these dishes down with fruit cocktails (prepared on the basis of natural yoghurt), fresh carrot juice, and bottled birch leaf juice. ■

✉ *ul. Mikołajska 14*
☎ *+48 12 4311027*
🕐 *Mon–Fri 10am–10pm, Sat 11am–9pm*
Ⓑ *124, 152, 424, 502, 522, 902, 904 (Dworzec Główny)*
Ⓣ *1, 7, 10, 12, 13, 19, 24, 40 (Poczta Główna); 2, 4, 7, 10, 12, 13, 14, 15, 19, 20, 24, 40 (Dworzec Główny)*

Vega

A vegetarian restaurant right by the Planty (➤ 53). Tables are covered with white tablecloths. A piano and a wooden chest of drawers contribute to an elegant ambience. The monotony of orange walls is broken with a few paintings. Among the many dishes on offer, there are appetising salads, a wide choice of cutlets (made of soya beans, millet groats and processed cheese, lentils and vegetables, etc.), more than ten types of savoury and sweet pancakes served with vegetables and feta cheese, pineapple, bananas… ■

✉ *ul. św. Gertrudy 7*
☎ *+48 12 4223494*
@ *www.vegarestauracja.pl*
🕐 *9am–9pm*
Ⓣ *3, 6, 8, 10, 18, 19, 40 (św. Gertrudy)*

✉ *ul. Krupnicza 22*
☎ *+48 12 4300846*
Ⓑ *124, 152, 304, 424, 502, 522, 601, 608, 618, 902 (Teatr Bagatela)*
Ⓣ *2, 3, 4, 8, 12, 13, 14, 15, 20, 24 (Teatr Bagatela)*

Beer and Stuff

The diversity of the city's drinking bars is truly impressive. Some are murky and atmospheric, others are up-to-the-minute and modern in style. Beer bars prevail in terms of number, but there is no lack of good places serving spirits.

Bars are abuzz with talk, and beer is flowing like water. People flock in not only on weekend nights, but also during the day. Visiting the most popular places, you might think that some people have turned hanging out there into their life philosophy. It is a good idea to sit in a garden pub in the Main Square (➤ 26) or in Kazimierz (➤ 68, ➤ 88) and – sipping beer – take a look at historic buildings, or just close your eyes, raise your face to the sun and enjoy the moment.

Cracow's bars, especially the ones in Kazimierz, are often peculiar examples of junk room aesthetics. Some say that opening a pub here is more than easy: it is enough to find a few old chairs and put up several candles without being bothered too much about the decrepit state of the walls. Obviously, this is an unfair oversimplification, but there is a grain of truth to it. Places like Eszeweria (➤ 193) have large groups of regulars, who feel at home there. Indeed, at some bars such as Absynt (➤ 192), the décor resembles that of an old apartment. Stylish furnishings contribute to a special ambience and give a nice and cosy feel. Wide sofas and armchairs (customers' favourite seats) allow one to sit back comfortably and relax.

There are, however, many places that defy this convention. After all, Cracow is a city that combines the past with the present. Modern-style bars include Paparazzi (➤ 194) and Łódź Kaliska (➤ 193). Some places, such as Pierwszy Lokal (➤ 194), have a minimalist, even ascetic décor.

You can order beer at every single bar: it is unquestionably Poland's No. 1 alcoholic beverage. The most popular Polish beer brands are Żywiec, Lech and Tyskie; top foreign brands include Czech-produced Pilsner Urquell and Dutch-produced Heineken. Some bars, mainly Irish pubs, serve Guinness; check out, for example, Nic Nowego (➤ 193). There are also drinking places where you can taste lesser-known types of beer, made in small breweries. In Cracow, connoisseurs can find delicious beers from Poland (Omerta ➤ 194), the Czech Republic and Lithuania (Non Iron ➤ 193), and from all over the world in general (House of Beer ➤ 193).

Recently, drinks have been gaining in popularity. They are a more costly option, but a growing number of bars that specialise in serving drinks (such as Paparazzi) are established every year. As the city of the decadent Young Poland movement, Cracow cannot but serve flaming absinthe as well. ∎

€€€ **up to PLN 7**
€€€ **PLN 7–9**
€€€ **over PLN 9**
Each price bracket covers a pint of beer.

PUBS AND BARS

Absynt €€€

The "Absinthe" bar certainly has a decadent feel to it. The main hall with a relatively low ceiling looks like the living room of an old apartment with its paintings, musical instruments, knitted tablecloths, a shaded lamp and an antique typewriter. You can take a wooden chair or lounge in a large, comfortable armchair or a sofa. Absinthe is served as it was in the past, with a sugar cube set ablaze and then dropped into the glass. ∎

✉ *ul. Miodowa 28*
☎ *+48 605240397*
🕐 *Mon–Thu 10am–midnight, Fri–Sat from 10am until the last customer leaves*
🚊 *7, 9, 11, 13, 24, 50, 51 (Miodowa)*

Eszeweria

A perfect example of the distinctive style of bars in Kazimierz: second-hand wooden chairs and tables, old cupboards, paintings and photographs on the walls, candles burning in semi-darkness. These ingredients are sometimes considered to be the essence of an atmospheric drinking place. Eszeweria serves draught beer, vodka and drinks. Live music (usually experimental or improvised sounds) is performed on Tuesdays and Thursdays. ■

✉ *ul. Józefa 9*
☎ *+48 12 2920458*
🕐 *from 11am until the last customer leaves*
🚊 *7, 9, 11, 13, 24, 50, 51 (Miodowa)*

House of Beer

The name speaks for itself. Guests can choose between nearly 200 different brands, including the ones from the Czech Republic, Austria and Lithuania, as well as those produced in small Polish breweries (the brands to be recommended are Maćkowe honey beer, Lubuskie green beer and the traditional double-malt beer from Jabłonowo). Behind the counter, bottles are arranged like chocolates in a box, each in a separate compartment. This greatly facilitates the choice: it is enough to point to the bottle you want, or the one with a label that has caught your eye. Some beers are also offered on tap. ■

✉ *ul. św. Krzyża 13*
☎ *+48 888511515*
🕐 *2pm–2am*
🚌 *124, 152, 424, 502, 522, 601, 605, 608, 609, 610, 614, 618, 902, 904 (Dworzec Główny)*
🚊 *2, 4, 7, 10, 12, 13, 14, 15, 19, 20, 24, 40 (Dworzec Główny)*

Łódź Kaliska

The bar is named after a legendary *avant-garde* artistic group, established in Łódź in 1979; one of its founders now lives in Cracow. Go inside to see bizarre chandeliers, sofas made to imitate the Baroque style, décor made of glass, mirrors and metal, as well as reproductions of works created by the Łódź Kaliska group. The bar holds concerts and dance events (to the sounds of electro, funky, jazz, and disco music). ■

✉ *ul. Floriańska 15*
☎ *+48 12 4227042*
🕐 *5pm–5am*
🚌 *124, 152, 424, 502, 522, 601, 605, 608, 609, 610, 614, 618, 902, 904 (Dworzec Główny)*
🚊 *2, 4, 7, 10, 12, 13, 14, 15, 19, 20, 24, 40 (Dworzec Główny)*

Nic Nowego

As the owner explains, the name ("Nothing New") comes from a common Polish reply to the question "What's up?" This modern-style Irish pub has an aesthetic appearance and friendly staff. It boasts a wide selection of drinks and an impressive choice of snacks and salads for breakfast, lunch and dinner. Above all, Nic Nowego is one of the few places in Cracow where you can get draught Guinness (PLN 15). ■

✉ *ul. św. Krzyża 15*
☎ *+48 12 4216188*
@ *www.nicnowego.com*
🕐 *until the last customer leaves, Mon–Fri from 7am, Sat–Sun from 10am*
🚌 *124, 152, 424, 502, 522, 601, 605, 608, 609, 610, 614, 618, 902, 904 (Dworzec Główny)*
🚊 *2, 4, 7, 10, 12, 13, 14, 15, 19, 20, 24, 40 (Dworzec Główny)*

Non Iron

Excellent beer certainly makes up for the rather mediocre décor and atmosphere. On offer are some light and dark beers (also on draught) from the Czech

Republic, Lithuania and Germany, e.g. the delicious Velkopopovicky Kozel Cerny, Primator, Skalak, Erdinger. Like in the best Czech taverns, beer is served in beer mugs up to 1 litre in volume. ▪

✉ *ul. św. Marka 27*
☎ *+48 12 4294198*
🕐 *Mon–Fri 2pm–midnight,*
   Sat–Sun noon–midnight
🚌 *124, 152, 424, 502, 522, 601, 605, 608,*
   609, 610, 614, 618, 902, 904 (Dworzec
   Główny)
🚊 *2, 4, 7, 10, 12, 13, 14, 15, 19, 20, 24, 40*
   (Dworzec Główny)

Omerta

The bar takes its name from *omertà*, the code of silence enforced by organised crime groups. The walls display stills from *The Godfather* and an inscription that reads: "Join the Corleone Family." There is a large selection of beers from large and small Polish breweries, e.g. the already legendary Ciechan honey beer, Dawne and Żywe natural beers – a good choice for those who would like to try more than two or three most popular Polish brands, available in every single bar around Cracow. Omerta also offers other alcoholic beverages, liqueurs, and coffee served in several different ways. ▪

✉ *ul. Warszauera 3*
☎ *+48 501648478*
@ *www.omerta.com.pl*
🕐 *Mon–Thu, Sun 4pm–11pm,*
   Fri–Sat 4pm–3am
🚊 *7, 9, 11, 13, 24, 50, 51 (Miodowa)*

Paparazzi

A smart modern-style club with comfortable sofas, chairs and tables. Music celebrities and film stars look down from the walls. There is a wide selection of drinks and cocktails; even more importantly, they are expertly prepared by bar staff. Paparazzi is an ideal place for those who prefer more refined beverages to beer. The club specialities include Mojito (Havana Club rum, fresh mint,

sugar syrup and lime juice), Katarinka (pear vodka, blackberry liqueur, pear mousse, sugar syrup, lime juice and fresh mint) and Kraków Martini (pure vodka, cherry vodka, freshly squeezed red grapefruit juice and sugar syrup). ▪

✉ *ul. Mikołajska 9*
☎ *+48 12 4294597*
@ *www.paparazzi.com.pl*
🕐 *Mon–Fri 11am–1am, Sat–Sun 4pm–1am*
🚌 *609, 614, 904 (Poczta Główna)*
🚊 *1, 7, 10, 12, 13, 19, 24, 40*
   (Poczta Główna)

Pauza

One of the most fashionable places in Cracow. It is in vogue to take a "pause" on a white sofa in the first-floor bar overlooking ul. Floriańska. The second floor accommodates a gallery that presents (mostly photo) exhibitions. The basement consists of seating room and a dance hall, where DJs mix ultra-modern rhythms at the weekends. ▪

✉ *ul. Floriańska 18*
☎ *+48 12 4224866*
@ *www.pauza.pl*
🕐 *10am–midnight, Sun noon–midnight*
💶 *gallery: free*
🚌 *124, 152, 424, 502, 522, 601, 605, 608,*
   609, 610, 614, 618, 902, 904 (Dworzec
   Główny)
🚊 *2, 4, 7, 10, 12, 13, 14, 15, 19, 20, 24, 40*
   (Dworzec Główny)

Pierwszy Lokal na Stolar-skiej po lewej stronie idąc od Małego Rynku €€€

"The First Bar on the Left Side of ul. Stolarska when Walking from Mały Rynek" – this name may seem too long and difficult to remember, but, paradoxically, it has become a real asset. Pierwszy Lokal is widely recognisable. The minimalist décor and discreet background music create a perfect setting for conversations over beer from the local microbrewery (try e.g. Smocza Głowa). ▪

✉ ul. Stolarska 6–1
☎ +48 12 4312441
🕐 8.30am–11pm, Sun 9.30am–11pm
🚊 1, 3, 6, 8, 18 (Plac Wszystkich Świętych)

Ulica Krokodyli 🔴🔴Ⓔ

The "Crocodile Street" is furnished in the retro style, characteristic of drinking establishments in Kazimierz (➤68). The design resembles a street, with lamp posts and inscriptions in Polish and Yiddish, imitating the shop signs and advertisements of the old Jewish quarter. On Fridays and Saturdays, a small room in the basement turns into a dance floor with music from the 1960's, 70's and 80's (admission is free). ■

✉ ul. Szeroka 30
☎ +48 12 4310516
🕐 Mon–Thu, Sun 9am–1am,
Fri–Sat 9am–3am
🚊 7, 9, 11, 13, 24, 50, 51 (Miodowa)

Pierwszy Lokal tempts passers-by with its home-made beer.

Sweet and Bitter

There is hardly anything better to raise your spirits than a sweet bite and a cup of good coffee. Cracow boasts a lot of places where you can treat yourself to a dessert, an ice-cream, or a cup of delicious hot chocolate.

Coffee served in Cracow's many cafés is always a real treat, whether in the morning or in the afternoon. It allows Cracovians to escape for a moment the hustle and bustle of busy streets, provides a pretext for families to meet downtown, and assists students in flicking through their notes, writing essays and debating more or less important issues. The air in the cafés is usually filled with the magnificent aroma of freshly brewed coffee, hot chocolate, cakes and desserts. You can take a rest here before or after dining (Siesta Cafe ➤ 198), browse through newspapers and books, or just have a quick cup of coffee and continue on your way to work, classes, or on a sightseeing tour.

Some cafés do not limit their offer to sweet things. They also serve beer and wine (Cafe Szafe ➤ 196), not to mention savoury snacks (Cheder Cafe ➤ 197). Closing time is usually about 8pm, but more and more places stay open even until midnight, which makes them a good alternative to bars and restaurants.

Yet another interesting option is a café combined with a bookshop. Apart from buying a book, you can take a bite or have a read with a glass of wine (Bona. Książka i Kawa ➤ 196) or a cup of coffee (Massolit Books&Cafe ➤ 198).

The ever-popular hot chocolate may turn out to be a disappointment if you choose the wrong café. Hot chocolate served at tried and tested places is delicious, and has a thick consistency that requires eating with a spoon instead of drinking. You can be assured of being served with a high quality product in the Wedel Chocolate Lounge (➤ 199). Also to be recommended are Camera Cafe (➤ 196) and Nowa Prowincja (➤ 207). At other places, it is better to make sure before ordering if the "hot chocolate" they list in the menu is not in fact a thin drink similar to instant cocoa. ▪

€€€ up to **PLN 12**
€€€ **PLN 12–18**
€€€ over **PLN 18**

Each price bracket covers a cup of coffee and a cake.

CAFÉS

Cafe Szafe €€€

A very cosy place with orange walls, a parquet floor, an old tile stove, wooden chairs and an old wardrobe adapted to hold dining seats. Cafe Szafe is so much more than a traditional café serving hot and cold drinks. Like a cultural centre, it hosts meetings with writers such as Etgar Keret, photo exhibitions, and debates. A truly intriguing venue. ▪

✉ *ul. Felicjanek 10*
☎ *+48 663905652*
@ *www.cafeszafe.com*
🕐 *Mon–Thu from 9am until the last customer leaves, Fri–Sun from 10am until the last customer leaves*
🚌 *304, 522 (Filharmonia); 109, 114, 124, 144, 164, 169, 173, 179, 194, 409, 424, 608, 610 (Jubilat)*
🚊 *1, 2, 3, 6, 8, 18 (Filharmonia); 1, 2, 6 (Jubilat)*

Bona. Książka i Kawa

Located in one of the most picturesque streets of the Old Town (➤ 50), this exceptional coffee bar has two rooms: a bookshop and a café. It is a great option

for those who want to start reading right after buying a book. You can order coffee, tea or wine to have an even better time. Snacks are also on offer, not only cake, *tiramisù* and gingerbread cookies, but also savoury specialities: salmon tartare and canapés. You are welcome to sit down, eat, drink, and immerse yourself in reading… ▪

✉ *ul. Kanonicza 11*
☎ *+48 12 4305222*
@ *www.ksiegarnia.bonamedia.pl*
🕐 *10am–7pm*
🚊 *1, 3, 6, 8, 18 (Plac Wszystkich Świętych)*

Cafe Camelot €€€

A very atmospheric, romantic place: small tables, paintings on the walls, an old stove in the corner of one of the rooms. The most popular seats (often taken by young couples) are at a table for two placed in the window, above the other tables. The menu is comprehensive and includes not only desserts, but also breakfast meals, salads and pastas. Cakes – especially cheesecake and apple pie – are in great demand, and so is the delicious coffee to go with them. On cold days, it is possible to warm oneself up with mulled beer or wine. Every Friday, the basement holds shows of the Loch Camelot cabaret, recitals, or concerts. ▪

✉ *ul. św. Tomasza 17*
☎ *+48 12 4210123*
🕐 *9am–midnight daily; cabaret: Fri at 8.15pm*
€ *cabaret: PLN 30; concerts: PLN 20–40*
🚌 *124, 152, 424, 502, 522, 601, 605, 608, 609, 610, 614, 618, 902, 904 (Dworzec Główny)*
🚊 *2, 4, 7, 10, 12, 13, 14, 15, 19, 20, 24, 40 (Dworzec Główny)*

Camera Cafe €€€

The modern-style interior is decorated in pastel colours. The filmmaking allusion in the name is not accidental: silent films, mostly from the 1920's, are pro-

The Art Nouveau-style Jama Michalika restaurant used to wine and dine Polish modernist artists.

jected on a wall as a sort of background scenery. You can choose between coffee, tea and hot chocolate (served in a number of ways). In addition, Camera Cafe offers a wide selection of desserts and cakes, such as *tiramisù*, apple pie with ice-cream and pear tart.

- ✉ ul. Wiślna 5
- ☎ +48 601190381
- 🕐 Mon–Thu 10am–10pm, Fri–Sun 10am–11pm
- Ⓢ 304, 522 (Filharmonia)
- 🚊 1, 2, 3, 6, 8, 18 (Filharmonia); 1, 3, 6, 8, 18 (Plac Wszystkich Świętych)

Cheder Cafe €€€

The building was home to a Jewish prayer house of Chevra Ner Tamid (Fraternal Society of Eternal Light) until the outbreak of WWII. Today, it houses one of the city's most interesting cafés. Its name – *cheder* – denotes a Jewish school, and for good reason: the place hosts educational projects on Jewish culture. There are a lot of theme-related books, also in English, that guests can take from the shelf and read. You will be served Israeli coffee in a brass coffee pot called

finjan, tea, or kosher wine. Snacks can be sweet (cake) or savoury (*hummus*).

- ✉ ul. Józefa 36 (entrance from ul. Jakuba)
- ☎ +48 12 4311517
- @ www.cheder.pl
- 🕐 11am–10pm daily
- 🚊 7, 9, 11, 13, 24, 50, 51 (Miodowa)

Jama Michalika €€€

The interesting interior of Michalik's Den, one of Cracow's best-known cafés (see also: Ulica Floriańska ➤22), can be admired while you enjoy your coffee or an alcoholic beverage. Cakes (for example, cheese tart and Pischinger cake) are also worth a try; after all, Jama Michalika started as a *patisserie*. It now offers breakfast and dinner dishes as well.

- ✉ ul. Floriańska 45
- ☎ +48 12 4221561
- @ www.jamamichalika.pl
- 🕐 Sun–Thu 9am–10pm, Fri–Sat 9am–11pm
- Ⓢ 124, 152, 424, 502, 522, 601, 605, 608, 609, 610, 614, 618, 902, 904 (Dworzec Główny)
- 🚊 2, 4, 7, 10 12, 13, 14, 15, 19, 20, 24, 40 (Dworzec Główny)

Massolit Books&Cafe

An exceptionally interesting and unique place. It is not just a café, but also (or rather, first of all) Cracow's greatest shop with new and second-hand English books, comprising about 20,000 titles. Take a seat, browse through a book or a newspaper, and have some coffee, tea or wine. The café also serves small snacks; apple and blueberry pies, a choice of bagels, etc. ■

- ✉ *ul. Felicjanek 4*
- ☎ *+48 12 4324150*
- @ *www.massolit.com*
- ⌚ *Mon–Thu, Sun 10am–8pm, Fri–Sat 10am–9pm*
- Ⓑ *304, 522 (Filharmonia); 109, 114, 124, 144, 164, 169, 173, 179, 194, 409, 424, 608, 610 (Jubilat)*
- Ⓣ *1, 2, 3, 6, 8, 18 (Filharmonia); 1, 2, 6 (Jubilat)*

Noworolski €€€

The café has been housed in the Sukiennice (➤28) for over a century. It was founded in 1910 by Jan Noworolski, who moved here from Lviv. The Noworolski café soon gained the renown of being one of Cracow's best, and has enjoyed a good reputation ever since. In the stylish interior, you can savour the chocolate *Sacher-Torte*, warm apple pies, cream slices and fruit salad. Breakfast meals and dinner courses are also served here. The chef's specialities include lamb chops in nut liqueur sauce, herb and mushroom *conchiglioni*. ■

- ✉ *Rynek Główny 1 (Sukiennice)*
- ☎ *+48 12 4224771*
- @ *www.noworolski.com.pl*
- ⌚ *9am–midnight*
- Ⓑ *124, 152, 424, 502, 522, 601, 605, 608, 609, 610, 614, 618, 902, 904 (Dworzec Główny)*
- Ⓣ *2, 4, 7, 10, 12, 13, 14, 15, 19, 20, 24, 40 (Dworzec Główny)*

Siesta Cafe €€€

Siesta Cafe is situated close to the Dominican Basilica (➤31) and numerous embassies. It is a perfect place to take a rest and enjoy a tasty dessert. A cup of coffee and some apple pie with or without whipped cream or ice-cream will surely help to restore one's energy and good spirits. Everyone feels at home here: students, adults, and old-age pensioners. ■

- ✉ *ul. Stolarska 6*
- ☎ *+48 12 4311488*
- ⌚ *Mon–Fri 9am–midnight, Sat 11am–midnight, Sun 11.30am–midnight*
- Ⓣ *1, 3, 6, 8, 18 (Plac Wszystkich Świętych)*

Sara €€€

The café is located in the Centre for Jewish Culture (➤87). Tables and spacious armchairs are arranged within the walls painted in leaves, with ivy hanging down from upper floors. Guests can also sit at café tables in the second-floor terrace, which can be reached by a flight of stairs. It is really difficult to decide where to have your coffee and dessert: in the cosy interior, or in the open with a view over pl. Nowy (➤86, ➤225). Both of these places have a charm of their own. ■

- ✉ *Centrum Kultury Żydowskiej, ul. Meiselsa 17*
- ⌚ *Mon–Fri 10am–8pm, Sat–Sun 10am–2pm*
- Ⓣ *7, 9, 11, 13, 24, 50, 51 (Miodowa)*

OTHER

Vanilla €€€

This little cake shop in Kazimierz sells cakes mostly to take away, but there are also two small tables for guests who order an espresso or a cup of tea – to wash down some fresh cake, of course! These are prepared as individual pieces, or cut off from

cakes sold by weight (with cream, chocolate, or fruit). In the summer, check out
the raspberry tart – it tastes heavenly! ■

✉ ul. Brzozowa 13
☎ +48 602790988
🕐 Mon–Fri 9am–7pm, Sat 9am–6pm,
   Sun 9am–5pm
🚊 7, 9, 11, 13, 24, 50, 51 (Miodowa)

Czajownia €€€

As the name of the "Chai Place" seems
to promise, tea reigns supreme here. The
selection is really impressive. You can
choose between many different varieties such as white, yellow, red, dark, and
blue-green (for example, *ali shan formosa
oolong* from Taiwan, voted the best tea of
2010 by the customers). Guests can sit
in wicker chairs, or go for the comfortable bean bags arranged on the carpets
around low wooden tables. ■

✉ ul. Józefa 25
☎ +48 664299306
@ www.czajownia.pl
🕐 Mon–Thu, Sun 1pm–10pm,
   Fri–Sat 1pm–11pm
€ approx. PLN 10 for a pot of tea
🚊 7, 9, 11, 13, 24, 50, 51 (Miodowa)

Wedel Chocolate Lounge €€€

A paradise on earth for all the great lovers of chocolate and those who have
a sweet tooth. Wedel offers hot chocolate
of different varieties (classic, milk, white)
with an addition of syrups or fruit. There
is also ice-cream served with whipped
cream and sprinkled with sweet chocolate, and hand-made pralines of different
flavours (for instance, marzipan, nougat
or hazelnut, honey, even whisky). You
will be truly spoilt for choice here. Your
taste buds can be reset with a cup of tea or
coffee. Those who want to take the special
Wedel taste home with them can make
some sweet purchases in the Chocolate
Shop before they leave. ■

Papal Cream Cake

**Polish cuisine boasts many differ-
ent types of cream cakes, but the
best-known ones, called "Papal"
(*kremówki papieskie*), come from
Wadowice – the birthplace of
John Paul II.**

Visiting Wadowice in 1999, the
late Pope remembered with affec-
t on his youth, mentioning the cream
cakes to which he and his friends
treated themselves in a cake shop
at the corner of Wadowice's Main
Square and ul. Mickiewicza. The
building now houses a bank, but
there is no shortage of cake shops
selling cream cakes – puff pastry with
a thick layer of vanilla cream, popular all over Poland. As a result of the
Pope's reminiscences, they are often
dubbed "Papal," and have become
a symbol of Wadowice (➤175).
Every year, Wadowice sells about
one million cream cakes to tourists!

✉ Rynek Główny 46
☎ +48 12 4294085
@ www.wedelpijalnie.pl
🕐 9am–midnight
🚌 124, 152, 424, 502, 522, 601, 605, 608,
   609, 610, 614, 618, 902, 904 (Dworzec
   Główny)
🚊 2, 4, 7, 10, 12, 13, 14, 15, 19, 20, 24, 40
   (Dworzec Główny)

Culture and Entertainment

The city's theatres, such as the Juliusz Słowacki Theatre (➤54, ➤203) and Bagatela (➤201), always play to full houses.

Classical Way

In Cracow, high culture stands strong. People frequently go to theatres, the Opera and the Philharmonic, attracted by varied repertoires and a large number of premieres. The offer from cinemas and cabaret clubs is also quite interesting.

The diversity of thematic content and means of artistic expression is immense. On Cracow stages, one can see marionette and actor shows (see: Groteska ➤202), light comedies and serious drama. Repertoires include classic titles, such as Shakespeare's plays, as well as recent dramatic works. Productions are directed by celebrated artists such as Krystian Lupa and Jan Klata; there is also room for newcomers, who are just starting their careers as directors. Cracovians are avid theatre-goers: tickets for the most interesting performances sell out well in advance.

Although the building of the city's Opera House (➤205) was built only in 2008, the story of the institution goes back to 1782. That year saw the first opera spectacle ever performed in Cracow, André Grétry's *Zémire et Azor* (1771). Operas were first staged in the Municipal Theatre, later called the Juliusz Słowacki Theatre (➤203). The Municipal Opera and Operetta Theatre (Miejski Teatr Muzyczny – Opera i Operetka) was established in 1958 and went through several changes before it finally evolved into the Cracow Opera House (Opera Krakowska) in 2001. It took seven years, however, before it could move into its own dedicated building.

In Cracow, there are also many art houses that screen interesting and ambitious films. They are much smaller than chain multiplex cinemas, but boast an incomparably wider repertory. Viewers can watch not only Hollywood's latest releases, but also some lesser-known films from all over the world, not to mention numerous thematic reviews. Many art houses feature small screening rooms that can seat only up to 100 spectators (Pod Baranami ➤204 and ARS ➤204), or less than 20 (Mikro ➤204) – this makes for a more comfortable watching experience.

However, Cracow is not all about gravity and solemnity. Visitors often come across cabaret shows, sketch revues and other events that represent student culture, staged in clubs and theatre houses (for example, Groteska and Rotunda). ■

THEATRE HOUSES

Bagatela

The theatre was founded in 1918. Before WWII, the building also housed one of the most stylish screening rooms in Cracow. Since 1972, the theatre has been named after Tadeusz Boy-Żeleński, a Polish writer, critic and translator. The repertoire includes classic titles such as Shakespeare's *Hamlet* and a stage adaptation of Kafka's *The Trial*. However, the audience appears to be most fond of comedies; the most popular, like Ray Cooney's *Mayday*, have been shown over 1,000 times! The theatre is a perfect choice for those looking for laughter and light entertainment. The main stage is located in; shows can be also seen at ul. Sarego 7. ■

✉ *ul. Karmelicka 6*
☎ *box office: +48 12 4245212*
@ *www.bagatela.krakow.pl*
🕐 *box office: Mon 10am–7.15pm (break: 12.45pm–1.30pm, 2.15pm–3.45pm), Tue–Sat 9am–7.15pm (break: 12.45pm–1.30pm, 2.15pm–3.45pm), Sun: 2 hours before the show*

201

€ PLN 30–60 (PLN 25–50)

Ⓑ 124, 152, 304, 424, 502, 522, 601, 608, 618, 902 (Teatr Bagatela)

Ⓣ 2, 3, 4, 8, 13, 14, 15, 20, 24 (Teatr Bagatela)

✉ ul. Sarego 7

🕑 box office: 60 minutes before the show

€ PLN 45–60 (PLN 35–50)

Ⓑ 128, 184, 609, 614, 904 (Starowiślna)

Ⓣ 3, 6, 8, 10, 18, 19, 40 (św. Gertrudy); 1, 7, 9, 11, 12, 13, 22, 24, 50, 51 (Starowiślna)

Groteska

This is the only marionette theatre in Cracow. Its stage adaptations of fairy tales create a lasting memory for children of all ages. Rainbow-coloured costumes and scenery transport the viewers (not only the youngest) into a fantasy world. The repertoire of the theatre consists of shows for children (such as *Little Red Riding Hood* and *Pinocchio*) as well as for adults (for example, *Don Quixote* and *The Master and Margarita*). The combination of live acting with expertly operated marionettes is an interesting alternative to traditional theatre. Note that shows are performed in Polish; language is not a barrier, however, during guest concerts of Polish artists, international theatre festivals hosted by the theatre, and the Great Dragon Parade (➤ 229). ■

✉ ul. Skarbowa 2

☎ box office: +48 12 6237959

@ www.groteska.pl

🕑 box office: Mon–Fri 8am–noon, 3pm–5pm and 60 minutes before the show

€ children's shows: PLN 14–17; adult shows: PLN 20–25 (PLN 15–20); guest shows, e.g. cabaret: up to PLN 60

Ⓑ 124, 152, 304, 424, 502, 522, 601, 608, 618, 902 (Teatr Bagatela)

Ⓣ 2, 3, 4, 8, 13, 14, 15, 20, 24 (Teatr Bagatela)

KTO

KTO is an interesting landmark on the city's theatre scene. Founded in 1977 by Jagiellonian University students, it gained the status of a municipal theatre only in 2005. Apart from indoor performances at ul. Gzymsików 8, KTO is famous for its outdoor productions staged all over the world (*The Blind*, *Quixotage*, and *The Fragrance of Time*). This is a modern version of the medieval popular theatre of strolling players. ■

✉ ul. Gzymsików 8

☎ ticket reservation: +48 12 6338947

@ www.teatrkto.pl

🕑 box office: 9am–4pm and 2 hours before the show

€ PLN 30 (PLN 20)

Ⓑ 114, 139, 159, 164, 169, 179, 192, 208, 292, 610 (Grottgera)

Scena STU

It is a well-known name to all Polish theatre fans. Founded in 1966 by the graduates of Cracow's Academy for the Dramatic Arts, it has gone through several changes. At first, it witnessed the growth of student culture, very *avangarde* and *engagé*. With time, it has become a professional theatre, touring the world with its shows. The STU Theatre is now used as a prestigious venue, without its own group of actors. One thing has not changed: viewers can still count on the shows staged here to be of as high a quality as they were 40 years ago. ■

✉ al. Krasińskiego 16-18

☎ +48 12 4222263

@ www.scenastu.com.pl

🕑 box office: on days without shows 9am–5pm, on show days 9am–7pm, Sat and Sun: 2 hours before the show

€ PLN 50–100

Ⓑ 109, 114, 124, 144, 164, 169, 173, 179, 194, 409, 424, 608, 610 (Jubilat); 109, 114, 124, 134, 144, 164, 169, 173, 179, 192, 194, 292, 409, 502, 608, 610, 618 (Cracovia)

Ⓣ 1, 2, 6 (Jubilat); 15, 18 (Cracovia)

People's Theatre

The People's Theatre (Teatr Ludowy in Polish) was established in 1955. Today, it stages mainly contemporary drama. There are also shows for children, presented in the morning. The theatre is based in Nowa Huta, but some performances can be also seen in the small stage room of Scena pod Ratuszem in the Town Hall Tower (➤ 30). See also: ➤ 130. ∎

✉ os. Teatralne 34
☎ box office: +48 12 6802111, customer service: +48 12 6802112
@ www.ludowy.pl
🕐 box office: Mon–Sat noon–6pm, Sun and holidays: 2 hours before the show
€ PLN 32–42 (PLN 22–32), children's shows: PLN 18
🚌 110, 122, 123, 139, 149, 153, 169, 202, 212, 222, 232, 604, 608 (Teatr Ludowy)
🚊 1, 5 (Teatr Ludowy)

✉ Rynek Główny 1
☎ box office: +48 12 4215016
🕐 box office: Mon–Sat noon–7pm, Sun and holidays: 2 hours before the show
€ PLN 32–42 (PLN 22–32)
🚌 124, 152, 424, 502, 522, 601, 605, 608, 609, 610, 614, 618, 902, 904 (Dworzec Główny)
🚊 2, 4, 7, 10, 12, 13, 14, 15, 19, 20, 24, 40 (Dworzec Główny)

Juliusz Słowacki Theatre

The theatre produces adaptations of classics as well as works by young playwrights. The fine interior decoration of the auditorium is an added value to watching performances shown on the Large Stage (Duża Scena, see also: ➤ 54). The Small Stage (Scena Miniatura), where actors perform at an arm's reach, boasts a repertoire that is often even more interesting than that of the Large Stage. On summer nights, you can watch performances in the open-air Stage by the Pump (Scena przy Pompie). The theatre also holds very popular poetry meetings, the so-called Cracow Poetry Salon (Krakowski Salon Poezji). For eight years, celebrated Polish actors have read poems in the theatre foyer on Sundays at noon. Free entry passes should be collected early on Saturdays. ∎

✉ pl. św. Ducha 1
☎ visiting: +48 12 4244525, box office: +48 12 4244526

@ www.slowacki.krakow.pl
🕐 box office: Mon 10am–2pm, 2.30pm–6pm, Tue–Sat 9.30am–2pm, 2.30pm–7pm, Sun (only on show days) 3pm–7pm
€ PLN 30–50 (PLN 25–35)
🚌 124, 152, 424, 502, 522, 601, 605, 608, 609, 610, 614, 618, 902, 904 (Dworzec Główny)
🚊 2, 4, 7, 10, 12, 13, 14, 15, 19, 20, 24, 40 (Dworzec Główny)

National Old Theatre

The National Old Theatre (Narodowy Stary Teatr) is named after Helena Modjeska, a famous 19th-century Polish and American actress. The oldest theatre in Cracow, it has achieved wide recognition and attracts crowds of spectators every year. It has been in operation for over two centuries, but the repertoire is by no means outdated, featuring modern *avantgarde* performances. Viewers flock to watch eminent Polish actors directed by acclaimed artists such as Jan Klata and Krystian Lupa. There are four stage rooms. The building in ul. Jagiellońska houses three of them, the largest of which can seat up to 350 spectators (for the most popular plays there are even more people, sitting on the stairs). A small stage room is located in ul. Starowiślna. ∎

✉ ul. Jagiellońska 1
☎ box office and ticket reservation: +48 12 4224040
@ www.stary.pl
🕐 box office: Tue–Sat 10am–1pm, 5pm–7pm and 2 hours before the show
€ PLN 50 (PLN 30)
🚌 124, 152, 304, 424, 502, 522, 601, 608, 618, 902 (Teatr Bagatela)
🚊 2, 3, 4, 8, 13, 14, 15, 20, 24 (Teatr Bagatela)

✉ ul. Starowiślna 21
☎ box office: +48 12 4284700
🕐 box office: Tue–Sat 10am–1pm, 5pm–7pm and 2 hours before the show
€ PLN 40–50 (PLN 25–30)
🚌 128, 184, 609, 614, 904 (Starowiślna)
🚊 1, 7, 9, 11, 12, 13, 22, 24, 50, 51 (Starowiślna)

CINEMAS AND ART HOUSES

ARS

The top cinemas in Cracow are ARS and Pod Baranami (described below). ARS is located close to the Main Square (➤26). It is frequented by students and fans of "ambitious" cinema. There are several screening rooms, including two really small ones. An interesting idea is the so-called Kiniarnia, an original combination of a cinema (in Polish, *kino*) and a café (*kawiarnia*): you can have a beer or coffee while watching a film. Food cannot be brought into other screening rooms, so no one is going to spoil your watching experience by slurping a Coke or chomping on popcorn. ▪

✉ ul. św. Jana 6
☎ +48 12 4214199
@ www.ars.pl
€ PLN 12–19 (PLN 12–14)
Ⓑ 124, 152, 424, 502, 522, 601, 605, 608, 609, 610, 614, 618, 902, 904 (Dworzec Główny)
Ⓣ 2, 4, 7, 10, 12, 13, 14, 15, 19, 20, 24, 40 (Dworzec Główny)

Mikro

The "micro-cinema" has been in operation in the city centre since 1984. The cinema is known for its interesting choice of films and thematic reviews. Apart from the main screening room, there is also a very cosy, blue-painted Mikroffala room, where up to 13 spectators can lounge comfortably on claret-coloured sofas and armchairs. Watching a film in such conditions is the essence of relaxation. A real highlight is the programme of monthly live broadcasts from London's National Theatre. ▪

✉ ul. Lea 5
☎ +48 12 6342897
@ www.kinomikro.pl
🕐 box office: 30 minutes before the first screening until 10pm

€ PLN 10–16 (PLN 10–13), National Theatre broadcasts: PLN 35–40 (PLN 30–35)
Ⓑ 114, 139, 159, 164, 169, 179, 192, 208, 292, 501, 601, 610 (Plac Inwalidów)
Ⓣ 4, 8, 13, 14, 20, 24 (Plac Inwalidów)

Pod Baranami

The "Under the Rams" cinema is situated in the same-named historic palace by the Main Square (➤26). It is one of the best film centres in Cracow and a member of the prestigious Europa Cinemas – the International Network of Cinemas for the Circulation of European Films. There are three screening rooms. The red one is large and stately, with a carved wooden ceiling. The smaller white room holds 30 wide armchairs. The cinema often hosts reviews of films from particular countries and directors, as well as theme festivals. There is a special offer for parents with babies, called "Lambs in Nappies" ("Baranki w pieluchach"): films are shown with the lights dimmed only slightly and the sound toned down so as not to wake up tiny tots. Yet another interesting idea is the midday "Heynal Screening" ("Seans z hejnałem"): a show of an interesting film, often a recent one, with tickets sold at moderate prices. ▪

✉ Rynek Główny 27
☎ +48 12 4230768
@ www.kinopodbaranami.pl
🕐 box office opens 30 minutes before the first screening; "Lambs in Nappies": Thu at 11am; "Heynal Screenings": daily at noon
€ PLN 11–19 (PLN 11–14); "Lambs in Nappies": PLN 10; "Heynal Screenings": PLN 11
Ⓑ 124, 152, 304, 424, 502, 522, 601, 608, 618, 902 (Teatr Bagatela)
Ⓣ 2, 3, 4, 8, 13, 14, 15, 20, 24 (Teatr Bagatela)

Sfinks

The "Sphinx" cinema is an interesting art house located in a Socialist-Realist building of Nowa Huta (➤118). Films are screened here twice or three times a day. The cinema is exceptional for the fact that it still keeps to the old tradition of showing a weekly newsreel before each screening. The newsreel always concerns Nowa Huta, presenting current events in the cultural and social life of the district. ■

- ✉ os. Górali 5
- ☎ +48 12 6442765
- @ www.kinosfinks.pl
- ⊘ box office opens 30 minutes before the first screening
- € PLN 12–13 (PLN 7–11)
- Ⓑ 110, 122, 123, 139, 149, 153, 169, 202, 212, 222, 232, 604, 608 (Teatr Ludowy)
- Ⓣ 1, 5 (Teatr Ludowy)

MUSIC

Cracow Philharmonic

The Cracow Philharmonic is named after Karol Szymanowski (1882–1937), a Polish composer and pianist. It has seen performances from eminent soloists and world-class symphony orchestras led by Polish and foreign conductors. Renowned musicians who have played here include one of the world's greatest violinists, Nigel Kennedy, a British artist who lives in Cracow with his Polish wife. Concerts in the Philharmonic are not limited to classical music; particularly memorable were those given by popular musicians such as Stanisław Soyka, Grzegorz Turnau, and Czech bard Jaromir Nohavica. Perfect acoustics and a large auditorium for almost 700 seats make this concert hall rank among the major ones in Cracow. ■

- ✉ ul. Zwierzyniecka 1
- ☎ box office: +48 12 6198721, +48 12 6198733; ticket reservation: +48 12 6198722
- @ www.filharmonia.krakow.pl
- ⊘ box office: Tue–Fri 11am–2pm, 3pm–7pm, Sat–Sun: 60 minutes before the concert
- € PLN 15–45

- Ⓑ 304, 522 (Filharmonia)
- Ⓣ 1, 2, 3, 6, 8, 18 (Filharmonia)

Cracow Opera House

The construction of the Opera House gave rise to a series of controversies: first concerning its projected location, then the architectural project, and finally the interior design. In spite of all the polemics involved, the Opera House immediately became one of the most popular places in Cracow. The facade of the building, as well as the interior (the auditorium walls, comfortable spacious armchairs, and the stage curtain), all have a vivid red colour scheme. There are 760 seats. Spectators suffering from a fear of heights should not go up to the top of the upper balcony; all others will find it an interesting experience. Seats are installed very high up, and the steep rows are secured by a pane of glass.

The Cracow Opera House has its own symphony orchestra, soloists, a choir and a ballet troupe. It is also a venue for guest performers. From time to time, it holds ballet shows and concerts; it has seen Bobby McFerrin and the jazz NDR Big Band, among other stars. The Opera House boasts very good acoustics. Viewers still follow the disappearing convention of wearing formal clothes to performances. Men in suits and women in evening dresses are a common sight. ■

- ✉ ul. Lubicz 48
- ☎ +48 12 2966100
- @ www.opera.krakow.pl
- ⊘ box office: Mon–Sat 10am–7pm, Sun: 2 hours before the show
- € PLN 20–250
- Ⓑ 124, 125, 128, 148, 152, 182, 184, 424, 501, 502, 522, 601, 605, 608, 609, 618 (Rondo Mogilskie)
- Ⓣ 4, 5, 9, 10, 12, 14, 15, 20, 40, 50, 51 (Rondo Mogilskie)

Cool and Trendy

Some places have their own devoted regulars not for the delicious cuisine they serve; their menus do not differ considerably from those of similar establishments. However, they have "that special something" which attracts crowds.

Never-ending heated debates and chatting long into the night – this is what Cracovians do when they stay up. And there are no places more suited to the purpose than atmospheric dimly-lit interiors. Some clubs are visited for the fame they have gained throughout the decades. Some provide an opportunity to rub shoulders with interesting guests, such as representatives of Cracow's artistic community. While many customers come here just to enjoy themselves, others do so with an ulterior motive to see the famous and the beautiful – and, who knows, maybe even bump into them and start a conversation, having mustered up courage with a drink. These clubs also host interesting cultural events and concerts; the ones given in small tight rooms are usually an unforgettable experience. ■

Alchemia

The chemistry of "Alchemy," the best-known club in Kazimierz, includes several ingredients. Old paintings, photographs, and mirrors on the walls. A wooden wardrobe through which you pass into another room. Antique tables and chairs from different sets (careful: some wobble or have broken seats). Wax-dripping candles, semi-dark interiors, and an ambience of mystery. On a weekend night, finding a free table can be a real challenge, and crowds of people besiege the bar. Go through all the rooms to reach the bizarrely furnished "kitchen," its walls displaying photographs by Tomasz Sikora. The club basement is the venue of frequently held discos and concerts (admission tickets usually sell out very quickly). Alchemia also hosts an annual jazz festival (➤231). ■

✉ ul. Estery 5
☎ +48 12 4212200
@ www.alchemia.com.pl
🕐 Mon 10am–4am, Tue–Sun 9am–4am
€ disco: free; concerts: PLN 20–70
🚌 128, 184, 609, 614, 904 (Stradom)
🚊 7, 9, 11, 13, 24, 50, 51 (Miodowa); 3, 6, 8, 10, 12, 18, 19, 22, 40 (Stradom)

Dym

A major asset of the "Smoke" bar is its convenient location in the narrow part of ul. św. Tomasza by a tiny yard, close to the Main Square (➤26) and the ARS cinema (➤204). The décor is ascetic in style. Regulars include the artists of Cracow and those who aspire to be part of that community. Cultural personalities often talk over beer or wine. Some say that the club attracts too many pretentious people who try to pose as trendy. Nevertheless, it is certainly worth a visit. ■

✉ ul. św. Tomasza 13
☎ +48 12 4296661
🕐 10am–midnight, Fri–Sat 10am–2am
🚌 124, 152, 424, 502, 522, 601, 605, 608, 609, 610, 614, 618, 902, 904 (Dworzec Główny)
🚊 2, 4, 7, 10, 12, 13, 14, 15, 19, 20, 24, 40 (Dworzec Główny)

Klub pod Jaszczurami

The "Lizards Club" is a legend. One of the oldest student bars in Cracow, it is housed in a graded historic building; the Gothic Hall (Sala Gotycka) has kept the original asymmetrical vaulted ceiling. The club is so much more than just a good place to have a mug of draught beer. It holds not only discos, but also many cultural events such as meetings with authors and scientists, debates, film screenings, concerts

---

and public slide shows. The programme is displayed in the window. ■

✉ Rynek Główny 8
☎ +48 12 2922202, +48 12 2922203
@ www.instytutsztuki.pl
Ⓑ 124, 152, 424, 502, 522, 601, 605, 608, 609, 610, 614, 618, 902, 904 (Dworzec Główny)
Ⓣ 2, 4, 7, 10, 12, 13, 14, 15, 19, 20, 24, 40 (Dworzec Główny)

Nowa Prowincja

The "New Province" was founded by Grzegorz Turnau, one of the best-known Polish singer-songwriters; it is located in ul. Bracka (➤58), the street that was the subject of one of his most popular songs. The bar serves delicious hot chocolate and tea. It is usually crowded, filled with the aroma of hot drinks, but there is also a quiet side to it: in the room upstairs, you can read a book, talk over a cup of strong tea, and see a temporary exhibition (in the past, artists such as photographer Tomasz Sikora and poet Ewa Lipska presented their works here). ■

✉ ul. Bracka 3-5
☎ +48 693770079
@ www.nowaprowincja.krakow.pl
Ⓒ 8.30am–11pm, Sun 9.30am–11pm
Ⓑ 124, 152, 424, 502, 522, 601, 605, 608, 609, 610, 614, 618, 902, 904 (Dworzec Główny)
Ⓣ 2, 4, 7, 10, 12, 13, 14, 15, 19, 20, 24, 40 (Dworzec Główny)

Piękny Pies

The already legendary "Beautiful Dog" moved here several years ago. The owners claim it was established for their own convenience, their families and friends, befriended artists and a few local "locos." A rather unimpressive décor is more than made up for by the (usually) good atmosphere. Discos and occasional concerts are held in the basement. Once a month, there is a presentation of the so-called "Talking Dog" ("Gadający Pies"), a sort of a sound magazine. This

is when you can listen to, and sometimes see, more or less interesting addresses to the audience made by representatives of Cracow's artistic community. ■

✉ ul. Sławkowska 6a
@ www.piekny-pies.pl
Ⓒ noon–2am, Fri–Sat noon–4am
Ⓑ 124, 152, 424, 601, 608, 610, 618, 902 (Basztowa LOT)
Ⓣ 2, 3, 4, 7, 13, 14, 15, 20, 24 (Basztowa LOT)

Piwnica pod Baranami

The "Cellar under the Rams" is a legendary cabaret venue, famous all around Poland. It was founded and headed by Piotr Skrzynecki (1930–1997). In the communist era, the club was a refuge for those looking for an artistic respite from the ubiquitous monotony. Performances of the Cellar's team are famous for wit, songs, and an unconventional stage style. Throughout the decades, the club has seen performances from well-known Polish actors, actresses, singers and musicians such as Ewa Demarczyk, Grzegorz Turnau and Krzysztof Komeda, who also gained popularity abroad. Cabaret shows can be seen every Saturday, while Thursdays see jazz concerts. In addition, jazz takes over the club every summer (see: Summer Jazz Festival ➤231). Remember that you are welcome to visit the club's bar even if no show is on. ■

✉ Rynek Główny 27
☎ +48 601739673
@ www.piwnicapodbaranami.krakow.pl
Ⓒ from 6pm until the last guest leaves; cabaret: Sat at 9pm; jazz concert: Thu at 9pm
€ cabaret: PLN 50; jazz concerts: PLN 15–40
Ⓑ 124, 152, 304, 424, 502, 522, 601, 608, 618, 902 (Teatr Bagatela)
Ⓣ 2, 3, 4, 8, 13, 14, 15, 20, 24 (Teatr Bagatela)
ℹ concert tickets can be bought in the club at least 60 minutes before the start of the show; cabaret tickets should be reserved in advance at tel. +48 12 4212500, and collected in the club management com-

pany at ul. św. Tomasza 26 (8am–3pm) or, by prior arrangement, in the club one hour before the start of the show

Singer

This is one of the first and best-known bars of Kazimierz. It was established at the time when the district was still quite an unwelcoming place, with few tourists coming here. The name derives from a well-known company that produces sewing machines (some fine old ones are even mounted on a few tables). The dimly lit interior is usually crowded with people, and when there are no more seats left, people stand by the bar. The party often gets out of hand and, even though Singer is no dance club, guests start moving to the music – for lack of space, even on the tables or on the bar. ■

✉ *ul. Estery 20*
☎ *+48 12 2920622*
🕐 *9am–3am, Fri–Sat 9am–6am*
🚊 *7, 9, 11, 13, 24, 50, 51 (Miodowa)*

Vis à Vis

Vis à Vis is one of the few places by the city's Main Square (➤26) that has resisted the easy design solutions necessitated by mass tourism: it has preserved its old character, with narrow tables and high chairs. It used to be the favourite bar of Piotr Skrzynecki, the late founder of the nearby Piwnica pod Baranami (➤207). Vis à Vis is now fronted by the bronze statue of Skrzynecki in his trademark hat, sitting by a table. Cracovians often put flowers into his hand, or sit next to him, looking towards the Main Square. The summer pavement café is frequented by Cracow artists. ■

✉ *Rynek Główny 29*
☎ *+48 12 4232255*
🕐 *8am–11pm*
🚌 *124, 152, 304, 424, 502, 522, 601, 608, 618, 902 (Teatr Bagatela)*
🚊 *2, 3, 4, 8, 13, 14, 15, 20, 24 (Teatr Bagatela)*

All That Jazz

Cracow has a long tradition of jazz music: the first association of jazz fans was established as early as 1926. Today, there are many places where you can listen to evening concerts, and the highly popular festivals dedicated to that genre of music are held on a cyclical basis.

Jazz has been present in Cracow for a long time. It was already taught at one of the city's music schools in the 1930's, when many jazz clubs, big bands and orchestras came into being. After WWII, the communist authorities tried to stamp out the "music of the capitalist enemy," and concerts were given mainly for closed circles of people at private apartments. Jazz came back to grace only in the mid-1950's. 1954 saw the first edition of Cracow's All Souls Jazz Festival (see: the Cracow Jazz All Soul's Day Festival ➤232), held annually ever since. The subsequent decades were the time of further expansion

of the jazz scene. Jazz concerts still enjoy an unwaning popularity.

This fact becomes evident on visiting the city's clubs. The best-known among them, U Muniaka (➤210), is located in a small cellar close to the Main Square (➤26). The club is named after its founder and owner Janusz Muniak, an excellent saxophonist who can be often heard performing there. Jam sessions and concerts are also held in the Harris Piano Jazz Bar (➤209). Even more stylish is Piano Rouge (➤209), a restaurant and jazz club that hosts concerts of jazz and pop music every night. Crowds come to take part in Cracow's festivals, such as the Summer Jazz Festival (➤231) organised by Piwnica pod Baranami (➤207), and Cracow Jazz Autumn (➤231) in Alchemia (➤206).

The story of jazz in Cracow features a lot of famous names. Concerts were given here by pianist Krzysztof Komeda (1931–1969), one of the best-known Polish composers of film music; he gained international acclaim with the famous theme he wrote for Roman Polański's *Rosemary's Baby* (1968). Komeda left behind a lot of jazz albums recorded with his band. The key jazz personalities of Cracow in the 1960's were violinist Zbigniew Seifert (1946–1979) and saxophonist Janusz Muniak (b. 1941), inspired by the then-*avantgarde* American music. Other renowned musicians connected with the city include guitarist Jarosław Śmietana (b. 1951) and the world-famous trumpeter Tomasz Stańko (b. 1942), a graduate of the Cracow Music Academy. ■

Harris Piano Jazz Bar

The bar is situated in the basement of a building in the Main Square (➤26). Concerts are held in one of the bar's three rooms. When a famous band is performing, there is practically no chance of finding a free seat without prior reservation. Fans of traditional jazz will have a great time here on Tuesday and Sunday evenings. Jam session nights are usually held on Mondays, Wednesdays or Thursdays. As you order a beer or a drink, be aware that you do so at one of the longest bars in the city. ■

✉ *Rynek Główny 28*
☎ *+48 12 4215741*
@ *www.harris.krakow.pl*
🕐 *Mon–Thu 9am–2am, Fri–Sat 9am–3am*
€ *concerts: PLN 10–20*
Ⓑ *124, 152, 304, 424, 502, 522, 601, 608, 618, 902 (Teatr Bagatela)*
Ⓣ *2, 3, 4, 8, 13, 14, 15, 20, 24 (Teatr Bagatela)*

Mile Stone

The club is housed in the exclusive Qubus hotel in Podgórze, close to pl. Bohaterów Getta (➤106). It is a place for those who prefer modern-style, spacious interiors to dimly lit cellars. Comfortable orange armchairs and sofas promise relaxation. Concerts (mostly jazz) are held on Fridays and Saturdays. ■

✉ *ul. Nadwiślańska 6*
☎ *+48 12 3745100, +48 12 3745186*
@ *www.mile-stone.pl*
🕐 *Fri–Sat 7pm–2am*
€ *concerts: up to PLN 35*
Ⓣ *7, 9, 11, 13, 24, 50, 51 (Plac Bohaterów Getta)*

Piano Rouge

Red-carpeted stairs lead to the club's three rooms. The interior design makes one think of castle chambers with old stone walls guarding comfortable sofas, wide chandeliers, carpets, and stylish lamps. An elegant restaurant by day, the place turns into a concert venue in the evening – every single night! The repertoire is mainly jazz, but it sometimes includes decent pop music. ■

✉ *Rynek Główny 46*
☎ *+48 12 4310333*
@ *www.thepianorouge.com*
🕐 *Mon–Thu, Sun noon–2am, Fri–Sat noon–4am; concerts at 9pm or 10pm*
€ *concerts: free on Mon–Tue, Sun, daily for restaurant guests; Wed–Thu PLN 10, Fri–Sat PLN 15*
Ⓑ *124, 152, 424, 502, 522, 601, 605, 608, 609, 610, 614, 618, 902, 904 (Dworzec Główny)*
Ⓣ *2, 4, 7, 10, 12, 13, 14, 15, 19, 20, 24, 40 (Dworzec Główny)*

Piec Art

The club is not called the "Oven Art" for no reason: it actually serves proper meals. This nice and cosy place near the Main Square (➤26) has a good reputation. Concerts are mostly held on Wednesdays and

Thursdays, but you should also check the weekend programme. The stylish interior design of the cellar is a perfect setting for live music. The photos hanging on brick walls portray jazz musicians, and candlelight makes for a truly special atmosphere. ■

- ✉ ul. Szewska 12
- ☎ +48 12 4296425
- @ www.piecart.pl
- 🕑 4pm–2am daily
- € concerts: PLN 5–35
- Ⓓ 124, 152, 304, 424, 502, 522, 601, 608, 618, 902 (Teatr Bagatela)
- Ⓣ 2, 3, 4, 8, 13, 14, 15, 20, 24 (Teatr Bagatela)

U Muniaka

The best-known jazz club in Cracow. It is housed in medieval cellars only a few steps away from St Mary's Basilica (➤23). Concerts are given almost every day by a number of Cracovian stars and musicians, often by the club founder Janusz Muniak himself. Muniak has participated in recording numerous albums as a soloist, a band member, and a guest musician. He has worked with big names such as Krzysztof Komeda, Tomasz Stańko and Jarosław Śmietana. ■

- ✉ ul. Floriańska 3
- ☎ +48 12 4231205
- 🕑 7pm–2am daily; concerts at 9.30pm
- € concerts: approx. PLN 20
- Ⓓ 124, 152, 424, 502, 522, 601, 605, 608, 609, 610, 614, 618, 902, 904 (Dworzec Główny)
- Ⓣ 2, 4, 7, 10, 12, 13, 14, 15, 19, 20, 24, 40 (Dworzec Główny)

Saturday Night Fever

There are hundreds of bars and clubs in Cracow. Many of them are turned into all-night party dens on the spur of the moment. Others put forward a specific party offer that consists of either recent or old hits of dance music.

Day or night, you will never get bored in Cracow. Local clubs invite you to dance to the modern electro sound (e.g. Cień ➤210) or hot salsa rhythms (El Sol ➤211). Very popular are dancing events to the disco hits from the 1980's and 90's, or even older ever-greens, held by clubs such as U Louisa (➤212) and Stajnia (➤212).

In Cracow, the clubbing scene is flourishing. Those who are lazy by nature should go to Wielopole 15 (➤212), a cluster of several clubs, which makes "club crawling" possible without even leaving the building. Yet another great party place is the Fashion Time (➤211), with each storey presenting a different genre of music. It is also a good idea to take a look inside some bars that do not host dance events on a regular basis. Random parties that develop spontaneously in narrow and crowded rooms are often as great a success as the organised ones. ■

CLUBS

Cień

For several years, the "Shadow" club has ranked among the most fashionable in Cracow. It is hard to pinpoint what exactly makes the place so highly regarded: its modern-style interior, club music played by DJs, or a wide selection of drinks. There is no doubt, however, that this is where one should put in an appearance to be seen as "trendy." No wonder, then, that the place can be packed with people. The line in front of the entrance may dampen your enthusiasm, but you will surely regain it once you step on the dance floor. Fans of modern electro music will be on top of the world, though a dense crowd of revellers will dishearten those keen on ballroom dancing. Bouncers select who can get in, and it is better not to wear sporty clothes. ■

✉ ul. św. Jana 15
☎ +48 12 4222177
@ www.cienklub.com
🕐 Tue–Sun 9pm–6am
€ free, for some events: PLN 10–20
Ⓑ 124, 152, 424, 601, 608, 610, 618, 902 (Basztowa LOT)
Ⓣ 2, 3, 4, 7, 13, 14, 15, 20, 24 (Basztowa LOT)

El Sol

A place for enthusiasts of hot rhythms: salsa, samba, bossa nova, and other dances that involve swaying one's hips. This is the first club in Cracow to have focused on latino music. Most guests really know how to move their bodies, but those who do not, need not worry. Dancing absorbs people to such an extent that no one notices if you miss a step or two. After all, it is only having good time that counts. ■

✉ ul. Batorego 1
☎ +48 506398476
@ www.elsol-krakow.pl
🕐 Mon–Wed 8pm–1am, Thu–Sat 8pm–4am
€ free
Ⓓ 601 (Batorego)
Ⓣ 4, 8, 13, 14, 20, 24 (Batorego)

Fashion Time

People who flock in here for all-night partying have three storeys to choose from. Each is different not only for the décor, but also the type of music that reigns on the dance floor: retro (all-time favourites), R'n'B, or house. The club interior is very modern in style, decorated with lots of trinkets, colourful lighting,

comfortable boxes where you can take a rest (booking is required, most seats are paid – each box is for exclusive use), and well-stocked bars to boot. ■

✉ ul. Tadeusza Kościuszki 3
☎ +48 607949976
@ www.krakow.fashiontime.pl
🕐 Thu–Sat from 9pm
€ Thu: ladies enter for free, men after 10pm: PLN 10; Fri after 10pm: PLN 10; Sat 9pm–11pm PLN 10, after 11pm: PLN 15; a private box (2–16 people): PLN 10–60
Ⓑ 109, 114, 124, 144, 164, 169, 173, 179, 194, 409, 424, 608, 610 (Jubilat)
Ⓣ 1, 2, 6 (Jubilat)

Forty Kleparz

The name of the club refers to the building where it was established – the 19th-century fort constructed by Austrian troops that occupied the city at that time. Like St Benedict's Fort (➤ 111), it was part of the Cracow Fortress. Characteristic red-brick walls, spacious rooms, concerts and dance events to the sound of various music genres (from latino to techno) are the distinguishing features of the place. ■

✉ ul. Kamienna 2-4 (entry from al. Słowackiego, through the car park)
☎ +48 607949976
@ www.fortykleparz.pl
🕐 open only for events
€ mostly free; concerts: PLN 20–40
Ⓑ 114, 115, 130, 132, 139, 154, 159, 164, 169, 179, 192, 208, 257, 277, 292, 501, 610, 904 (Nowy Kleparz)
Ⓣ 3, 7 (Nowy Kleparz)

Prozak

The popular modern-style "Prozac" club is housed in the basement of a building in pl. Dominikański. Two storeys accommodate as many as three dance floors, each with its own DJ mixing club beats together (electro, funk, chillout, etc.). The "all you can drink" nights with the open bar offer are held on Tuesdays. ■

Wielopole 15

With its three clubs, the grey shabby-looking tenement at Wielopole 15 is one great entertainment factory. Although the interiors are not much different from the facade, they are teeming with party crowds who enjoy themselves here until the small hours every weekend.

Caryca, Łubu-Dubu and Kitsch rank among the best-known party places in Cracow. Some come here to dance the night away; for others, it is just a stop on their club crawl from the Main Square (➤26) to Kazimierz (➤68, ➤88) – or the other way round. Because of its location in between the two nightlife destinations, the building is usually packed with people. The décor of Łubu-Dubu is modelled on the old socialist style: a cold shelf for a DJ stand, leatherette armchairs, a few dated knick-knacks, and a plastic letter board similar to those in milk bars, but displaying the names of drinks available from the bar. The old-school disco of the 1970's and 80's is played here. The Kitsch club looks exactly how the name promises: colourful door frames, fairy lights, spotted pelt by the bar. More recent music is played in Caryca. Though these are three separate clubs, guests wander about the building, looking for the best music and the least crowded places.

✉ Wielopole 15
☎ +48 694461402 (Łubu Dubu)
@ www.kitsch.pl, www.lubu-dubu.pl
⏱ daily from 7pm until the last customer leaves
Ⓣ 1, 7, 10, 12, 13, 19, 24, 40 (Poczta Główna)
Ⓑ 609, 614, 904 (Poczta Główna)

✉ pl. Dominikański 6
☎ +48 12 4291128
@ www.prozak.pl
⏱ from 8pm until the last customer leaves
€ free; on Tue ladies PLN 25, men PLN 35
Ⓑ 609, 614, 904 (Poczta Główna)
Ⓣ 1, 3, 6, 8, 18 (Plac Wszystkich Świętych); 1, 7, 10, 12, 13, 19, 24, 40 (Poczta Główna)

Stajnia

The "Mews" pub is one of the most intriguing dance places in Cracow. The courtyard alone boasts a special ambience, immortalised in films such as *Schindler's List*; in the summer, it turns into a beer garden. The place is also a restaurant, perfect to sit around and talk. Tuesday nights are dedicated to parties to the rhythm of Cuban salsa, and Wednesdays see couples embracing to Argentine tango. On Thursdays, Fridays and Saturdays, guests enjoy themselves to the biggest hits of the 1960's, 70's and 80's. A good time is guaranteed. ▪

✉ ul. Józefa 12
☎ +48 12 4237202
@ www.pubstajnia.pl
⏱ Mon–Thu, Sun 11am–1am, Fri–Sat 11am–3am
€ free; Fri and Sat PLN 8
Ⓣ 7, 9, 11, 13, 24, 50, 51 (Miodowa)

U Louisa

"Louis' Place" is a typical Cracow club: a narrow staircase, a cellar, medieval stone walls and vaulted ceiling. It is party time practically all week long. Amateur singers can sing their hearts out on Monday karaoke nights, while the dance floor is alive from Tuesdays to Fridays (Tuesdays: old-school disco and electro house, Thursdays: R'n'B). At the weekends, the club usually resounds with the ever-green hits that are great for dancing, and sometimes with electro music as well. ▪

✉ Rynek Główny 13
☎ +48 12 6170222
@ www.ulouisa.com
⏱ daily from 11am until the last customer leaves
Ⓑ 124, 152, 424, 502, 522, 601, 605, 608, 609, 610, 614, 618, 902, 904 (Dworzec Główny)
Ⓣ 2, 4, 7, 10, 12, 13, 14, 15, 19, 20, 24, 40 (Dworzec Główny)

Active Pursuits

When in Cracow, tourists who are used to active pursuits do not have to limit themselves to self-imposed tasks such as getting from one sight to another as quickly as possible, or taking walks in the Planty. If you feel like action, there are plenty of opportunities to choose from.

The city does not lie far from the high Tatra Mountains, and the Cracow Valleys Landscape Park is even closer. It is small wonder, then, that a lot of Cracow inhabitants have been bitten by the climbing bug. This sport, however, is seasonal, since it is very hard to go up snowy mountain walls. Those not fond of frosty winters can spend that time practising on indoor climbing walls in Reni-Sport (➤215) or the Forteca Climbing Centre (➤214). Both places are often packed with people of different ages and skills. Some regulars are highly advanced climbers, but for most the sport is just a hobby, fitness training or good fun: one does not need to be a demigod with supernatural strength to enjoy climbing!

Cracow is the hometown of Robert Kubica, the first Polish driver to take part in Formula One. This is where his racing career started with numerous successes in karting championships. Today, kart circuits can be found in the roofed WRT-Karting (➤215) and the summer race course in front of the former Forum hotel. The basement of this gloomy building features rooms for playing laser paintball (see: Laser Arena ➤215). There are no paint balls; instead, guns shoot infrared beams, which makes games safe and painless.

Polish Pilots' Park (Park Lotników Polskich) by the University School of Physical Education boasts one of the latest and most interesting attractions of Cracow: the Garden of Experiences (➤214). This modern open-air installation is a model example of combining education and fun in a truly intriguing way.

The pride of the city is one of Poland's newest aquaparks (➤213). More and more people come to play paintball and bowling at Fantasy Park (➤214). There are also many possibilities for children to blow off some steam in the colourful mazes, slides and ball pools of the playgrounds at Fantasy Park and Anikino. ▪

Anikino

Anikino is called the "Land of Children's Games." This adventure playground offers plenty of attractions for children, such as climbing nets and bars, exploring tunnels, slides, ball pools, and mazes. The décor has a vibrant colour scheme. Children can run and jump about, shout and laugh out loud as much as they want. Birthday parties are held in painted theme rooms (the jungle, the universe, a pirate island, etc.). ▪

✉ ul. Nieduża 4

☎ +48 12 4113007, +48 12 4134849, +48 601959022

@ www.anikino.pl

🕐 9am–9pm daily

€ PLN 12–14/hr, PLN 18–22/2 hrs, PLN 24–29 with no time limit

🚌 124, 424 (Wieczysta)

🚊 4, 5, 9, 10, 12, 15, 40 (Wieczysta)

Aquapark

Cracow's Aquapark (Park Wodny) boasts the largest swimming pool hall in Poland. Apart from its many swimming lanes, *jacuzzi* bathtubs and a sauna, the aquapark also features ten slides with a total length of approx. 800 m. Sliding down rainbow-coloured tubes is an exciting experience. Inside the black one, there is total darkness, with colourful lights going on as sliders descend. You can also go up a low climbing wall, risking only a plunge into water if you fall off. The aquapark has plenty of children's attractions, such as the Alligator family slide (wide enough for three people to slide side by side) and the Pirates' Island in the paddling pool. If you get hungry or thirsty, you can visit a bar on site. ■

✉ ul. Dobrego Pasterza 126
☎ +48 12 6163190
@ www.parkwodny.pl
🕐 8am–10pm daily
€ PLN 13–22 (PLN 11–19)/hr, PLN 27/hr + sauna (18 and up), PLN 30–32 (PLN 25–28)/2 hrs, PLN 43–49 (PLN 35–40)/with no time limit + sauna, family tickets: PLN 42–48/hr (3 people, each additional ticket PLN 14–16), PLN 72–81/2 hrs (3 people, each additional ticket PLN 24–27)
🚌 125, 128, 129, 132, 138, 139, 142, 148, 152, 169, 182 (Park Wodny)

Fantasy Park

This family entertainment centre has the best bowling alley in Cracow. Sixteen professional bowling lanes, bowling balls of different weights, a computer system that measures the speed of your throw… in such favourable conditions, a friendly game can easily turn into a true tournament. If you tire of bowling, you can try your hand at one of the pool tables or shove-halfpenny boards. Children up to 9 years of age will enjoy Fantasy Park's Softplay that features slides, miniature rope bridges, pools full of colourful balls and other attractions. Young ones frolic around under the watchful eye of the centre's staff members, while their parents can take a break and go for a cup of coffee or tea – or, perhaps, a game of billiards? … ■

✉ al. Pokoju 44
☎ +48 12 2909515

@ www.krakow.fantasypark.pl
🕐 10am–2am, Sun 11am–2am; playground Mon–Sat 10am–8pm, Sun 11am–8pm
€ bowling: PLN 54–94/hr, PLN 8–21 person/game; billiards: PLN 17–28/hr; playground: PLN 5–6/30mins, PLN 8–10/hr, PLN 15–18 with no time limit
🚌 1, 14, 22 (Kraków Plaza)
ℹ playground: free coffee or tea for child carers

Forteca Climbing Centre

With its 1,300 square metres of rock climbing walls (vertical and overhanging), 59 belay points, a 17-metre-tall tower with wrought iron holds and a bouldering panel, the "Fortress" Centre is a true paradise for climbers who do not want to stop practising because of bad weather or winter time. Climbing harnesses and shoes, as well as belay devices, are available for rental on the spot. Beginners are offered a free introduction training. The centre has sports and recreational sections, there is also a parachute section. ■

✉ ul. Racławicka 60
☎ +48 12 6328333
@ www.cwf.pl
🕐 10am–11pm daily
€ PLN 12–20 (PLN 9–15) with no time limit
🚌 130, 904 (Urząd Marszałkowski); 102, 130, 144, 194, 904 (Łobzów PKP); 102, 144, 194, 601 (Biprostal + 15 minutes on foot)
🚊 4, 8, 13, 14, 20, 24 (Biprostal + 15 minutes on foot)

Garden of Experiences

The Garden of Experiences (Ogród Doświadczeń) has a motto that goes: "What rules here? Physics does!" However, it is precisely those allergic even to the word "physics" who should drop in. The park is a perfect place to prove to anyone that this field of study can be truly fascinating. An area of 7 ha is home to a number of devices and installations which allow for a hands-on discovery of physical laws. Everyone may – and even should – act like a child, turning things around, peeping in, hitting and spilling. How could you ever get bored in the Garden of Experiences? ■

✉ *al. Pokoju 67*
☎ *+48 12 3641285*
@ *www.ogroddoswiadczen.pl*
🕐 *Apr 26–May: Mon–Fri 8.30am–7pm, Sat–Sun 10am–7pm; June–July: Mon–Fri 8.30am–8pm, Sat–Sun 10am–8pm; Aug: Mon–Fri 8.30am–7pm, Sat–Sun 10am–7pm; Sept: Mon–Fri 8.30am–5pm, Sat–Sun 10am–7pm; Oct: Mon–Fri 8.30am–3pm, Sat–Sun 10am–5pm*
€ *PLN 8 (PLN 5.50)*
🕐 *1, 14, 22 (M1 Al. Pokoju)*
ℹ️ *guided tours in English and French: PLN 15 (prior phone booking is necessary)*

Laser Arena

The basement of the former Forum hotel offers the possibility to play laser paintball. The game is completely safe. No paintballs are used; instead, guns shoot laser beams, which eliminates pain and bruises. Players wear special jackets with sensors that indicate every hit. An additional advantage is unlimited "ammunition." You can come here on your own, but it is always better to bring along a group of friends to make it even more fun. The gloomy atmosphere of the specially converted interior of an abandoned hotel is enhanced by flashing strobe lights and sombre music. By the hotel, there is a go-kart track (opened seasonally March–October, depending on the weather). ■

✉ *ul. Marii Konopnickiej 28 (former Forum hotel, entry from ul. Ludwinowska)*
☎ *+48 604423174, +48 664392681*
@ *www.laserarena.pl*
🕐 *noon–midnight daily (Mon–Fri noon–4pm and 10pm–midnight only upon prior reservation; Sat–Sun 10pm–midnight only upon prior reservation)*
€ *PLN 10–15/15 mins, PLN 20–25/30mins, PLN 30–40/hr*
🅑 *101, 112, 114, 116, 124, 128, 144, 156, 162, 164, 169, 173, 179, 184, 194, 424, 608, 609, 610 (Most Grunwaldzki)*
🕐 *12, 18, 19, 22 (Most Grunwaldzki)*

Reni-Sport

Though smaller than Forteca (➤214), the Reni-Sport climbing hall has many staunch regulars. It features vertical and overhanging walls, as well as a bouldering wall where there are no safety ropes but only crash pads. You can also practice… on the ceiling, which has holds and belay points. Children can start their climbing adventure with a low slab. It is possible to rent the equipment on site. Beginners are offered free introduction training. ■

✉ *ul. Czepca 11*
☎ *+48 12 6380734*
@ *www.renisport.pl*
🕐 *10am–11pm daily*
€ *PLN 10–20 (PLN 8–15)*
🕐 *4, 8, 13, 24 (Wesele)*

WRT-Karting

If you have ever dreamt of being a Formula One driver – just like Robert Kubica – you can practise some racing in Cracow's roofed karting track. It can hold up to six cars at a time; the fleet consists of Sodi karts with 6.5 horsepower engines. A ride takes eight minutes, but there should be no problem with arranging to make it longer. It is also possible to book a kart for an exact date and time. The disabled need permission from their legal guardians (accepted only in person). ■

✉ *ul. Nowolipki 3 (entry from ul. Makuszyńskiego)*
☎ *+48 511407247 (possible prior reservation)*
@ *www.krakow.wrt-karting.pl*
🕐 *Mon–Thu 2pm–11pm, Fri noon–11pm, Sat 11am–11pm, Sun 11am–10pm*
€ *PLN 20/8 mins, Mon–Thu: PLN 35/16 mins and PLN 50/24 mins*
🅑 *138, 182 (Nowolipki)*

Shopping

With its great shopping centres and bazaars, Cracow is a true paradise for buyers.

In Vogue

Some Cracow streets will practically make you dizzy with their multi-coloured shop windows. Shopping centres are always besieged with shoppers. There are also many boutiques with highly original vintage-style clothes.

The great popularity of Cracow's shopping centres is evidenced by their ever-growing number, and by the increasing crowds of shoppers. The centres are quiet in the morning, since most people come in the afternoon and at the weekend. You will find a variety of shops, from those offering youth fashion, through global chain stores, to luxury boutiques (especially at Galeria Krakowska ➤218). Galeria Kazimierz is the smallest and not as lively as the other centres, but you can end your shopping spree with a visit to the cinema; this is also possible at Bonarka City Center.

Most boutiques are clustered around Floriańska, Grodzka and Długa streets. Many shops sell largely the same selection of clothes and accessories, but there are also places with an unconventional assortment. Among such outstanding stores, one should mention Chorąży (➤218) – a hat and cap manufacturer. Today, it seems to be a sort of a living museum: since buying mass-produced headwear is easier and quicker, having hats and caps especially made to order is not common. Słoń Torbalski (➤219), in turn, offers quality handmade leather bags, recognised in Poland and abroad.

Fashion trends are often set by small shops with truly interesting products. Mulholland Drive (➤219) is a paradise on earth for vintage enthusiasts looking for old-style clothes and accessories. Treasures ferreted out from grandma's loft can be found at Maruna (➤219), a shop that sells handmade trinkets as well. Yet another stylish shop is Idea Fix Concept Store (➤218) with clothes created by young Polish designers (usually inspired by the clubbing culture). A totally differ-ent style – and price range – prevails at Likus Concept Store (➤218). This exclusive boutique in the Main Square (➤26) is a real treat for those who want to follow the latest trends. ∎

SHOPPING CENTRES

Bonarka City Center

The shopping facility is located in the converted building that housed a cement plant and then, after WWII, the Bonarka Chemical Works (closed in 2003). A factory chimney reminds one of the old industrial purpose of the place. The total surface area of the centre is as much as 234,000 square metres – almost six times the size of Cracow's Main Square (➤26). There is a cinema, 30 restaurants and over 250 shops (if you wanted to visit them all, it would certainly take a lot of walking). A major drawback is inconvenient access by public transport. ∎

✉ ul. Kamieńskiego 11
☎ +48 12 2986000
@ www.bonarkacitycenter.pl
🕐 10am–9pm daily
Ⓞ 164 (Puszkarska); 144, 173, 179, 184, 304 (Kamieńskiego)
ℹ free parking facility

Galeria Kazimierz

The two storeys of the shopping gallery in Kazimierz are brimming with shops selling clothes, jewellery, shoes, electronic appliances and cosmetics. Cracovians come here attracted by popular brands, the centre's convenient location, long opening hours, and the fact that it is cosier and less crowded than Galeria

Krakowska. The upper storey holds self-service restaurants and a cinema. ▪

✉ *ul. Podgórska 34*
☎ *+48 12 4330101*
@ *www.galeriakazimierz.pl*
🕐 *Mon–Sat 10am–10pm, Sun 10am–8pm*
🚌 *125, 128, 148, 184 (Rondo Grzegórzeckie)*
🚋 *1, 9, 11, 14, 20, 22, 50, 51*
   (Rondo Grzegórzeckie)
ℹ️ *free parking facility*

Galeria Krakowska

This is Cracow's largest shopping centre. It is tremendously popular and vibrant with life, always full of people because of the convenient location by the Local Coach Station and the Central Railway Station, and only a five-minute walk from the Main Square (➤ 26). The three storeys hold as many as 270 shops with electronic appliances, watches, jewellery, cosmetics and, above all, clothes of all sorts. The choice is impressive, from youth fashion, through sports shops, popular Polish and foreign brand stores, to luxury boutiques (Versace, Hugo Boss). The best bargains are offered in sales at the end of December and the beginning of January, when prices are reduced by 50 percent. ▪

✉ *ul. Pawia 5*
☎ *+48 12 4289900*
@ *www.galeria-krakowska.pl*
🕐 *Mon–Sat 9am–10pm, Sun 10am–9pm*
🚌 *124, 152, 424, 502, 522, 902, 904*
   (Dworzec Główny)
🚋 *2, 4, 7, 10, 12, 13, 14, 15, 19, 20, 24, 40*
   (Dworzec Główny)
ℹ️ *1st hour of parking is free, 2nd hour:*
   PLN 2, each subsequent hour: PLN 4

AVANTGARDE STYLE

Chorąży Hat and Cap Workshop

The "Standard-Bearer" workshop is part of yesterday's Cracow that is slowly becoming a thing of the past. This particu-

lar shop dates from 1990, but the family business of hat and cap production has been in operation since the beginning of the 20th century. You can either buy ready-made headware or have it made to order by professional milleners. ▪

✉ *ul. Krakowska 35*
☎ *+48 12 4306114*
@ *www.czapkichorazy.prv.pl*
🕐 *Mon–Fri 10am–5pm*
🚌 *304, 522, 904 (Plac Wolnica)*
🚋 *3, 6, 8, 10, 40 (Plac Wolnica)*

Idea Fix Concept Store

The place where you can find clothes fashioned by young Polish designers (T-shirts, tops, caps, etc.). Other products include colourful high trainers, handmade accessories, vinyls and CDs with Polish music, books… a real hotch-potch of merchandise. ▪

✉ *ul. Józefa 20*
☎ *+48 12 4275643*
@ *www.ideafix.pl*
🕐 *Mon–Fri noon–8pm, Sat–Sun noon–5pm*
🚋 *7, 9, 11, 13, 24, 50, 51 (Miodowa)*

Likus Concept Store

Lovers of luxury and splendour should visit Likus Concept Store – the chic boutiques in the basement of a building in the Main Square (➤ 26). There is a vinotheque, a restaurant and a delicatessen, as well as a shop with exclusive clothes, including brands such as Viktor&Rolf, Yves Saint Laurent and D&G. Prices are as high as could be expected. ▪

✉ *Rynek Główny 13*
☎ *+48 12 126170210*
@ *www.likusconceptstore.pl*
🕐 *Mon–Sat 11am–9pm, Sun 11am–6pm*
🚌 *124, 152, 424, 502, 522, 902, 904*
   (Dworzec Główny)
🚋 *2, 4, 7, 10, 12, 13, 14, 15, 19, 20, 24, 40*
   (Dworzec Główny)

Maruna

A colourful shop selling all sorts of things: female clothing and vintage-style handbags, old plush toys, handmade jewellery (strings of beads, brooches, earrings – even made from felt or Lego blocks). Most have been produced by artists that cooperate with Maruna. A place where you can buy a remarkable souvenir. ■

- ✉ ul. Miodowa 2
- ☎ +48 609916199
- @ www.maruna.pl
- 🕐 11am–7pm, Sun 11am–3pm (sometimes closed)
- Ⓑ 128, 184, 904 (Stradom)
- Ⓣ 3, 6, 8, 10, 12, 18, 19, 22, 40 (Stradom)

Mulholland Drive

Not long ago, the shop was housed on the first floor of a tenement located outside the tourist area of Kazimierz, but it soon gained sufficient popularity to move to the very centre of Cracow. Drop in to see an assortment of retro- and vintage-style clothes (both for men and women) – second-hand, but carefully selected and of very high quality. Nice and competent staff. ■

- ✉ ul. Sienna 1
- @ www.mulholanddrivestore.com
- 🕐 11am–8pm
- Ⓣ 1, 7, 10, 12, 13, 19, 24, 40 (Poczta Główna)

Słoń Torbalski

This outstanding shop with leather handbags is named after Słoń Trąbalski – an elephant character from a children's book – whose name was modified to include the word *torba* (Polish for "bag"). All the products sold here are handmade, which ensures their durability and a careful finish. Graduates of Cracow's Academy of Fine Art work on the design. The choice is truly impressive: you can choose between traditional and folk-style bags, rectangular and round-shaped. Some are plain and have a toned-down dark shade, other dazzle with an extravaganza of colour and pattern. Men's bags are also on offer. ■

- ✉ ul. Sławkowska 4
- ☎ +48 12 4216626
- @ www.slontorbalski.com
- 🕐 Mon–Fri 10am–7pm, Sat 10am–3pm
- Ⓑ 124, 152, 424, 902 (Basztowa LOT)
- Ⓣ 2, 3, 4, 7, 13, 14, 15, 20, 24 (Basztowa LOT)

Souvenirs to Bring Home

In search of souvenirs, most tourists head straight for the stalls inside the Sukiennice. But there are many more places in Cracow that offer interesting mementos, such as unique coffee-table books, posters and CDs.

Like centuries ago, the Sukiennice (➤28, ➤220) **is abuzz with activity and teeming with people.** It is mostly visited by tourists. The building that once served to sell cloth is now full of souvenirs, regional products and trinkets. It is also a good idea to leave the Main Square and head for places such as ul. Józefa (➤220) in Kazimierz. The street is a cluster of small shops and galleries that sell interesting paintings, jewellery, and unusual everyday items. In the city, there are also opportunities for buying antiques (e.g. ESTE Gallery of Curiosities ➤221), as well as products made of porcelain (see: Mila ➤220) and amber.

Ulica Józefa

Ul. Józefa is one of the most attractive streets in the Kazimierz district, a true paradise for lovers of colourful knickknacks, souvenirs, and pieces of art.

The street accommodates a number of shops with original handmade jewellery (earrings, rings, necklaces, etc.). It is amazing how many charming ornaments can be created from odd pieces of fabric, building blocks, felt and wood. Ul. Józefa is also home to antique shops, galleries (for example, the motley-coloured Galeria d'Art Naif) and functional art stores, where everyday items such as metal mugs with imprints are given a soul of their own. A walk down the street is like a journey into another, rainbow-coloured world.

🕐 7, 9, 11, 13, 24, 50, 51 (Miodowa)

In the Middle Ages, Cracow was the intellectual centre of Poland. 1364 saw the establishment of Poland's first university; 1473 was the year that the first Polish print shop was founded. Forty years later, in 1513, the first book written entirely in Polish was published. From the 15th century to the first half of the 17th century, Cracow was the only Polish town to sell books – a luxury at that time. A historic building in the Main Square has been home to Europe's first bookshop (now Matras Bookshop ➤ 222). The Main Square has more places related to literature: a few houses away, there is the Hetmańska Bookshop (➤ 221), which features a medieval vaulted ceiling. The House of Albums (➤ 222), in turn, has a modern-style interior and a wide offer of picture album publications in many different fields.

Cracow also boasts Poland's best shop with artistic posters. The Cracow Poster Gallery (➤ 221) is certainly one of the most original places in the city. Music fans will not get bored, either (see: Music Corner ➤ 222). Those fond of plush toys should definitely visit the Bukowski Gallery (➤ 221). For a laugh, go see the cartoons at the Andrzej Mleczko Gallery (➤ 221). ▪

SOUVENIRS

Mila

The shop specialises in ceramic, porcelain, faience and crystal ware. It offers a wide choice of service sets, also in single pieces, from recognised producers in Poland and abroad. There are also artistic items (for example, decorated with Swarovski crystals). ▪

✉ ul. Sławkowska 14
☎ +48 12 4224082
@ www.mila.zaprasza.net
🕐 Mon–Fri 10am–6pm, Sat 10am–2pm
Ⓞ 124, 152, 424, 902 (Basztowa LOT)
🚊 2, 3, 4, 7, 13, 14, 15, 20, 24 (Basztowa LOT)

Sukiennice Stalls

A great number of souvenir stalls attracts a lot of tourists, and the atmosphere enchants even the most reluctant of shoppers. A great variety of products to choose from, sparkling trinkets on offer, and – above all – enthusiastic crowds make one inadvertently join in the shopping spree. You can be sure of the good quality of merchandise, whether made of leather, glass, or wood. There are a lot of paintings, regional costumes, tablecloths and tableware, not to mention a vast assortment of jewellery (with amber and other stones). ▪

✉ Rynek Główny
🕐 9am–8pm
Ⓞ 124, 152, 424, 502, 522, 902, 904 (Dworzec Główny)
🚊 2, 4, 7, 10, 12, 13, 14, 15, 19, 20, 24, 40 (Dworzec Główny)

GALLERIES

Andrzej Mleczko Gallery

Andrzej Mleczko is one of the best-known satirists in Poland, famous mostly for his cartoons. In 1982 (the time of Martial Law), he could not publish them, so he decided to found his own gallery in Cracow. On offer are Mleczko's original works as well as their reproductions – also on mugs, cushions, T-shirts, and even boxer shorts. The author himself appears at the gallery quite often, and you can ask for his autograph on the purchased product. ■

✉ ul. św. Jana 14
☎ +48 12 4217104
@ www.mleczko.pl
🕓 Mon–Fri 10am–6pm, Sun 10am–3pm
Ⓑ 124, 152, 424, 902 (Basztowa LOT)
Ⓣ 2, 3, 4, 7, 13, 14, 15, 20, 24 (Basztowa LOT)

Bukowski Gallery

The company specialises in the production of plush toys, recognised all around Europe. The sheer number of toy animals makes one feel dizzy, and it is not only children that get a bit carried away here. You will be spoilt for choice among the (more or less) fluffy teddy bears, bunnies, elks, kittens and puppies of different sizes. Bears are handmade, and every model has a name of its own. ■

✉ ul. Sienna 1
☎ +48 12 4338855
@ www.galeriabukowski.pl
🕓 Mon–Fri 10am–7pm, Sat–Sun 10am–6pm
Ⓣ 1, 7, 10, 12, 13, 19, 24, 40 (Poczta Główna)

Cracow Poster Gallery

The only shop in Poland that specialises in posters designed by Polish artists. There are over 2,000 titles in different thematic categories (cinema, theatre, opera, exhibitions, political and social campaigns, archive materials). You will find here works by internationally acclaimed Polish artists such as Henryk Tomaszewski, Franciszek Starowieyski, Jan Lenica and Waldemar Świerzy. ■

✉ ul. Stolarska 8-10
☎ +48 12 4212640
@ www.cracowpostergallery.com
🕓 Mon–Fri 11am–6pm, Sat 11am–2pm
Ⓣ 1, 3, 6, 8, 18 (Plac Wszystkich Świętych)

ESTE Gallery of Curiosities

The name perfectly sums up the character of the place. The products on offer do not fall under one category. They include both antiques and recent artistic works, created mostly on paper (such as drawings and prints), as well as jewellery and shells. ■

✉ ul. Grodzka 36
☎ +48 12 4291984
🕓 Mon–Fri 10am–6pm, Sat 10am–2pm
Ⓣ 1, 3, 6, 8, 18 (Plac Wszystkich Świętych)

BOOKSHOPS AND MUSIC STORES

Hetmańska Bookshop

Go inside even if you are not keen on books – the shop is located in one of the oldest preserved houses in the Main Square (➤26). It still boasts the original Gothic vaulted ceiling and the decorative keystones that date from the latter 14th century. This is certainly an extraordinary setting for buying a book (album titles are also available). ■

✉ Rynek Główny 17
☎ +48 12 4302453
🕓 Mon–Sat 9am–9pm, Sun 11am–9pm
Ⓑ 124, 152, 424, 502, 522, 902, 904 (Dworzec Główny)
Ⓣ 1, 3, 6, 8, 18 (Plac Wszystkich Świętych); 2, 4, 7, 10, 12, 13, 14, 15, 19, 20, 24, 40 (Dworzec Główny)

House of Albums

Among the many bookshops in Cracow, this place is one of the kind: it sells only album titles. The subject matter varies between architecture, travelling, fashion, religion, dancing, photography, etc. The choice is very impressive. Even more importantly, all the publications are characterised by the highest editing quality. There is a large offer of books in English. Prices are rather high, but it is a good idea to drop in for the pure pleasure of browsing. ■

- ✉ ul. Zwierzyniecka 17
- ☎ +48 12 4291363
- @ www.houseofalbums.pl
- 🕐 Mon–Sat 11am–7pm
- Ⓑ 304, 522 (Filharmonia)
- Ⓣ 1, 2, 3, 6, 8, 18 (Filharmonia)

Matras Bookshop

At No. 23 in the Main Square (➤26), books were sold as early as 1610; it was probably the first regular bookshop in Europe. The site is still home to a book-selling facility which holds strong in spite of the generally diminishing reading statistics. Shelves are groaning under the weight of paper- and hardbacks, and the place is always crowded with fans of many different types of literature

(including specialist and album publications). A small table in the first room holds books autographed by Polish authors. ■

- ✉ Rynek Główny 23
- ☎ +48 12 4226089
- 🕐 Mon–Fri 9am–8pm, Sat 10am–6pm, Sun 11am–5pm
- Ⓑ 124, 152, 304, 424, 502, 522, 902 (Teatr Bagatela)
- Ⓣ 1, 3, 6, 8, 18 (Plac Wszystkich Świętych); 2, 3, 4, 8, 13, 14, 15, 20, 24 (Teatr Bagatela)

Music Corner

This is probably the best music shop in Cracow, very well stocked with CDs that represent practically every type of music. Particularly impressive is the choice of rock (in all its various forms) and jazz albums. Vinyls are also available. Exceptionally competent staff members will help you make the most of your visit. ■

- ✉ ul. św. Tomasza 4
- ☎ +48 12 4220803
- @ www.musiccorner.pl
- 🕐 Mon–Sat 11am–8pm
- Ⓑ 124, 152, 424, 902 (Basztowa LOT)
- Ⓣ 2, 3, 4, 7, 13, 14, 15, 20, 24 (Basztowa LOT)

Culinary Specialities

There is more to the local cuisine than Cracow bagels. The city is known for other products that will please gourmet palates: *lisiecka* sausage, chocolate treats, and all sorts of food made with traditional recipes.

Cracow has many shops that offer specialities prepared according to the old tried-and-tested recipes. The market has been taken by storm by the Krakowski Kredens food brand, bringing back the historic taste of Galicia. Other highly popular products are the so-called Produkty Benedyktyńskie, prepared in the Benedictine Abbey in Tyniec (➤167); the monks certainly know their art, and the recipes they guard are often centuries' old. The Benedictines offer preserves, cheese, tinctures, etc.

Almost any *charcuterie* shop sells two types of sausage, both named after Cracow. The first one (usually dry and dense) is simply called *krakowska*, which is an adjective derived from the Polish name of the city. The other one, *podwawelska* (derived from Wawel), is good for heating in a frying pan or a bonfire. Yet another type is *lisiecka* sausage, produced in the village of Liszki near Cracow. The meat processing plant located there managed to survive the post-war regime, hostile to private businesses. Equally highly valued is the sausage produced by the company of Stanisław Mądry in Nowa Wieś Szlachecka. Its characteristic flavour is the result of using not minced, but chopped meat. Thus, the sausage consists of relatively large chunks of lean meat, seasoned with garlic. This product is available at some deli and health food shops.

Wawel designates not only the hill topped with Poland's best-known castle. It is also the name of a company that has been producing sweets and chocolate products for more than a century (➤ 224). Franz Joseph of Austria himself was said to appreciate the taste of Wawel chocolates, giving them to his grandchildren. Those with a sweet tooth should also visit a café shop called Ciasteczka z Krakowa, popular with Cracovians and tourists alike. ▪

Ciasteczka z Krakowa

Handmade "Cracow pastries" are not only a delicious treat to go with your after-dinner coffee; they are also an interesting gift or souvenir from the city. There is a very wide choice (jam, chocolate, hazelnut, etc.), and most types of pastries can be bought by weight. At your request, the staff will provide a special packaging decorated with photos of Cracow. On site, you can also take a seat in a small café to savour the pastries you have just bought, washing them down with a cup of tea or coffee. ▪

✉ *ul. św. Tomasza 21*
☎ *+48 12 4232227*
@ *www.ciasteczkazkrakowa.pl*
🕐 *Mon–Sat 9am–8pm, Sun 10am–8pm*
🚌 *124, 152, 424, 502, 522, 902, 904 (Dworzec Główny)*
🚊 *2, 4, 7, 10, 12, 13, 14, 15, 19, 20, 24, 40 (Dworzec Główny)*

Krakowski Kredens

The "Cracow Pantry" chain offers high quality food products, mostly prepared by small family companies – often to the special order of the Krakowski Kredens brand. They are very tasteful in terms of flavour (attributable to the old Galician recipes) as well as packaging. On offer are *charcuterie* and dairy products, fruit and vegetable preserves, liqueurs, sweets, and many other delicacies. ▪

✉ *ul. Grodzka 7*
☎ *+48 12 4238159*
@ *www.krakowskikredens.pl*
🕐 *Mon–Fri 10am–8pm, Sat 11am–7pm, Sun 11am–6pm*
🚊 *1, 3, 6, 8, 18 (Plac Wszystkich Świętych)*

Produkty Benedyktyńskie

The monks at the Benedictine Abbey in Tyniec (➤ 167) certainly know a thing or two both about the matters of spirit and the well-being of the body. Their shops offer several hundred products: cheese, *charcuterie*, jam, pasta, beer, tinctures, all made with natural ingredients. Of course, it is not just the monks who are involved in the preparation of these goodies, which are also made by individuals and small private companies in accordance with old traditional recipes under the supervision of the Benedictines. ▪

✉ *ul. Krakowska 29*
☎ *+48 12 4220216*
🕐 *Mon–Fri 9am–6pm, Sat 9am–2pm*
🚌 *128, 184, 904 (Stradom)*
🚊 *3, 6, 8, 10, 12, 18, 19, 22, 40 (Stradom)*

Szambelan

The "Chamberlain" is an off-licence with a difference. Its impressive stock includes mead, tinctures and liqueurs prepared in accordance with traditional formulas. Alcohol is kept in demijohns and poured into bottles of different shapes and sizes upon purchasing. Teetotallers can buy quality olive oil and vinegar. ■

✉ ul. Gołębia 2
☎ +48 12 6287093
@ www.szambelan.pl
🕐 Mon–Thu 10am–9pm, Fri–Sat 10am–10pm, Sun 11am–7pm
🚋 1, 3, 6, 8, 18 (Plac Wszystkich Świętych)

Wawel

This confectionery company ranks among the best-known in Poland. Dating back to 1898, it is now an up-to-date listed company, specialising mainly in chocolate products. You should try excellent filled pralines, especially the vastly popular Malaga and Kasztanki varieties. Equally delicious are Wawel hard candies, such as Raczki and Kukułki (with cocoa and liquor filling). ■

✉ Rynek Główny 33
☎ +48 12 4231247
@ www.wawel.com.pl
🕐 10am–7pm
🚌 124, 152, 304, 424, 502, 522, 902 (Teatr Bagatela)
🚋 2, 3, 4, 8, 13, 14, 15, 20, 24 (Teatr Bagatela)

The Fair-Tale of Cracow

The city's public markets were first mentioned in the 12th century. Merchants used to trade in the Main Square. Today's marketplaces are visited by crowds of people and can still compete with the ever-expanding hypermarkets.

The smell of fresh vegetables, multi-coloured flowers, tasty *charcuterie* and dairy products – each of these is reason enough to go to a marketplace, a shopping option that is still very popular among Cracovians who look for quality food. Some stallholders offer home-grown produce (e.g., in the Old Kleparz ➤16, ➤225). You will find it hard to resist fine fruit piled up on stands, or stop thinking about a delicious soup or salad when the air is filled with the aroma of fresh vegetables. Other merchandise includes flowers (in New Kleparz ➤225) and household articles. An additional advantage of some marketplaces is their convenient location. Pl. Nowy (➤86, ➤225), for example, is like the centre of the Jewish Kazimierz, equally charming as the Old Kleparz (hemmed in by tenement houses).

On particular weekdays, some of the squares of Cracow are taken over by flea markets. Traders arrange their goods on stalls, makeshift counters constructed with tables or wooden boxes, and blankets spread on the grass. You will find here a variety of things you probably did not know you needed at all: old bathroom fittings, bikes, lamps, paintings, mirrors, candlesticks, and many other second-hand products. Expert "treasure hunters" can find genuine gems. Squeezing through the crowd, looking for bargains and haggling over the price is a memorable though peculiar experience. If you want to live it, go on a Saturday morning to pl. Nowy in Kazimierz, or on a Sunday morning to Unitarg – a popular "market hall" in the Grzegórzki district.

Potential customers should take into account the fact that the opening hours given below are only approximate. If a marketplace begins to empty before the closing time, stallholders leave as well. It is better to come before lunchtime if you want to see a marketplace at its busiest, with most stands open, not closed. ■

New Kleparz

New Kleparz (Nowy Kleparz) was founded much later than the Old Kleparz. It is also considerably more modern in style with its rows of small shops. The choice of goods on offer, however, is definitely conventional: fruit, vegetables, and dairy produce. There is also an assortment of wicker and household products. Looking from the direction of al. Słowackiego, you will see the trademark view – flower stalls located close to the main entrance of the marketplace. ■

🕐 Mon–Fri 7am–6pm, Sat 7am–4pm
🚌 114, 115, 130, 132, 139, 154, 159, 164, 169, 179, 192, 208, 257, 277, 292, 501, 904 (Nowy Kleparz)
🚊 3, 7 (Nowy Kleparz)

Plac Nowy

Market traders arrange their wares on the canopied folding stalls around the square. Cracovians come here to buy fresh fruit and vegetables; dairy and meat products are sold in the square's round building (Okrąglak). On summer afternoons, you can even buy jewellery, sunglasses, and second-hand books. Tuesday and Friday mornings (6am–9am) see the selling of small animals such as doves, a scene that is becoming more and more rare. Antique fairs are held on Saturday mornings, while Sunday mornings attract those interested in clothes, including second-hand bargains. See also: ➤ 86. ■

🕐 6am–3pm
🚊 7, 9, 11, 13, 24, 50, 51 (Miodowa)

Old Kleparz

The long and narrow alleyways of Old Kleparz (Stary Kleparz) are lined with tables and boxes with piles of tomatoes, aubergines, broccoli, cranberries, apples, pears and figs. Vivid colours and strong aromas of fruit and vegetables that fill the air put one in a mood for shopping. There are also dairy stands selling different types of regional cheese specialities: curd cheese, oscypek (smoked cheese made of salted sheep milk), and bunc (mild sheep milk cheese); stallholders give their word that all these "delicacies" are homemade. In addition, the marketplace offers meat and charcuterie products, as well as freshly picked mushrooms (seasonally). See also: ➤ 16. ■

🕐 Mon–Sat 7am–6pm; on Sun, some stalls do not open, and the rest close early in the afternoon
🚌 124, 152, 424, 902 (Basztowa LOT)
🚊 2, 3, 4, 7, 13, 14, 15, 20, 24 (Basztowa LOT)

Unitarg

For Cracovians, Unitarg is simply the "market hall." From Monday to Friday, the place is like any other marketplace, selling fresh vegetables, fruit, sweets, meat and dairy products; you will also find a lot of flowers to choose from. Unitarg is usually quite crowded, but most people are attracted by Sunday morning flea markets, when they can take a look at antiques, second-hand items, household goods, knick-knacks, and bikes. ■

✉ ul. Grzegórzecka
🕐 6am–4pm daily
🚌 128, 184 (Hala Targowa)
🚊 1, 9, 11, 22, 50, 51 (Hala Targowa)

Festivals and Events Calendar

JANUARY

Grand Finale of the Great Orchestra of Christmas Charity

On the first or the second Sunday each year, the charity foundation called Wielka Orkiestra Świątecznej Pomocy (WOŚP) organises free concerts in towns and cities all over Poland. Throughout the day, WOŚP volunteers collect money to purchase specialist equipment mainly for the infant wards at Polish hospitals, to finance medical tests and education programmes. The main concert venue in Cracow is the Main Square (➤ 26). Crowds gather despite the (usually) freezing temperatures. ■

✉ Rynek Główny

Ⓑ 124, 152, 424, 502, 522, 601, 605, 608, 609, 610, 614, 618, 902, 904 (Dworzec Główny)

Ⓣ 2, 4, 7, 10, 12, 13, 14, 15, 19, 20, 24, 40 (Dworzec Główny)

FEBRUARY

Shanties, the International Sailors' Song Festival

Cracow's shanty festival has rocked the boat every last week of February for over 30 years. Most concerts are held in the Rotunda club. The music of "sea dogs," streams of beer (and rum) make the participants' high spirits even higher. The festival is attended by the best Polish and foreign bands. It remains a mystery why it is Cracow, so far from lakes, seas and oceans, that has become the venue for one of the greatest shanty festivals not only in Poland, but the whole of Europe. Still, why should location matter more than a high artistic level? ■

✉ most concerts are held in the Rotunda club at ul. Oleandry 1

@ www.shanties.pl

€ concert ticket: PLN 20–40, festival pass: approx. PLN 220

Ⓑ 109, 114, 124, 134, 144, 164, 169, 173, 179, 192, 194, 292, 409, 502, 608, 610, 618 (Cracovia)

Ⓣ 15, 18 (Oleandry)

MARCH

Animated Films Festival

The Polish National Festival of Authors' Animated Films (Ogólnopolski Festiwal Autorskich Filmów Animowanych, OFAFA) has been held in Cracow since 1993. This is a very prestigious event for Polish artists. Among the participants, one can find names such as Marek Skrobecki, a co-creator of the Oscar-winning *Peter & the Wolf* (2006). ■

@ www.ofafa.pl

Three Elements – the Travellers' Festival

For three days in mid-March (from Friday to Sunday), those keen on exploring the Earth – from the air, the water and the land – meet in the Nowa Huta Cultural Centre to listen to talks, meet experienced Polish

---

The City's What Where When

Cracow boasts a large number of cultural events: festivals, concerts, shows, film reviews, exhibitions, meetings with important personages, fairs… You will need some help finding your way through the impressive offer.

The exact dates of most cyclical events are set well in advance; they usually change slightly every year. Naturally, Cracow also holds less celebrated one-time events. If you want to check for the upcoming happenings and be well informed on their exact time and place, take a look inside the *Karnet* magazine (available free at many restaurants, cafés, hotels, museums and InfoKraków points), or visit their website.

@ www.karnet.krakow.pl

globetrotters, watch travel films and vote for the best one. Other attractions include exhibitions of photos from far and away, and a number of workshops (photography, among others). ∎

- ✉ al. Jana Pawła II 232
- ☎ +48 12 6440266
- @ www.3zywioly.pl
- € 1-day ticket: PLN 15–30; 3-day pass: PLN 65; some events are free
- Ⓑ 121, 163, 174, 463, 501, 502, 522, 601, 608, 609 (Plac Centralny)
- Ⓣ 4, 15, 16, 17, 21, 22 (Plac Centralny)

The March of the Living on the anniversary of the Ghetto liquidation ends in the former Płaszów Camp (➤ 116).

March of the Living

Every year, on the Sunday closest to March 14 – the anniversary of the Ghetto liquidation – the March of the Living sets off from pl. Bohaterów Getta (➤ 106). The route runs along the following streets: Na Zjeździe, Lwowska, Limanowskiego, Jerozolimska. The end is the former Płaszów Camp (➤ 116), where the *Kaddish* – the Jewish prayer for the dead – is said at the foot of the Monument to the Nazi Victims. People who take part are ordinary Cracovians, representatives of the city authorities, and foreign visitors (from Israel, for example). The exact time and date of the March are announced in advance on posters put up around the city. ∎

- ✉ pl. Bohaterów Getta
- Ⓣ 7, 9, 11, 13, 24, 50, 51 (Plac Bohaterów Getta)
- ✉ former Płaszów Camp
- Ⓑ 144, 173, 184 (Makowa); when the celebrations end, a dedicated free bus service runs back to pl. Bohaterów Getta; 108, 127, 158, 163, 174, 178, 522 (Powstańców Wielkopolskich); 107, 143, 174, 243, 301, 463, 522 (Dworcowa); 144, 173, 179, 184, 304 (Kamieńskiego)

APRIL

Misteria Paschalia Festival

This is a major European festival devoted to Renaissance and Baroque music. It is linked to the celebrations of Easter – the central Christian feast: concerts are held during Holy Week leading up to Resurrection Sunday. The festival features famous conductors and acclaimed early music ensembles. The venues are the Cracow Philharmonic (➤ 205), the salt mine in Wieliczka (➤ 172), and some of the city's churches such as the one devoted to St Catherine (➤ 96). Tickets always sell like hot cakes. ∎

- @ www.misteriapaschalia.pl
- 🕐 concerts start between 7pm and 10pm
- € PLN 80–200

Cracow Philharmonic (Filharmonia)
- ✉ ul. Zwierzyniecka 1
- Ⓑ 304, 522 (Filharmonia)
- Ⓣ 1, 2, 3, 6, 8, 18 (Filharmonia)

Salt Mine in Wieliczka (Kopalnia Soli „Wieliczka")
- ✉ ul. Daniłowicza 10
- Ⓑ 204, 244, 304, 904 (Wieliczka Kopalnia Soli)

Anniversary of the Death of John Paul II

At 9.37pm on April 2 – the anniversary of the death of John Paul II – crowds gather under the "Pope's Window" at ul. Franciszkańska 3 (➤ 33) to commemorate the late Polish-born Pontiff. They pray and sing together, lighting candles in front of the Franciscan Basilica (➤ 33). ■

✉ ul. Franciszkańska 3
🕐 1, 3, 6, 8, 18 (Plac Wszystkich Świętych)

Off Plus Camera – the International Festival of Independent Cinema

The festival is gaining popularity every year, boasting such big-name attendees as director Peter Weir and actor Tim Roth. Polish and foreign feature films (also from continents other than Europe and America) are shown mostly in small art houses. You should also check out the particularly attractive rooftop screenings. ■

@ www.offpluscamera.com

MAY

Juwenalia

The beginning of the month (the week following the Polish national holiday of May 3) sees the annual student festival of Juwenalia. The first festival concerts in clubs around Cracow take place on Tuesday, but it is only on Friday that the municipal authorities hand the city keys over to students (who wield symbolic power until Sunday). The ceremony is preceded by a colourful procession of students from the car park in ul. Reymonta to the Main Square (➤ 26). Participants wear weird costumes; in the past, one could see, for example, Superman, Vikings, and huge bees. There are also open-air concerts. The festival programme is usually very varied. ■

@ www.juwenalia.krakow.pl
📍 the procession starts on Friday at 10am
🚌 the car park in ul. Reymonta can be reached on bus lines Nos. 139, 144, 159, 173, 194, 208 (Kawiory)

St Stanislaus Procession

This procession is one of the oldest traditions in Cracow. It has been held since the canonisation of the patron of Poland in 1253. The only time the processions did not take place was WWII, when they were banned by the Nazis.

Every year on the first Sunday following May 8 (St Stanislaus Day), the faithful proceed through the city carrying the Saint's relics. They start in Wawel Cathedral (➤ 46), where St Stanislaus is buried, and head for the Pauline Basilica on Skałka Hill (➤ 95) where he is believed to have been murdered. The holy relics of St Hyacinth, St Florian, St Faustina (among other saints) are also carried in the ceremonial procession. Among the believers you will see people wearing Cracovian costumes and members of a shooting association called the Brotherhood of the Rooster (Bractwo Kurkowe) in their traditional robes. ■

Wawel Cathedral (Katedra na Wawelu)
🕐 3, 6, 8, 10, 18, 19, 40 (Wawel)

Pauline Basilica on Skałka Hill (Bazylika Paulinów na Skałce)
✉ ul. Skałeczna 15
🚌 304, 522, 614, 904 (Plac Wolnica)
🕐 3, 6, 8, 10, 40 (Plac Wolnica)

Photomonth

At the end of May and the beginning of June, for a whole month, Cracow turns into the Polish capital of photography. The programme includes meetings with famous photographers, as well as photo exhibitions, vernissages and film screenings at Cracow's galleries, clubs and the Museum of the History of Photography. You can also submit your portfolio for professional

On the first Saturday of June, Cracow is taken over by dragons who parade the streets.

assessment and take part in photography and photo editing workshops (prior online registration is required). ■

Photomonth (Miesiąc Fotografii)
@ www.photomonth.com

Muzeum Historii Fotografii im. Walerego Rzewuskiego (Walery Rzewuski Museum of History of Photography)
✉ ul. Józefitów 16
☎ +48 12 6345932
@ www.mhf.krakow.pl
🕐 Wed–Fri 11am–6pm, Sat–Sun 10am–3.30pm
€ PLN 8 (PLN 5), free on Sun
Ⓑ 114, 139, 159, 164, 169, 179, 192, 208, 292, 501, 601, 610 (Plac Inwalidów)
Ⓣ 4, 8, 13, 14, 20, 24 (Plac Inwalidów)

JUNE

Great Dragon Parade

You had better watch out – dragons walk the streets of Cracow on the first Saturday of June. They advance along ul. Grodzka to the Main Square (➤ 26). The tradition was started by a marionette theatre called Groteska (➤ 202). Also schools and community centres present their own self-made dragons, often of enormous dimensions. The finest one is chosen in the Main Square. In the evening, there are open-air light and sound shows by the Vistula's bend (in Bulwary Wiślane, close to Wawel Hill). Dragons, of course, play the main part. ■

@ www.paradasmokow.pl
🕐 parade: about noon–2pm; show by the Vistula's bend: about 9.30pm
Ⓑ Main Square: 124, 152, 424, 502, 522, 902, 904 (Dworzec Główny)
Ⓣ Rynek: 2, 4, 7, 10, 12, 13, 14, 15, 19, 20, 24, 40 (Dworzec Główny); vicinity of the boulevards: 3, 6, 8, 10, 18, 19, 40 (Wawel)

St John's Fair and Midsummer Night Festival

Around St John's Night (June 23–24), Cracow holds a several-day fair called Jarmark Świętojański. Bulwary Czerwieńskie near Wawel Hill (➤ 40) turn into a medieval village. Tourists can observe the armour making process, shoot with a bow, learn dancing and swordsmanship, and dine on roast meat. The culmination of the festival is the so-called Wreaths (Wianki) – one big open-air Midsummer Night party in Bulwary Wiślane. It combines the tradition of the Slavic pagan Kupala Day – when

The Jewish Culture Festival is a real treat for music lovers.

young people would float flower wreaths topped with candles down the river – and the Christian St John's Night. An open-air show and a free concert (given by big names such as Lenny Kravitz) is held by the Vistula's bend. ■

✉ *Bulwar Czerwieński and the Vistula's bend*
@ *www.wianki.krakow.pl*
🕐 *from 11am until dusk*
🚃 *3, 6, 8, 10, 18, 19, 40 (Wawel)*

Jewish Culture Festival

The festival in Cracow – one of the largest of its kind in the world – takes place at the end of June and the beginning of July. For ten days, Kazimierz (➤68) plays host to thousands of international visitors.

Numerous concerts make the district resound with a variety of tunes, from klezmer to contemporary music. The festival ends with the open-air concert called the Shalom in Szeroka Street (Szalom na Szerokiej), attended by crowds of people. You can also take part in meetings, presentations, workshops (dancing and singing in the Yiddish language,) as well as Jewish-interest sightseeing tours. ■

✉ *Kazimierz*
@ *www.jewishfestival.pl*
€ *workshops, tours, concerts, etc.: PLN 10–200*
🚃 *7, 9, 11, 13, 24, 50, 51 (Miodowa)*

Małopolska Air Picnic

The festival for aviation fans of all ages. The

last weekend of June sees a two-day air picnic held by the Polish Aviation Museum at the otherwise closed airfield in Czyżyny (approx. 9 km to the east of the city centre). New and vintage aircraft are presented. The most awaited attraction is, of course, a show of aerobatic manoeuvres. ■

✉ *Muzeum Lotnictwa Polskiego (Polish Aviation Museum), al. Jana Pawła II 39*
☎ *+48 12 6409960*
@ *www.pikniklotniczy. krakow.pl*
€ *PLN 15 (PLN 8)*
🚌 *124, 424, 601 (Wieczysta), 159, 172, 501 (Bora-Komorowskiego)*
🚃 *4, 5, 9, 10, 12, 15, 40 (Wieczysta)*

JULY

International Festival of Street Theatre

For a few days in July, Cracow's Main Square (➤26) becomes the setting for street art shows from Poland and abroad. Some are also staged in Mały Rynek (➤57) and the Planty (➤53). Performances are held during the day and in the evening. Breaking with standard theatrical conventions, using the open-air scenery of the Main Square, and combining spectacles with interactive elements are some of the features that make the festival a memorable experience. ▪

✉ Main Square, Mały Rynek, Planty

Ⓑ 124, 152, 424, 502, 522, 601, 605, 608, 609, 610, 614, 618, 902, 904 (Dworzec Główny)

Ⓣ 2, 4, 7, 10, 12, 13, 14, 15, 19, 20, 24, 40 (Dworzec Główny)

Summer Jazz Festival

The programme of the one-month festival comprises several dozen concerts given by musicians from Poland and abroad. The central venue is the legendary Piwnica pod Baranami (➤207). Concerts are held in the city's other clubs as well, the final ones are also performed in the Cracow Opera House (➤205). ▪

@ www.cracjazz.com
€ concerts: PLN 20–60

AUGUST

Pierogi Festival

On a mid-August weekend, Mały Rynek (➤57) is filled with the appetising aroma of boiled and fried Polish dumplings (*pierogi*). The restaurants of Cracow compete for an annual challenge prize of Casimir the Great, awarded by the public, and the jury-awarded prize of St Hyacinth with *Pierogi* (the statuette depicts a white-robed friar holding a bowl of dumplings). The festival is a great chance to try this traditional Polish speciality served in a variety of ways: sweet, sour, savoury, spicy (PLN 1.5–2 per dumpling). ▪

✉ Mały Rynek

Ⓑ 609, 614, 904 (Poczta Główna); 124, 152, 424, 502, 522, 601, 605, 608, 609, 610, 614, 618, 902, 904 (Dworzec Główny)

Ⓣ 1, 7, 10, 12, 13, 19, 24, 40 (Poczta Główna); 2, 4, 7, 10, 12, 13, 14, 15, 19, 20, 24, 40 (Dworzec Główny)

Coke Live Music Festival

Held towards the end of August, the Coke Live Music Festival ranks among the largest in Poland. It targets especially those music fans who stay up to date on global trends in popular music. The festival has seen performances from the Chemical Brothers, 50 Cent, Muse and The Prodigy. There are three stages, and almost 30 hours of concerts in just two festival days. ▪

✉ grounds of the Polish Aviation Museum at al. Jana Pawła II 39

@ www.livefestival.pl

€ 1-day ticket: PLN 125; 2-day pass: PLN 225

Ⓑ 159, 172, 501 (Bora-Komorowskiego)

SEPTEMBER

Cracow Jazz Autumn

Jazz in Cracow stays strong, as borne out by an enormous popularity of the Jazz Autumn. The organiser is the Alchemia club (➤206), evidently inspired by Piwnica pod Baranami and its Summer Jazz Festival (➤231). The Cracow Jazz Festival usually begins in mid-September and lasts until the end of November. During that time, a large number of excellent concerts are given by Polish and international jazz stars. This is a real feast for music lovers and enthusiasts of atmospheric bar concerts. ▪

✉ ul. Estery 5

☎ +48 12 4212200

@ www.alchemia.com.pl

€ PLN 35–60

Ⓣ 7, 9, 11, 13, 24, 50, 51 (Miodowa); 3, 6, 8, 10, 12, 18, 19, 22, 40 (Stradom)

Sacrum Profanum

This is one of the most interesting and original festivals in Cracow. It combines 20th century classical music with other genres (represented, for example, by Aphex Twin, Jonny Greenwood of Radiohead and Adrian Utley of Portishead). Each edition focuses on a different country and its composers. The venues themselves are worth a visit: the Museum of Urban Engineering, the Łaźnia Nowa Theatre, and the Electrolytic Tinning Plant at the Arcelor Mittal Poland (the former Tadeusz Sendzimir Steelworks ➤ 122). ■

@ www.sacrumprofanum.com
€ PLN 40–180

Museum of City Engineering (Muzeum Inżynierii Miejskiej)
✉ ul. Wawrzyńca 15
Ⓑ 304, 522, 614, 904 (Plac Wolnica)
Ⓣ 3, 6, 8, 10, 40 (Plac Wolnica); 7, 9, 11, 13, 24, 50, 51 (Św. Wawrzyńca)

Łaźnia Nowa Theatre (Teatr Łaźnia Nowa)
✉ os. Szkolne 25
Ⓑ 113, 123, 132, 139, 142, 153, 163, 172, 463, 501, 601 (Struga)
Ⓣ 4, 16, 21, 22 (Struga)

Arcelor Mittal Poland
✉ ul. Ujastek 1
Ⓑ 117, 132, 138, 139, 142, 149, 163, 172, 174, 211, 242, 463, 501, 601, 604, 609 (Kombinat)
Ⓣ 4, 16, 21, 22 (Kombinat)

OCTOBER

Organ and Harpsichord Music Days

Four days in late October see a series of concerts presenting classical and contemporary works that highlight the qualities of both instruments, from solo recitals to oratorios. Some events are accompanied by wine tastings. ■

Cracow Philharmonic (Filharmonia Krakowska)
✉ ul. Zwierzyniecka 1
@ www.filharmonia.krakow.pl
€ PLN 15–35
Ⓑ 304, 522 (Filharmonia)
Ⓣ 1, 2, 3, 6, 8, 18 (Filharmonia)

Cracow Jazz All Souls' Day Festival

The tradition of the so-called Krakowskie Zaduszki Jazzowe dates back to 1954; concerts are also held in the neighbouring towns. An integral element and the finishing touch of the festival is a Catholic Mass celebrated for late musicians at the Dominican Basilica (➤ 31). The musical setting is provided by jazz artists. ■

@ www.krakowskie-zaduszkijazzowe.xt.pl
€ PLN 30–60, Mass: free

Dominican Basilica (Bazylika Dominikanów)
✉ Stolarska 12
Ⓣ 1, 3, 6, 8, 18 (Plac Wszystkich Świętych)

NOVEMBER

Conrad Festival

Held at the beginning of November, the Joseph Conrad International Festival of Literature explores the connections between literary works and film, theatre, music and art. It is a chance to meet eminent guests from abroad, such as Nobel Prize-winning German writer Herta Müller and Israeli novelist Amos Oz. For a few days, the Town Hall Tower (➤ 30) looks like a lighthouse – it emits light beams. ■

@ www.conradfestival.pl

Audio Art Festival

The festival, co-organised by Cracow's Academy of Music, combines sound and visual arts into experimental forms. Traditional and *avantgarde* music is performed by artists from all over the world. ■

@ www.audio.art.pl

Etiuda&Anima Festival

Held since 1994, the festival of short and animated films has gained a reputation in Poland and abroad. The prizes of Golden, Silver and Bronze Dinosaurs are awarded to students and professors of film schools from around the world. ■

@ www.etiudaandanima.com

DECEMBER

Christmas Fair

Wooden stands appear in the Main Square (➤ 26) on the last days of November and stay open until Christmas. The annual fair (called *targi bożonarodzeniowe*) is one of the city's most colourful traditions. It puts people in the mood for Christmas and offers a choice of Christmas tree trinkets, such as hand-painted baubles, little angels, and jewels. If you get cold, get some mulled wine served from a stand shaped like a huge barrel. ■

✉ *Main Square*
Ⓑ *124, 152, 424, 502, 522, 601, 605, 608, 609, 610, 614, 618, 902, 904 (Dworzec Główny)*
Ⓣ *2, 4, 7, 10, 12, 13, 14, 15, 19, 20, 24, 40 (Dworzec Główny)*

Christmas Cribs Competition

Cracow's cribs often represent not only the Nativity Scene, but also the city's old architecture. The Cracow competition for the title of the finest goes well back in time: 2011 saw its 69th edition. A recent element is the Cribs Procession in the Main Square (➤ 26) and their display upon a special stage by the Sukiennice at the beginning of December (usually Dec 2). There are different-size categories, from miniatures of up to 15 cm to models over 1.2 m in

height. Next, the cribs are taken to the Krzysztofory Palace, where the jury selects the most beautiful ones. The exhibition in the palace lasts from the second week of December until mid-February. ■

Krzysztofory Palace (Pałac Krzysztofory)
✉ *Rynek Główny 35*
☎ *+48 12 6192300*
🕐 *Mon–Thu, Sun 9am–5.30pm, Fri–Sat 9am–6.30pm; closed on Dec 24 and 25*
€ *Mon: PLN 3, Tue–Sun: PLN 8 (PLN 6)*
Ⓑ *124, 152, 424, 502, 522, 601, 605, 608, 609, 610, 614, 618, 902, 904 (Dworzec Główny)*
Ⓣ *2, 4, 7, 10, 12, 13, 14, 15, 19, 20, 24, 40 (Dworzec Główny)*

Cracow Nights

Throughout the year, there are some special occasions when the city's theatres and museums stay open at night. Visitors can also listen to concerts and take part in other events.

The first "Cracow Night" of the year takes place in the city's museums in May. You can choose between a number of sights: from the Barbican (➤ 19), through the Underground Trail (➤ 26), to the National Museum (➤ 151). Museum admission is free or costs a symbolic PLN 1, for which you get a commemorative coin.

During the Theatre Night in June, you can watch performances for free in the city's theatres; for some shows, free entrance tickets have to be collected well in advance. Jazz enthusiasts have their music night feast in July. Free concerts are held on stages located in, for example, the Main Square, Mały Rynek (➤ 57), and in numerous clubs around the city.

The last event of that kind is the so-called *Cracovia Sacra* Night, held in August, when visitors can tour Cracow's finest churches and historic monasteries. Sites that are usually closed for visiting become accessible just for one night. Admission is free, but for some sights you will need to collect entrance tickets at one of the InfoKraków Tourist Information Offices. Visit the website for detailed information on events and entrance tickets.

@ *www.krakowskienoce.pl*

Divine Comedy International Theatre Festival

The first half of December is the time of the festival called Boska Komedia (Divine Comedy). An international jury chooses and awards the best Polish performance of the past season. The programme comprises the season's major productions, shows by young artists and special guests. They are staged in theatres around Cracow. ■

@ *www.boskakomedia.pl*
€ *shows: PLN 15–180*

Practical Information

AIRPORT

Cracow is served by the International Airport in Balice (www.krakow-airport.pl), located about 15 km to the west of the city. The fastest way to reach the centre is by train. It takes less than 20 minutes and costs PLN 10 (tickets are available at railway stations, from the conductor, ticket machines on the trains, and in the T1 Terminal at the airport).

The bus connection to the airport is provided by the public transport bus lines Nos. 208 and 292; their terminal is the Dworzec Główny Wschód stop (close to

Smoking is banned at public transport stops.

the Central Railway Station, at the back of the Galeria Krakowska shopping centre and by the lower level of the Local Coach Station). The 902 night service runs only 3 times a night (it departs from Dworzec Główny Wschód and stops, among others, at the Central Railway Station and Basztowa-LOT). If you use public transport on the route, you need an agglomeration ticket. ■

RAILWAY AND COACH STATIONS

The Central Railway Station (PKP Kraków Główny, www.krakownowyglowny.pl) and the Local Coach Station (Regionalny Dworzec Autobusowy, RDA, www.rda.krakow.pl) are situated in close proximity of each other, by Galeria Krakowska (➤ 218) and the Dworzec Główny Tunel station of the Cracow Fast Tram (by the Galeria). They are within a 5-minute walking distance from the Main Square (➤ 26). The Central Railway Station building – with its numerous ticket windows – is located on the right, southern side of the Galeria (open between 5am and 11pm). From here, trains depart for the airport in Balice.

The main entrance into the Local Coach Station is from ul. Bosacka, east of Galeria Krakowska (behind the tracks). ■

PUBLIC TRANSPORT

In Cracow, there are two zones: the city and the agglomeration (encompassing the suburban area). Most of the above-described sights are located within the city zone, with the exception of the Ojców National Park (➤ 168), Wieliczka (➤ 172), Wadowice (➤ 175), Kalwaria Zebrzydowska (➤ 174) and Auschwitz (➤ 176).

Two types of fares apply: regular and discount. Passengers entitled to discount tickets include foreign students up to 26 years of age (only on presentation of a valid ISIC, EURO<26 Student World or EURO<26 Student card).

For the city zone, there are tickets for a single trip (regular: PLN 3.20, discount: PLN 1.60), two trips (PLN 6 and PLN 3 respectively), a 15-minute trip (PLN 2 and PLN 1), a 30-minute trip (PLN 3.20 and PLN 1.60), a 60-minute trip (PLN 3.60 and PLN 1.80), a 90-minute trip (PLN 5.20 and PLN 2.60). The above time tickets entitle the holder to travel and unlimited changes. There is also a 24-hour pass (regular: PLN 12, discount: PLN 6), a 48-hour pass (PLN 20 and PLN 10 respectively), a 72-hour pass (PLN 30 and PLN 15) and a weekly pass (PLN 40 and PLN 20). It is also possible to buy a single trip ticket for a group up to 20 people (regular: PLN 30, discount: PLN 15) and a weekend family ticket (PLN 12)

Tickets can be bought at newsagents and ticket vending machines installed at public transport stops as well as on some buses and trams. In vehicles without the machines, you can buy tickets from the driver for no extra charge (exact change is required; there are usually no passes available).

Those who head for a performance at the Opera House, the Philharmonic or a theatre, are entitled to free travel on public transport 2 hours before the event and 5 hours after its start (only on presentation of a valid event ticket).

For the current timetable, updates and a journey planner, visit www.mpk.krakow.pl.

Tram

Getting around the city by tram is the most convenient option: thanks to their (mostly) sectioned off lines, trams do not get stuck in traffic jams. Tram lines are marked with one- or two-digit numbers. The Cracow Fast Tram (Krakowski Szybki Tramwaj) consists of lines Nos. 50 and 51, which have three underground stops (e.g., Dworzec Główny Tunel in Level -1 of Galeria Krakowska ➤ 218). The 50 and 51 trams are all low-floor; the rest of Cracow's tram stock is being gradually modernised.

Passengers push a button to open the doors and to signal that they want to get off at the next on-demand stop.

Bus

Bus lines are marked with three-digit numbers, usually starting with "1." Lines Nos. 501, 502 and 522 are express services that stop only at key locations. The numbers of night services begin with "6." The same tariff and ticket types apply on all the above bus lines.

Numbers that begin with "2" indicate that the bus runs along a so-called agglomeration line, to the outskirts of Cracow. If you move around on these lines within the limits of Cracow, you need a ticket for the city zone (the same as above). If you want to go beyond the city limits, you need an agglomeration ticket (tariff border stops are marked on timetables). ■

It is best to get around Cracow by tram.

CAR

Driving a car in Cracow, especially in the city centre, may be difficult because of frequent traffic jams. Congestion is particularly heavy around the Planty (➤ 53) and in al. Trzech Wieszczów. There are three zones of limited traffic: A (the Main Square and some streets around it), where only pedestrians and cyclists are allowed; B (some streets of the Old Town within the Planty and pl. Na Groblach), accessible by car only for residents with parking badges, speed limit of 20 km/h and parking allowed only in specified areas; C (the belt

Cracow has a lot of bicycle paths.

around the Planty as far as al. Trzech Wieszczów and ul. Dietla) – a vehicle-accessible paid parking zone.

The edge of the paid parking zone is marked with a white "P" letter on a blue background (the D-44 sign). Parking charges apply Monday to Friday 10am–8pm. On parking, remember to buy a ticket in a parking meter (exact change only). Charges: PLN 1 for 20 minutes, PLN 3 for the first hour of parking, PLN 3.50 for the second hour, PLN 4.10 for the third hour, and PLN 3 for each subsequent hour. The zone C car parks that are situated closest to the Main Square can be found by pl. św. Ducha and behind the Francis-

can Basilica (a privately-owned car park that closes at 10pm, entry from ul. Franciszkańska); however, they are usually full. There is also a 24/7 car park with approx. 600 parking lots, located under pl. Na Groblach. Here, the rate is PLN 7 for the first hour of parking, the same amount for the second hour, and PLN 6.50 for each subsequent hour (PLN 66.50 for 24 hours). ■

TAXI

There are many taxi companies in Cracow; only the members of taxi associations are allowed to display the "TAXI" sign on the roof. The average starting fare is PLN 7, and the rate is about PLN 2.50 per kilometre. Most companies have night rates even up to 50 percent higher than daytime rates, so you had better ask about the cost before you order a taxi. Naturally, the taximeter must be switched on at the start of the journey to ensure fair pricing. Companies that can be recommended include Barbakan Taxi (+48 12 19661), City Taxi (+48 12 19621), Radio Taxi Dwójki (+48 12 19622), Radio Taxi Lajkonik (+48 12 19628), Euro Taxi (+48 12 19664).

Even though offering the so-called przewóz

osób (transportation of passengers) without a taxi licence has been made illegal in Cracow, there are still drivers trying to sidestep the law. Avoid suspicious-looking signs and pointers, and people who accost you offering their services. Always ask about the approximate price of the ride to your destination (the margin of error is a few złoty) before getting in a car; the rates of dishonest drivers' services can be horrendous. ■

BICYCLE

It is a real pleasure to ride around the Main Square (➤26) and its sur-roundings (zone A), the little streets of Kazimierz (➤68, ➤88), Bulwary Wiślane, and along the picturesque bicycle path at the foot of Wawel Hill ➤40. Some streets have special bicycle lanes.

There are several bike rentals, e.g. at ul. św. Anny 4 (www.bike-rental.pl) near the Main Square, and in Kazimierz at ul. Józefa 5 (dwakola.internetdsl.pl). The rental fee is about PLN 5 per hour, PLN 30–35 for one day. Self-service rental is also possible: 16 points with blue bicycles are located all around the city within the so-called second ring road of Cracow (e.g., in the Old Town and Kazimierz).

First register and log in at www.bikeone.pl, where you can find detailed information and make the payment, thus loading your account to use the service. A subscription for 7 days is PLN 15, 30 days cost PLN 35. Within the subscription, each ride shorter than 30 minutes is free. You can return the bike at any of the 16 rental points. ■

ACCOMMODATION

Cracow boasts a wide tourist accommodation offer, with a variety of choices at any price range. Luxurious 5-star hotels close to the Main Square (➤ 26), such as Copernicus, Grand and Sheraton, charge c. PLN 900 for one night in a double room. The same type of accommodation at a 4-star hotel is c. PLN 500–800; at a 3-star facility: PLN 250–500; lower-class hotels situated further from the city centre charge PLN 200–300. However, it is worthwhile looking for good offers, since one can find real bargains even close to the Main Square (visit www.hotelewkrakowie.pl).

A good alternative to hotels are the city's apartments, conveniently located in the Old Town (➤ 50, www.krakow-apartamenty.biz, www.apartmentskrakow.eu) and in Kazimierz(➤ 68,➤ 88,www.apartamenty-kazimierz.

The signposts with addresses and distances make it easy to get to the city's major sights.

com). Prices vary from PLN 100 for renting a studio to PLN 400–500 for a 4–6-person apartment. Cracow also has a lot of hostels (PLN 40–150 per person), a few of which – such as Mama's Hostel (www.mamashostel.com.pl) – have been awarded in international competitions. Equally commendable are Hostel Flamingo (www.flamingo-hostel.com) and Travellers Inn (www.travellersinn.pl). Motorised tourists can consider staying at a 3-star Clepardia camping at ul. Pachońskiego 28 A (high season: PLN 24 per adult person, PLN 12 per child, PLN 20 for a camper, PLN 15 for a caravan, PLN 120-190 for a bungalow). ■

TOURIST INFORMATION

The network of InfoKraków points is dense and well laid-out. You will find here not only competent advice, but also a lot of free publications such as maps, leaflets and brochures. Most InfoKraków offices can be found in the Old Town (➤ 50): in the Wyspiański Pavilion at pl. Wszystkich Świętych 2 (May–Oct 9am–7pm, Nov–Apr 9am–5pm), at ul. Szpitalna 25 (May–Oct 9am–7pm, Nov–Apr 9am–5pm), ul. św. Jana 2 (May–Oct 9am–7pm, Nov–Apr 10am–6pm), and in the Main Square: in the Sukiennice (May–Oct 9am–7pm, Nov–Apr

Cracow's ul. Floriańska is a must-see.

9am–5pm). In Kazimierz (➤68, ➤88), visit the InfoKraków office at ul. Józefa 7 (May–Oct 9am–7pm, Nov–Apr 9am–5pm). Other offices are located at the foot of Wawel Hill (➤40) at ul. Powiśle 11 (May–Sept 9am–7pm, Oct 10am–6pm, Nov–Apr 9am–5pm), and at the International Airport in Balice (9am–7pm). ∎

ORGANIZED TOURS

Only licensed guides with official badges are allowed to lead tours in Cracow. If you are interested in their offer, visit one of the many tourist guide operators or book through a website.

High-quality service is provided by the Tourist Guides Association (Stowarzyszenie Prze-wodników Turystycznych at ul. Sienna 5, www. przewodnik-krakow.pl); a 3-hour guided tour on a selected route costs PLN 180–200. Operators that organise tours in and around Cracow for English-speaking tourists include Point Travel (pl. Szczepański 7, www. krakow-tours.pl), Cracow Tours (ul. Krupnicza 3, www.cracowtours.pl), See Krakow (ul. Floriańska 6, www.seekrakow.com) and Cracow City Tours (ul. Floriańska 44, www. cracowcitytours.pl). A trip to the salt mine in Wieliczka (➤172) costs approx. PLN 125–130, to Auschwitz (➤176): approx. PLN 100–120. ∎

DISCOUNT PASS

TI offices sell the Cracow Tourist Card, which entitles its holder to free travel on public transport (both day and night services), free admission to 30 museums, and discounts at many shops and restaurants. The option for 2 days is PLN 50, 3 days cost PLN 65. The list of museums, shops and restaurants that accept the card can be found at www.krakowcard.com.

Some bars, museums and hostels also accept ISIC and EURO<26 cards. You will certainly need one of them if you are a foreign student below 26 years of age and want to be entitled to discount tickets when using the city's public transport. ∎

IMPORTANT PHONE NUMBERS

European Emergency Number: 112
Police: 997;
+48 12 6157317 (24/7, Rynek Główny 29, ➤26);
+48 12 6157711 (ul. Sze-roka 35, Kazimierz ➤73)
Ambulance: 999;
+48 12 4222999 (Rynek Podgórski 2, ➤102); +48 12 6444999 (Nowa Huta ➤118); private emergency service: +48 12 4289999 (ul. Łazarza 14)
Fire brigade: 998
Municipal Police: 986
Travel safety:
0800200300 for landline phones (toll free), +48 22 6015555 for foreign-based mobiles (in English and German, 8am–midnight)
Directory Enquiries in English: 118 811

SAFETY

Cracow is a safe city as long as you keep to some basic rules. Steer clear of dark streets and gateways. If anyone tries to taunt you, ignore them. When in a crowd, watch out for pickpockets (especially on public transport). It is risky to venture on your own after dusk into some areas of Nowa Huta (➤118), though this is the case with more recent estates rather than the ones described in the present guidebook. Men should beware of young attractive women who accost passers-by around the Main Square (➤26): they are hired by bars and night clubs that follow unfair practices. A drink bought for a beautiful new acquaintance may cost even more than ten times the regular price. ■

CHILDREN

Most museums and tourist attractions offer discounts for their youngest visitors. Moreover, children up to 4 years of age travel on public transport for free. Not every restaurant possesses baby chairs, and if you need one for your child you should ask before taking the table. Moms with babies can see a film at a cinema called Pod Baranami (➤204): screenings take place in special mother-friendly conditions. Older children will enjoy a visit to the Groteska theatre (➤202), which stages marionette and actor performances. Young ones may also blow off some steam in Jordan Park (➤150). Scientists-to-be can have their fun finding things out and experimenting at the Garden of Experiences (➤214). ■

INTERNET

Cracow has a few free hot spots in places such as the Main Square (➤26) and pl. Nowy (➤86). A lot of bars and restaurants offer free Internet access (you need your own laptop) – just look for establishments with the Wi-Fi sign on the entrance door. There is also a small number of Internet cafés (approx. PLN 3 for 30 minutes); in the vicinity of the Main Square, you can visit Nandu at ul. Wiślna 4 (Mon–Sat 8am–11pm, Sun 9am–11pm). ■

POST

Post offices are usually open Monday–Friday from about 9am to 6pm, on Saturday from about 9am to 3pm. The Main Post Office is located in the city centre at ul. Westerplatte 20 (Mon–Fri 7.30am–8.30pm, Sat 8am–2pm). There is also a post office open around the clock (also on Sundays and holidays) at ul. Lubicz 4, close to the Central Railway Station. ■

PUBLIC TOILETS

There are not many public toilets in Cracow. A few are situated in the Old Town, for example, in ul. Sienna

There are many postboxes in the city centre.

(close to the intersection with ul. św. Gertrudy), near ul. Straszewskiego (in the Planty ➤53), and in the Sukiennice (➤28). The charge amounts to PLN 1–2, the opening hours are usually 6.30am–10.30pm. Public toilets can be also found in the Central Railway Station and the Local Coach Station (approx. PLN 2), as well as in shopping centres. ■

City Atlas

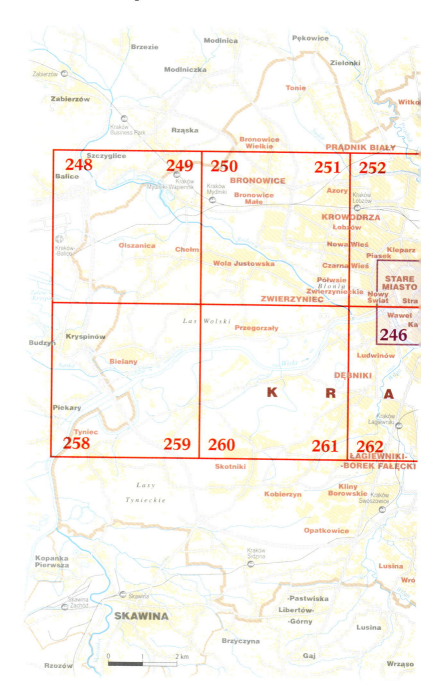

scale 1:12 000   scale 1:22 000

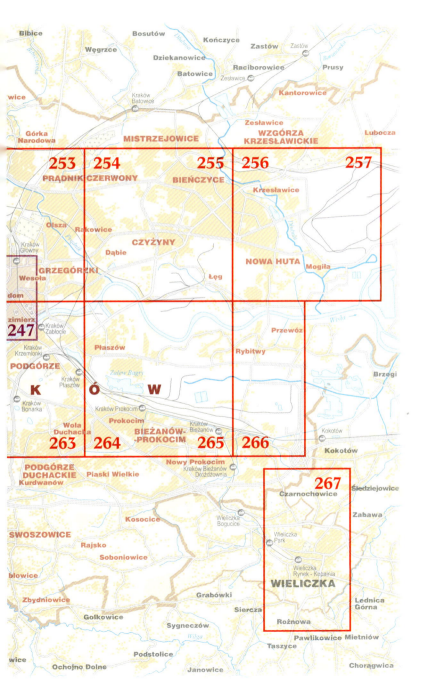

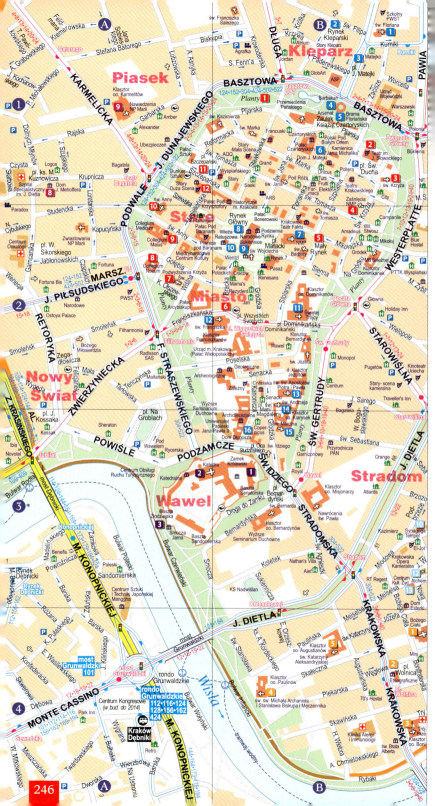

Key to city atlas symbols

1:12 000

0 ━━━━━━━━━━━━━ 500 m

(pp. 246–247)

1:22 000

0 ━━━━━━━━ 500 m

(pp. 248–267)

━ ━ ━	administrative boundaries
▬▬▬	motorways
▬▬▬	arterial streets
▬▬▬	main streets
▬▬▬	other streets
▬▬▬	pedestrian zone
▬▬▬	unpaved roads
▬▬▬	footpaths
Kraków Główny	railways; railway stations
●━━━●	tram routes; stops
●━━━●	bus routes; stops
▬▬▬	paid parking zone boundary
🚦	traffic lights
🚌	bus stations
P ⛽	car parks; filling stations
✚ ⊕	hospitals; pharmacies
Ⓟ ✉	police; post offices
🏛 ♀	museums; theatres
🎬	cinemas
🏨 🏠	hotels; youth hostels
⛺	camping sites
✝ ☦ ✡	churches; Eastern Orthodox churches; synagogues
⚓ 🏊	water bus stops; swimming pools
◆ ◆	historic buildings; public buildings
13 75	built-up areas; house numbers
	industrial areas
	cemeteries
	parks
	allotments
	forests

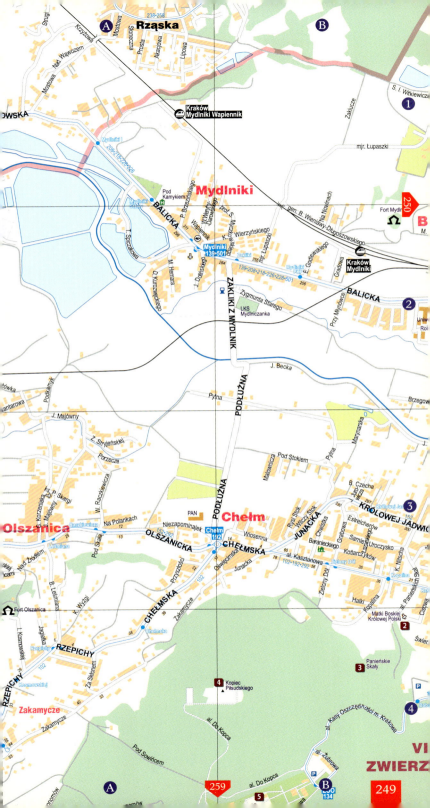

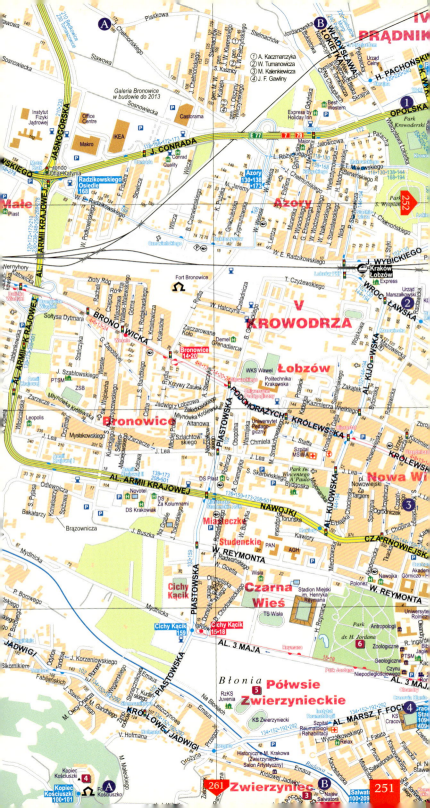

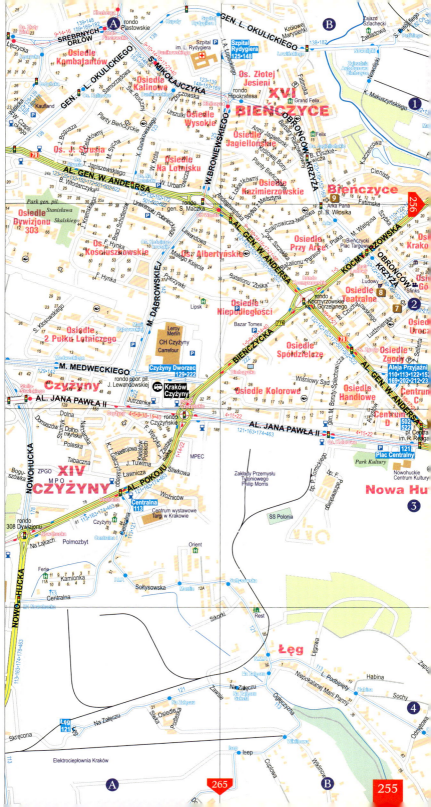

ArcelorMittal Poland

(dawna Huta im. T. Sendzimira)

XVIII
NOWA HUTA

Mogiła

Na Błoniach

Kępa

Fort Grębałów
Wzgórza
Krzesławickie

Cmentarz Grębałowski

Kraków
Lubocza
(nieczynna)

Walcownia
16•22

Agencja Kraków Wschód

Elektromontaż

MPK
Zajezdnia
Tramwajowa

UJASTEK

Mrozowa

Centrum
Medyczne
Ujastek

Kombinat

Kombinat
117•132•138•139•149•163
172•174•211•242•463•501

JB

UJASTEK MOGILSKI

Kopiec Wandy

Kopiec
Wandy
17

Fort Mogiła

IGOŁOMSKA

J. Bardosa

Bardosa

KIEGO

Hala Sportowa
Tomex

Kępska

Brama nr 4

Brama nr

211•Kombinat

Jeżynowa

J. Giedroycia

Kopaniec

Na Niwach

Jeżynowa

S. Samostrzelnika

Podbagnie

Żaglowa

Jeżynowa

J. Giedroycia

Jeżynowa

Zakranie

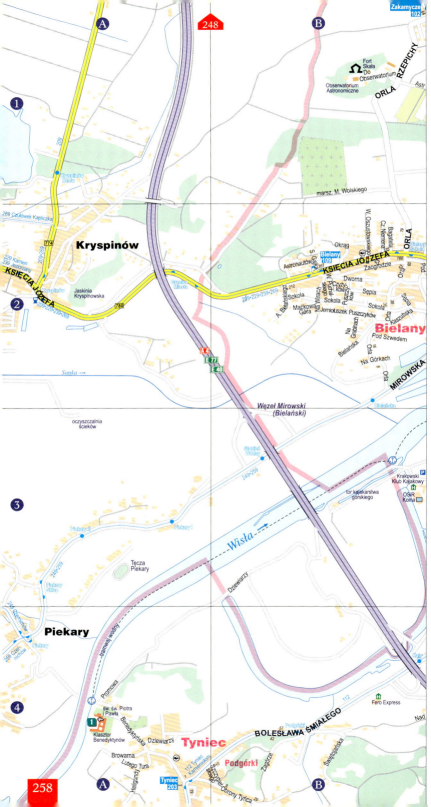

Pod Sowińcem

al. Do Kopca

al. Borowa

P

ZOO
134

5
Ogród Zoologiczny

Astronomów

al. Pustelnika

al. Żubrowa

al. Żubrowa

Astronomów

al. Wędrowników

1

Rędzina

Col.
Pole

L a s   W o l s k i

al. Konarowa

Przegc

260
209
245

Kozłówka

Czujówka

Ks. Kmędula

Szkolna

109•209•229•239
239•269

al. Wędrowników

6
Klasztor
Kamedułów

780

287

Pawilon

109•209•229•239
249•259•269

118

Bielany Klasztor

Daleka

134

Krucza

269

178

299

Fort
Krępak

Wodociągi

Bażancia

Przepiórcza

Zakręt

Czajek

Strzelna

249•259

tramwaj wodny (kursuje w sezonie letnim)

2

50

Fallita

Kostrze

**Koło
Tynieckie**

Kolna

Kolna

Elfów
Granitowa
Krzemowa
Gronowa

Widłakowa

Kaktusowa

Kolarzy

Fallista

Pustelnia

LZS Kostrze

Krzewowa

3

155

Tor kajakowy
(112)

(112)

124

Kostrze
Szkoła

144

163

112•162

Wały Wiślane

112

Kostrze
OSP

Z. Jachimeckiego

Tyniecki

H

Bona

H

Kostrze
Toplisko

TYNIECKA

173

Kostrzecka

152

Dąbrowa

Bobrowa

112

Dąbrowa

Dąbrowa

Orzask

33

Fort
Winnica

Wały Wiślane II

26

J. Staszkiego

**Osiedle
Srebrne Uroczysko**

4

Bojanówka

Zbożna

*Uroczysko
Skotniki*

Fosa

Węzeł Tyniecki

Czerna

Kostrze

J. Fedkowicza

59

A4

E 40

162 Podgórki Tynieckie

Dąbrowa

E 77

A

B

A

B

al. Żubrowa

P

ZOO
134

al. Żubrowa

1

s k i

259

780

Colegium
Polonijne UJ

Przegorzały UJ
409

Zaklałe

Kozłarówka

Gajowa

245

Nr Przegaln.

Żywiczna

Olchowa

T. Kasprzyckiego
Borówczana

Klonowa

Nieto. cz. Uboczna

J. Dobrzyc-
kiego

J. Herzoga

Winowców

Kamedulska

K. Munchn

K. Muzyczki

Bruzdowa

Skibowa

Cygańska

Przegorzalska

Kamedulska

Przegorzały

K. Żemaitisa

St. Ja- ko-Bohusza

Smok

Pałęcza

Gliniki

Księcia Józefa

109•209
229•249•259

Zaklałe

114

Przegorzały

229•269

84

Rybna

— tramwaj wodny (kursuje w sezonie letnim) —

2

Bodzów

Widłakowa

Nierówna

Wielkanocna

57

Widłakowa

Bodzowska

13

Widłakowa

50

Pychowice II

Kostrze

Falista

Grabowa

Elfów

Krzewowa

Gronowa

Kaktusowa

Kosiłarzy

Falista

Widłakowa

Pustelnia

81

Ω Fort Bodzów

Osiedle
Felczaka

TYNIECKA
112•156•162

Kosiłza II

Pychowicka
Górka

Skotnicka

112
127 Rozl. m.

Kosiłza I

155

124

Kosiłza
Szkoła

112•162

Z. Jachimeckiego

Bobrowa

J. Sląskiego

Gronostajowa

171

Ω Fort Winnica

Fort Winnica

57

WINNICKA

168

VIII
DĘBNIKI

Przelotowa

Krajobrazowa

por. Emira

Podole

mjr Mochnaniec

Królowka

20

J. Unruga

Winnicka

J. Unruga

Dworski Ogród

Zamglona

Kresowa

A. Zelwerowicza

Skotnicka

Czwartaków

Mochnaniec

Obrońców Hełu

Braterstwa Broni

Mochnaniec

oczysko
otni.

4

Za Dworem

J. Unruga

63

57

Batalionów Chłopskich

Hufcowa

Skotniki
Szkoła
106•156

106 Skotn.Szkoła

SKOTNICKA

Domowa

Mochnaniec

39

271 Kr

127 Br

K. BUJN

Skotniki

B

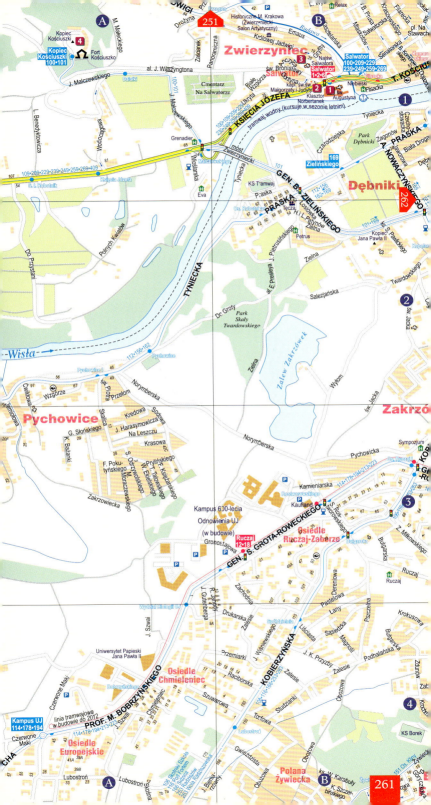

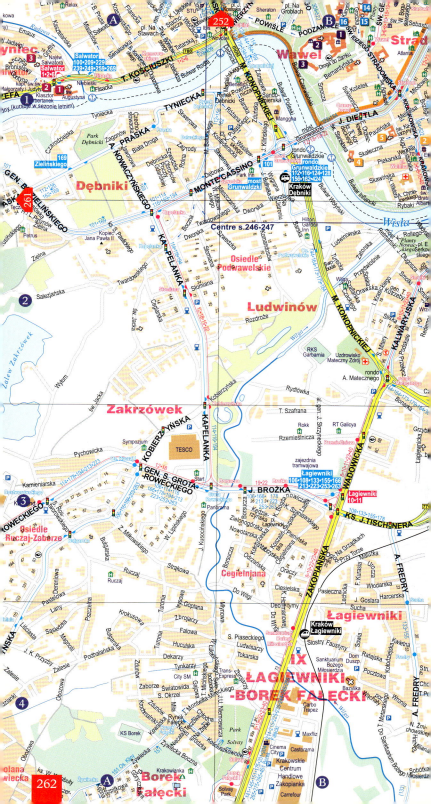

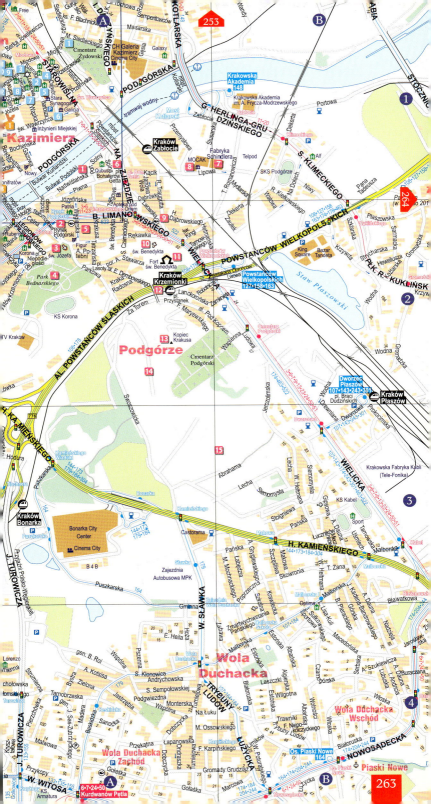

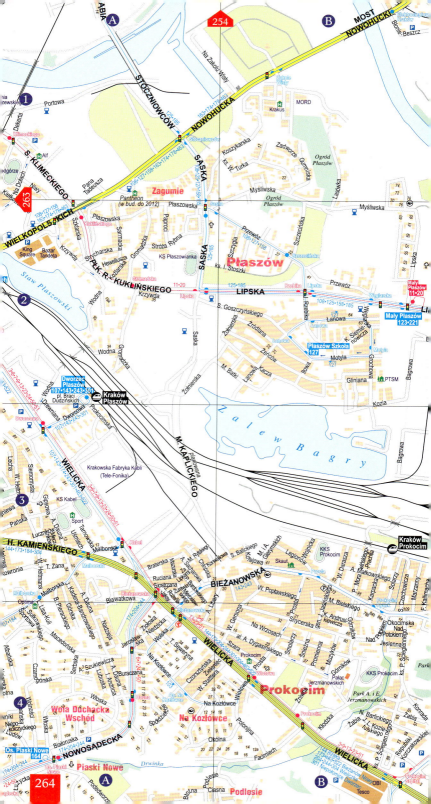

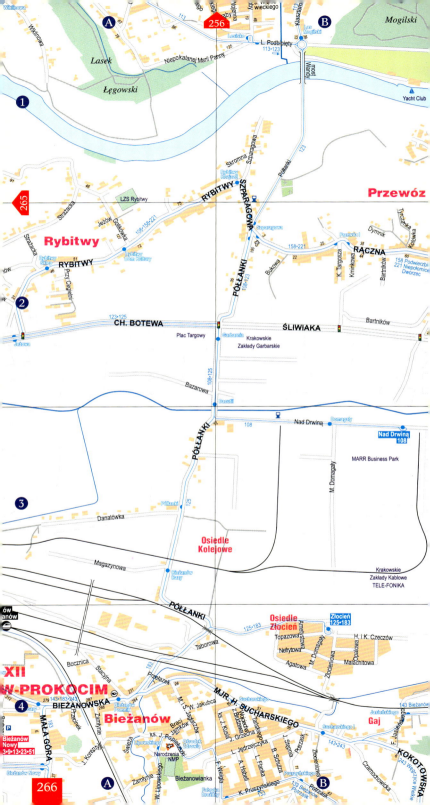

Cracow

Map & guide

Are you planning a romantic dinner in Paris? A business trip to Brussels or shopping excursion to London? Comfort! map & guide is a unique combination of a handy map and an informative guide. All the information you need for a short stay, presented in a practical and detailed yet concise manner. What-To's and How-To's in a nutshell. Ideal for people pressed for time and those who value practicality above all.

A map & guide publication includes:
- handy laminated map with rich tourist content and a user-friendly scale;
- matter-of-fact descriptions of all top sites (numbered for easy location on the map);
- useful information on public transport, money and weather;
- top things to eat and drink, places to go shopping;
- festivals and events calendar.

www.comfortmap.com